LEGENDARY LOCALS

OF

PACIFICA

CALIFORNIA

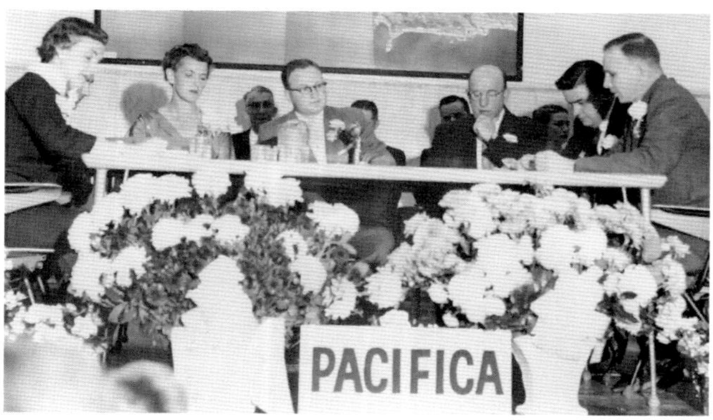

I0806129

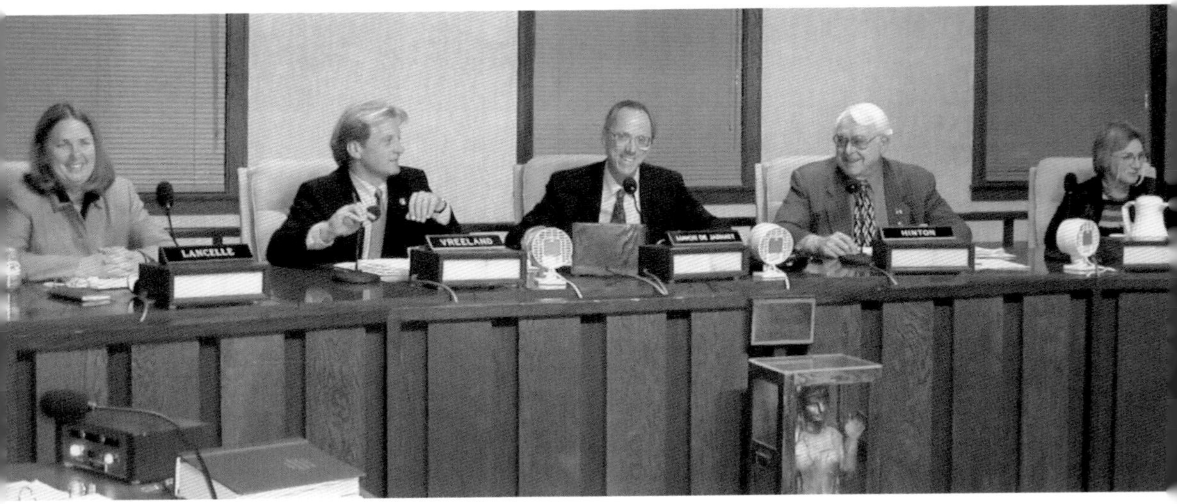

A Contemporary City Council

A recent city council, from the first decade of the 21st century, included (from left to right) Julie Lancelle, Jim Vreeland, Pete DeJarnatt, Cal Hinton, and Sue Digre. (Courtesy of the *Pacifica Tribune*.)

Page 1: **The First City Council**

The original 1957 city council for the new city of Pacifica consisted of, from left to right, (an unidentified non–council member) council members Jean Fassler, Gerry Schumacher, Harold Feyge, George Mason, and Don Miller. (Courtesy of the *Pacifica Tribune*.)

LEGENDARY LOCALS OF PACIFICA CALIFORNIA

CHRIS HUNTER

LEGENDARY LOCALS

ISBN 978-1-4671-0098-4

Legendary Locals is an imprint of Arcadia Publishing
Charleston, South Carolina

Printed in the United States of America

Library of Congress Control Number: 2013935349

For all general information, please contact Arcadia Publishing:
Telephone 843-853-2070
Fax 843-853-0044
E-mail sales@arcadiapublishing.com
For customer service and orders:
Toll-Free 1-888-313-2665

Visit us on the Internet at www.arcadiapublishing.com

Dedication

To those amazing girls in my family, my wife, Meg, and my two daughters, Mettlin and Brae, who supported me throughout my 17 years at the Pacifica Tribune *and continue to be a constant source of inspiration for my future projects.*

On the Cover: Clockwise from top left: Nick Gust and his family, proprietors of Nick's (Courtesy of the *Pacifica Tribune*; see page 18), Mildred Owen, artistic director of Pacifica Performances (Courtesy of the *Pacifica Tribune*; see page 30), Grace McCarthy, longtime Pacifica icon (Courtesy of the *Pacifica Tribune*, see page 20), Bill Drake, former owner, editor, and publisher of the *Pacifica Tribune* (Courtesy of the *Pacifica Tribune*; see page 72), Jerry Barrish, found object artist (Courtesy of the *Pacifica Tribune*; see page 38), Lucy Muir, disabled activist and artist (Courtesy of the *Pacifica Tribune*; see page 115), John Stanley, author (Courtesy of John Stanley; see page 27), and Russ Conroy, longtime director of the North Coast County Water District (Courtesy of the *Pacifica Tribune*; see page 22).

On the Back Cover: From left to right: Pacifica's famous "All-Woman City Council," which included Barbara Carr, Vi Gotelli, Bonnie Wells, Julie Lancelle, and Ellen Castelli (Courtesy of the *Pacifica Tribune;* see page 12), Rob Schneider giving a kiss to his mother, Pilar Schneider (Courtesy of the *Pacifica Tribune;* see page 26).

CONTENTS

Acknowledgments 6

Introduction 7

CHAPTER ONE Pacifica Politics 9

CHAPTER TWO Pacifica Arts and Music 25

CHAPTER THREE Pacifica Educators 47

CHAPTER FOUR Pacifica Science 59

CHAPTER FIVE Pacifica Business 63

CHAPTER SIX Pacifica Sports 81

CHAPTER SEVEN Pacifica Community Leaders 101

Index 127

ACKNOWLEDGMENTS

First and foremost I must gratefully acknowledge the support of the *Pacifica Tribune* and its parent company, the Bay Area News Group, for allowing me the freedom to search through file cabinets, photograph folders, an ancient microfilm reader, and countless stacks of loose photographs. Editor and publisher Elaine Larsen gave me free rein to go back in time and relive the nearly two decades I spent working at the newspaper with her as a colleague. Many of the photographs I examined that were from the 1990s and 2000s turned out to have been taken by me. Reporter Jane Northrop helped me look up a few items and even took the spare time to take a photograph for me. Bay Area News Group publisher Steve Paterson offered his unconditional support as well, which was crucial since the vast majority of the photographs in this book came from the *Pacifica Tribune*. I also must thank Horace Hinshaw, the once and future sports editor of the *Tribune*, whose unwavering support of all things sporting in Pacifica and his creation of the Pacifica Sports Hall of Fame provided a wealth of material and backgrounds on individuals included in this book. I am sure he would have been happy to see the entire book filled with sports figures! The Pacifica Historical Society, with its comprehensive files, was made available thanks to Kathleen Manning and Jerry Crow, both fantastic local historians in their own right, as well as fellow Arcadia authors. I thank them for their inspiration and support in this project. I appreciate the time Jerry Crow spent looking through his files and sharing some ideas.

All of the photographs are courtesy of the *Pacifica Tribune* archives, unless otherwise noted in the individual caption.

INTRODUCTION

Other than its spectacular scenery, ranging from the Pacific Ocean beaches to its rugged hills and valleys, the city of Pacifica really only has one other claim to fame: the interesting characters who grew up in this bedroom community just south of San Francisco. The people of Pacifica—from active local politicians to multitalented artists and just about everyone in between—have established their little coastal town as a beachfront haven that some consider a veritable "Brigadoon," conveniently hidden from the rest of the world by fog and fortress-like hills.

With the nickname "Scenic Pacifica," this California town is beloved by its residents and relatively unknown by everyone else. Its proximity to San Francisco, combined with a somewhat less-expensive housing market than other places on the peninsula, has made it a popular place to raise a family and sometimes disappear from the hectic pace of the region.

This book does not purport to showcase every famous, successful, or accomplished person who ever lived in or traveled through Pacifica. It can only scratch the surface of chronicling the community celebrities, political powerhouses, and personalities who have somehow been connected to the coastal city. In fact, because of its ease of commuting to San Francisco and Silicon Valley, there have always been high-profile people who kept a low-profile presence in town. Some have even been known to simply drive out of Pacifica every morning without ever engaging the community in any way. A California Supreme Court Justice, for example, once lived in town without ever being interviewed in the local weekly newspaper. There have also been rumors of baseball players and movie stars living under the radar in Pacifica.

There are, however, enough prominent people and active citizens to fill several books about local legends. Unlike typical tourist towns in California, Pacifica is more of a residential enclave with a public beach and a public pier. There are no longer any car dealerships or magnet shopping centers that attract people from "over the hill." The primary sales tax generators are the grocery stores and the gas stations. That is a formula that is not common for cities of 40,000 people.

The natural beauty and extensive open space that is liberally sprinkled throughout Pacifica has had an impact on the way people behave in Pacifica. Everyone seems to agree that they love Pacifica, if only this or that specific thing could be changed. Usually, the only ongoing local debate centers on how much development should be allowed or supported. It is a decades-long dialogue in Pacifica and it shows no signs of changing.

School communities were the original building blocks of Pacifica, which had a neighborhood school within walking distance of just about every home during the early growth years. To have 11,000 children going to 15 schools in 1975 meant everyone knew everyone else. By 2000, the number of students had dropped to about 2,000 and there were seven elementary schools. Pacifica began to morph into a different kind of city, with fewer large families and more young commuters.

Whatever else one says about Pacifica, it is clear that the city's natural beauty, oceanfront allure, and community connections are universally beloved. The individuals who are profiled in this book all share some level of Pacifica predilection, and their stories—whether involving politics, sports, arts, or education—tend to have some intersection with their personal involvement with Pacifica itself.

CHAPTER ONE

Pacifica Politics

Politics is truly a spectator sport in Pacifica, with back-and-forth battles between folks who would like the city to have a vibrant economic personality and those who prefer to keep the city a bedroom community with strong environmental protection. There have been successful recall elections removing council members who promoted special tax measures followed by the election of officials with similar political philosophies as those recalled. Debates on development extend for decades, with multiple public votes showing the public leans away from more typical development agendas. An underlying affection for the community, however, seems to connect nearly all politically active personalities. Battle cries of who loves Pacifica the most and who has lived there the longest are voiced by all sides of the political spectrum.

Every person who puts his or her neck on the line to become a city council member, a school board trustee, or a water district director deserves to be called a legendary Pacifican. The handful of selections of this compendium is a sampling of the people who have made a difference by their public service. Some have served on multiple boards or made a unique impact. Some had a quirky incident happen to them or are known for a specific achievement.

In any case, there have always been interesting, dedicated people who have been willing to step up and serve their city. The folks identified here are representative of all the good people who have wanted to be leaders and who asked the public to let them try.

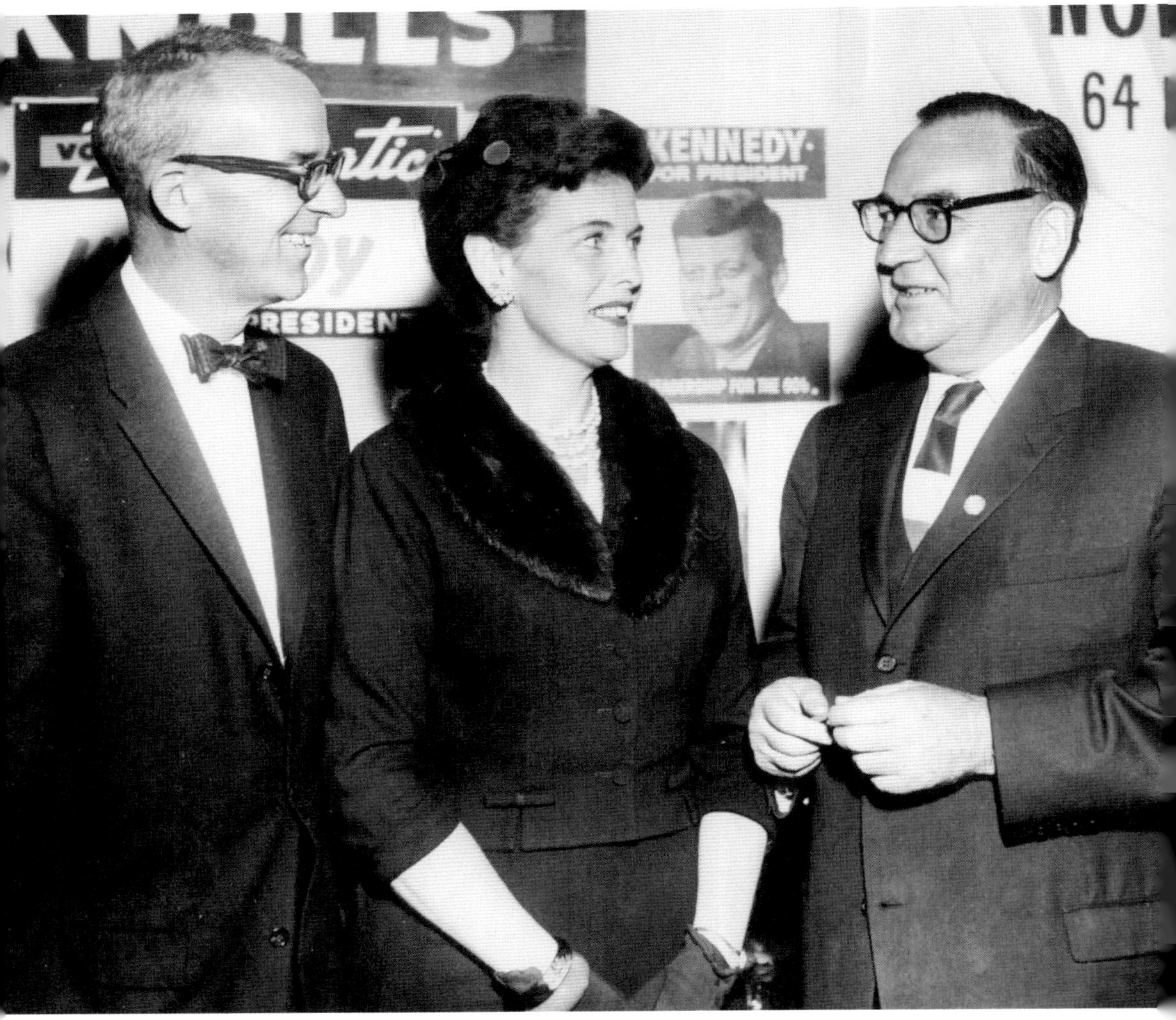

Jean Fassler (ABOVE AND OPPOSITE PAGE)

Jean Fassler was the very first mayor of Pacifica, advancing from a neighborhood activist promoting the original incorporation of Pacifica as a city to one of its most prominent political leaders. Meetings in her famous yellow house on the Linda Mar beach went on late into the night as locals gathered to discuss their dreams for a future city made up of the small unincorporated villages tucked into the hills and valleys between Daly City and the Devil's Slide area of Highway 1. In 1957, by a small margin, voters agreed with Jean, and Pacifica was born. The same voters put Jean on the new city council and she became the first mayor. This established a tradition in Pacifica of strong female leaders: while there has been one instance of an all-women city council, there has never been an all-men council in the city's 55-year history. Jean Fassler went on to be elected to the San Mateo County Board of Supervisors, where she served three terms stretching through the 1960s and early 1970s. No other Pacifica politician has ever been elected to the board of supervisors to this day. A major artery connecting Highway 1 to the Linda Mar Valley was named Fassler Avenue to honor Jean Fassler, and while she moved away from Pacifica, her name and contributions have continued to resonate through the years. In the above photograph, Fassler is meeting with Gov. Pat Brown. The picture on the top of the opposite page shows Fassler under the new sign for the street named after her. The photograph on the bottom of the opposite page is Fassler (at right) with another legendary Pacifica woman, Grace McCarthy.

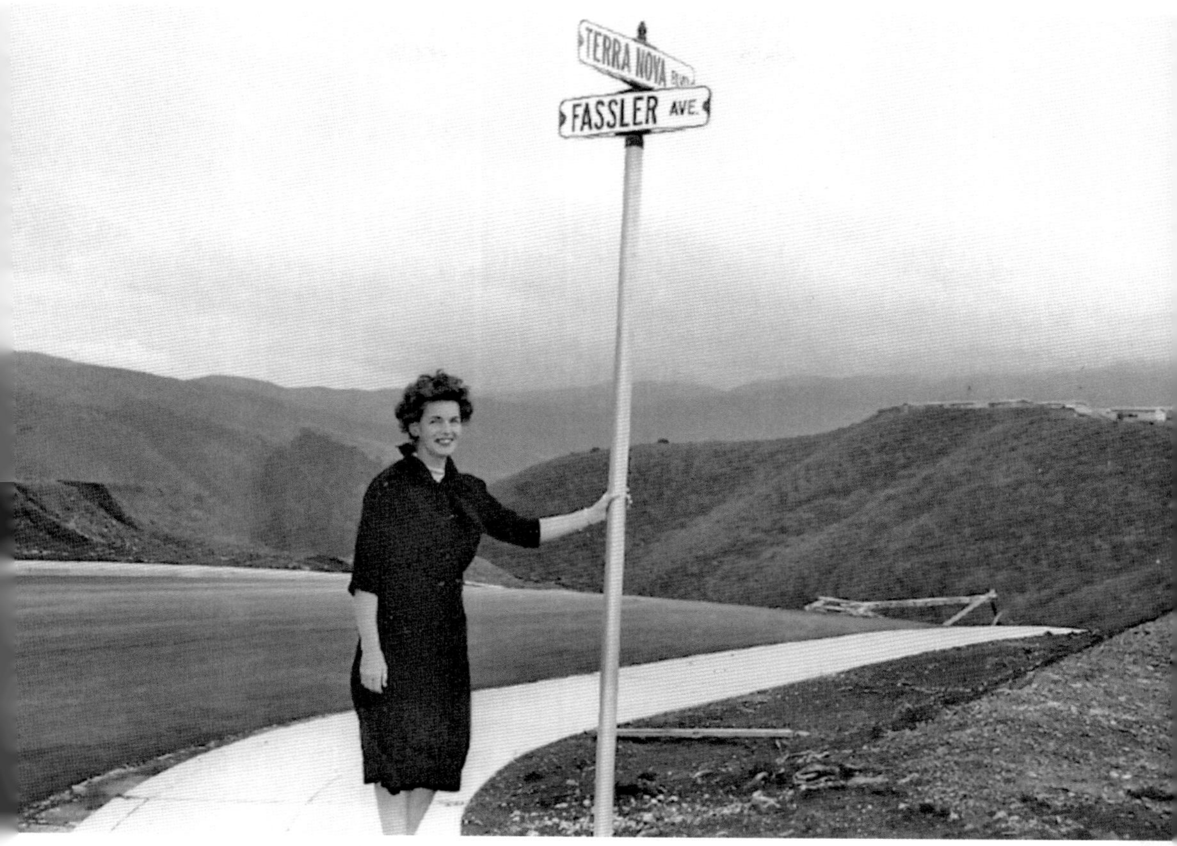
TERRA NOVA
FASSLER AVE.

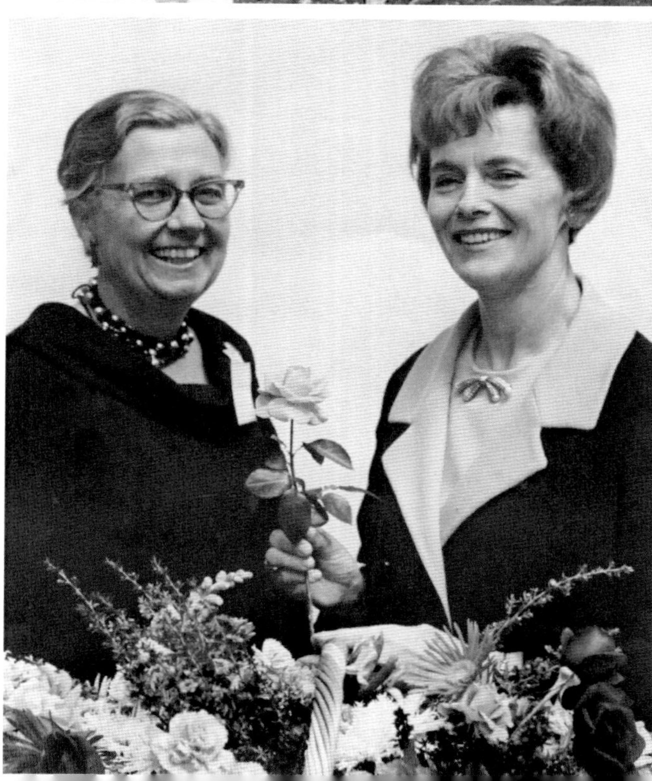

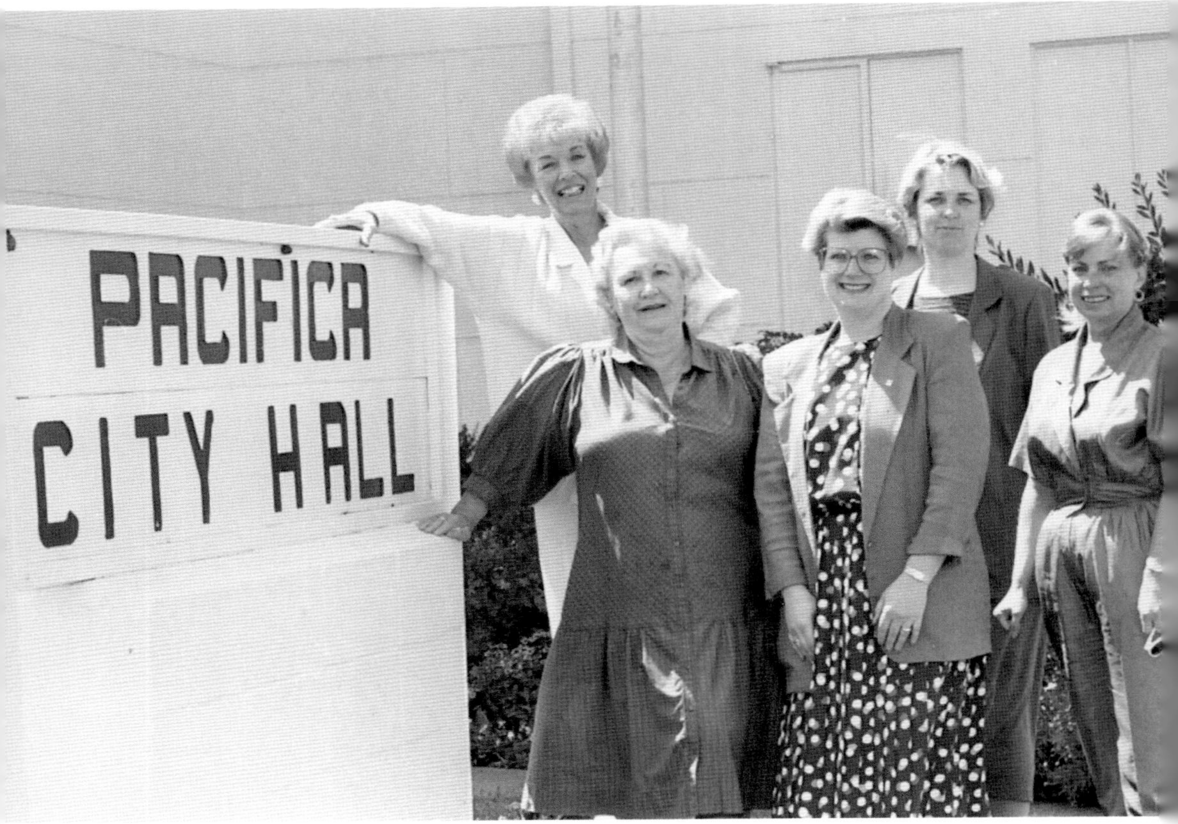

The Famous All-Woman City Council

Following a recall election in 1992, the city council was reconstituted with all women. Bonnie Wells, a member of the previous council, was the only politician to sense the anger of a large number of voters and changed her mind about a controversial Lighting and Landscaping Tax being implemented by the council. She voted against it and was spared when the subsequent recall successfully removed four of her fellow council members from office. In the following replacement elections, Barbara Carr, Ellen Castelli, Julie Lancelle, and Vi Gotelli were voted into office. This created one of the only all-women city councils in the country and the media had a field day writing about it. Even a supermarket tabloid covered the story, as if it had true celebrity magnetism. The incoming council wound up being relatively balanced, with pro-recall advocates like Ellen Castelli, Barbara Carr, and Vi Gotelli being joined by Julie Lancelle, who opposed the recall. The mixture of personalities, while eliminating the tax, created a relatively moderate council. Barbara Carr, a realtor, was famously quoted as joking that city hall might explode if all five women were having PMS at the same time. It was a decidedly non-PC joke that went nationwide. Ironically, the city of Pacifica never has had an all-man city council since its incorporation in 1957. That detail of political history is often overlooked when the all-woman city council is brought up as a unique anomaly. Pictured are, from left to right, Barbara Carr, Vi Gotelli, Bonnie Wells, Julie Lancelle, and Ellen Castelli.

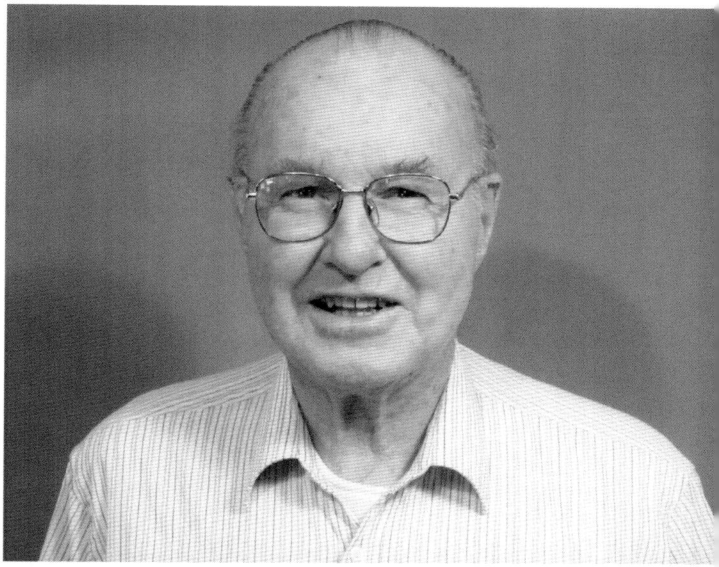

Karl Baldwin

Karl Baldwin was the very first city manager for the newly incorporated City of Pacifica. Unlike many other professional city managers, he did not follow a career of doing the same kind of work in other cities. His term in Pacifica lasted from 1958 through 1966. Instead of getting another job as a city manager, Baldwin went to Vietnam as a USAID representative. He and his wife, Eileen, returned to Pacifica in retirement and became involved as an active citizen of the city he helped to create. In the below photograph, Karl Baldwin meets with Lydia Azevedo to discuss the "Little Brown Church" project.

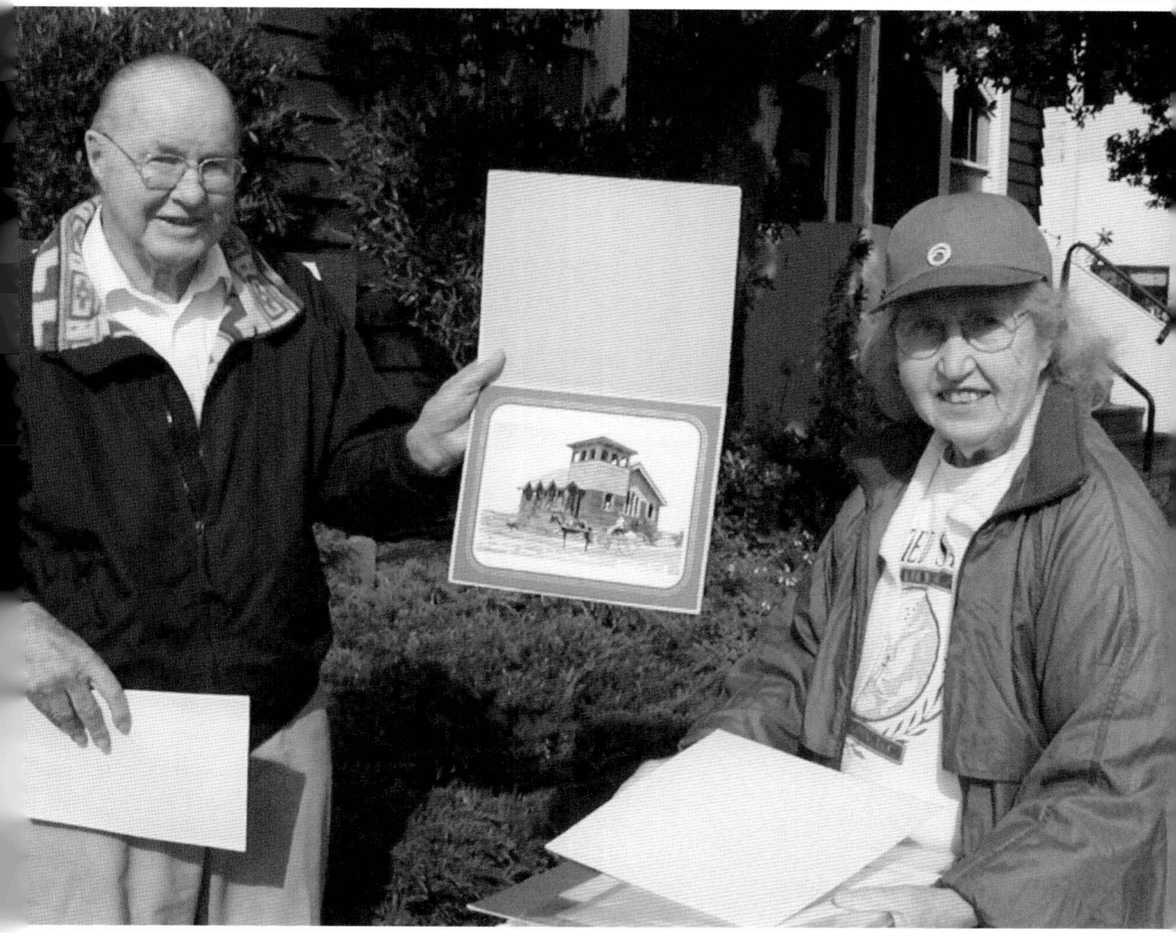

May Gee

North Coast County Water District board member May Gee was also one of the founding mothers of Pacifica, serving on the local organization committee that eventually placed the successful ballot measure for incorporation in front of the voters in 1957. While she never sat on the Pacifica City Council, although she did run, her political career as a longtime member of the water district kept her active and aware of the city she helped create. During World War II, May Gee worked in the boatyards in San Francisco, earning her place as one of those women known by the nickname "Rosie the Riveter." A Chinese American pioneer in many ways, May Gee forged a path for those who followed her and never gave up her love of Pacifica. At one time, she owned and operated a Chinese food shop in Pacific Manor Shopping Center. She and her husband, Ed, owned and operated seven different businesses through the years, including the Muffin Mine and the Pacifica Ice Creamery. However, May Gee always worked hard as a volunteer and a Water District board member to make Pacifica the unique coastal community it grew to be. She is shown here at the Vietnam War Memorial traveling replica when it came to Pacifica.

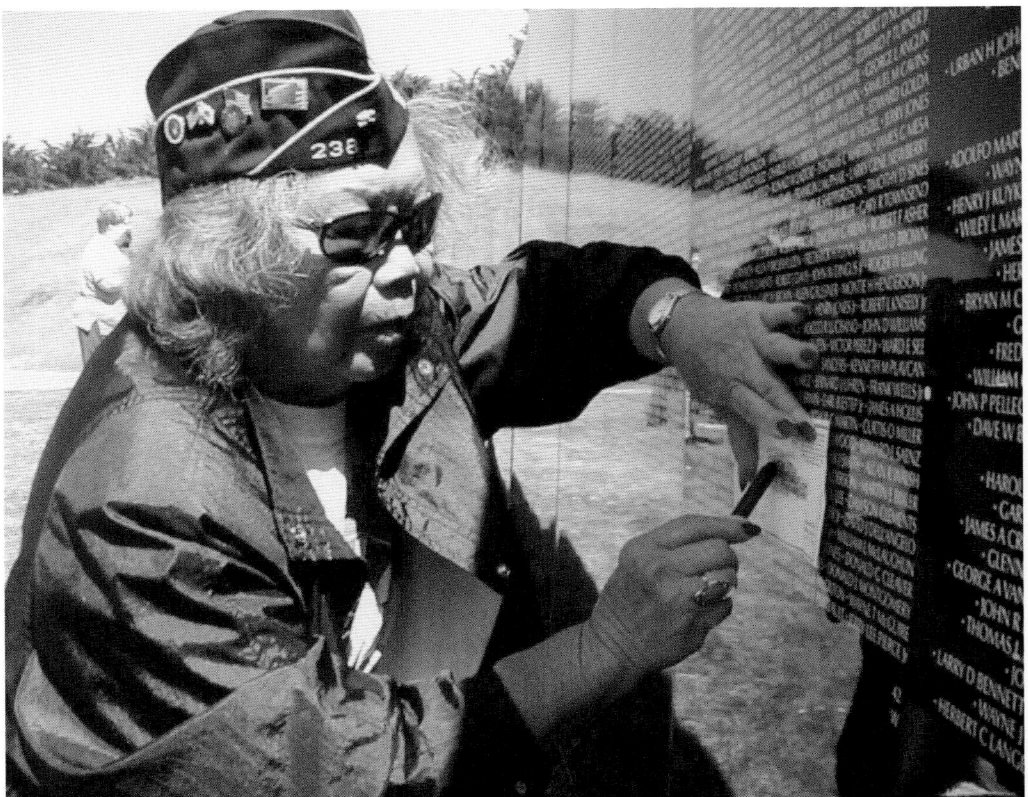

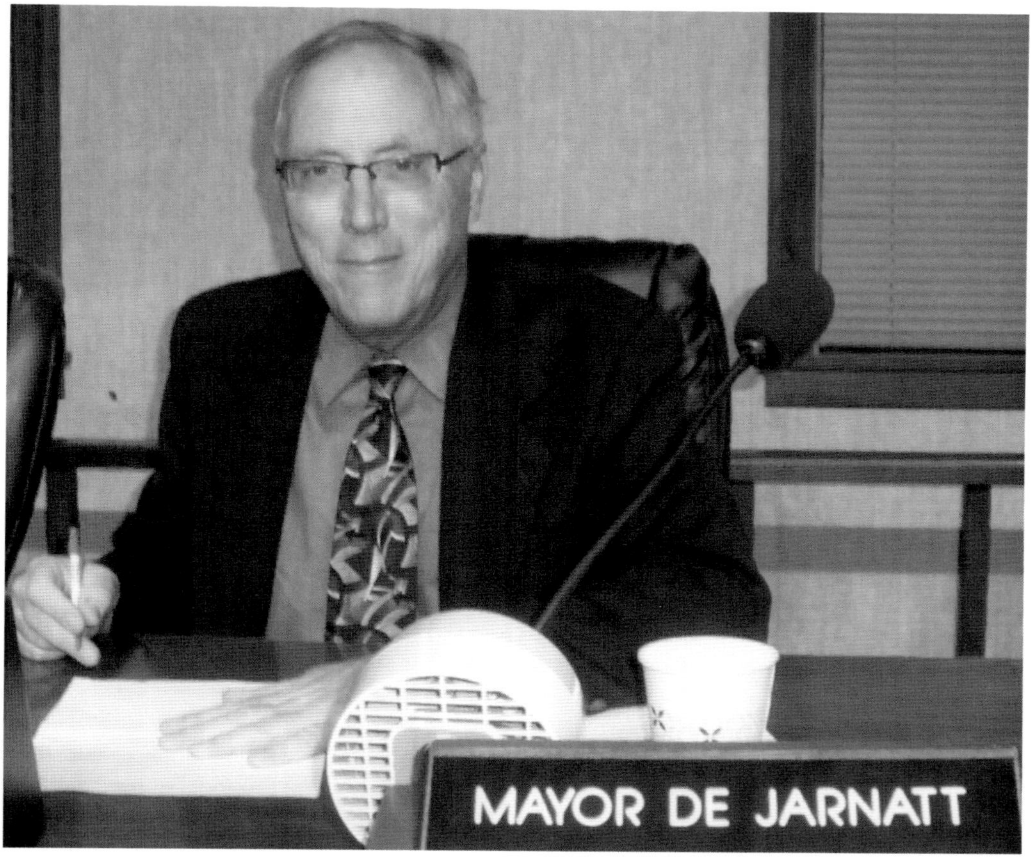

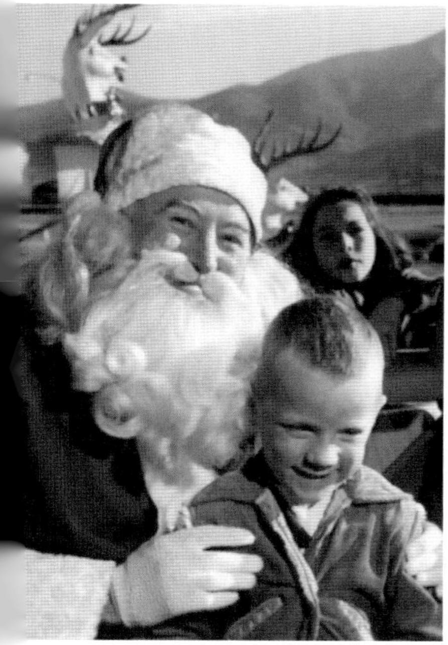

Pete DeJarnatt

Like many politicians, Pete DeJarnatt was inspired to run for office because of opposition to a specific issue. The proposed development of land on Milagra Ridge in Northern Pacifica spurred him to work with a community group known as "Concerned Manor Residents" and eventually win a seat on the council. Then, he stayed through four elections and served 16 years in office. During that time, he was mayor of Pacifica four times, a record matched only by Nick Gust from a prior generation. With the advent of term limits, there will never again be someone who serves as long, although Sue Digre, a fellow member of the Concerned Manor Residents has the potential, having served 12 years. After ending his tenure in 2012, DeJarnatt said that the constant battles over development in Pacifica were stressful and he was not going to miss being the center of attention for his critics. His continuing reelection to office showed that more people supported him than fought with him. A lifelong resident of Pacifica, DeJarnatt suffered from a back injury, which forced him to stand up during city council meetings that lasted long hours. A true native son, DeJarnatt appeared in the newspaper with Santa Claus when he was just a little boy.

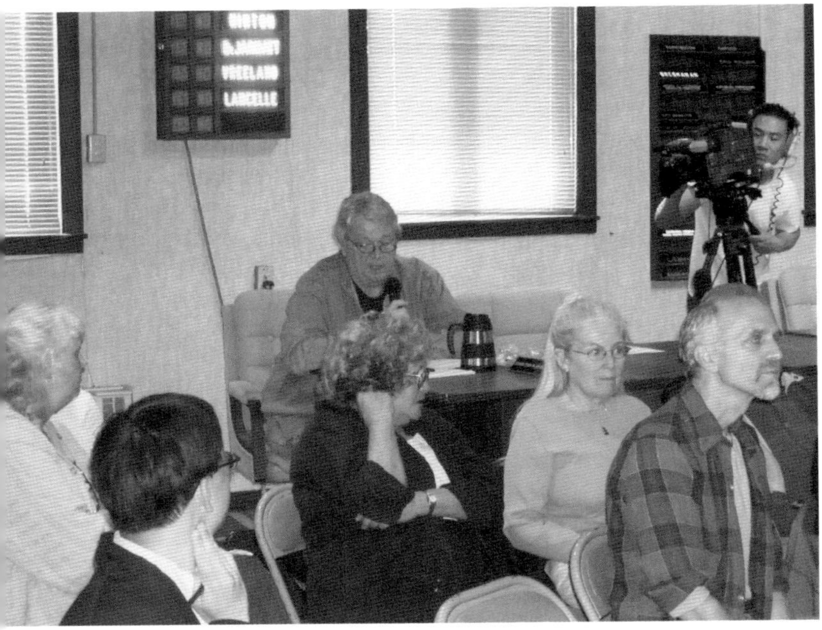

John Curtis

John Curtis was at the right hand of quite a few political candidates for many years, running campaigns for longtime city council member Pete DeJarnatt and being a supportive consultant for various other campaigns. While he served on the planning commission, Curtis never ran for office himself, but his influence was widespread and he was known for his forceful opinions on development issues, which he shared readily through the pages of the *Pacifica Tribune*.

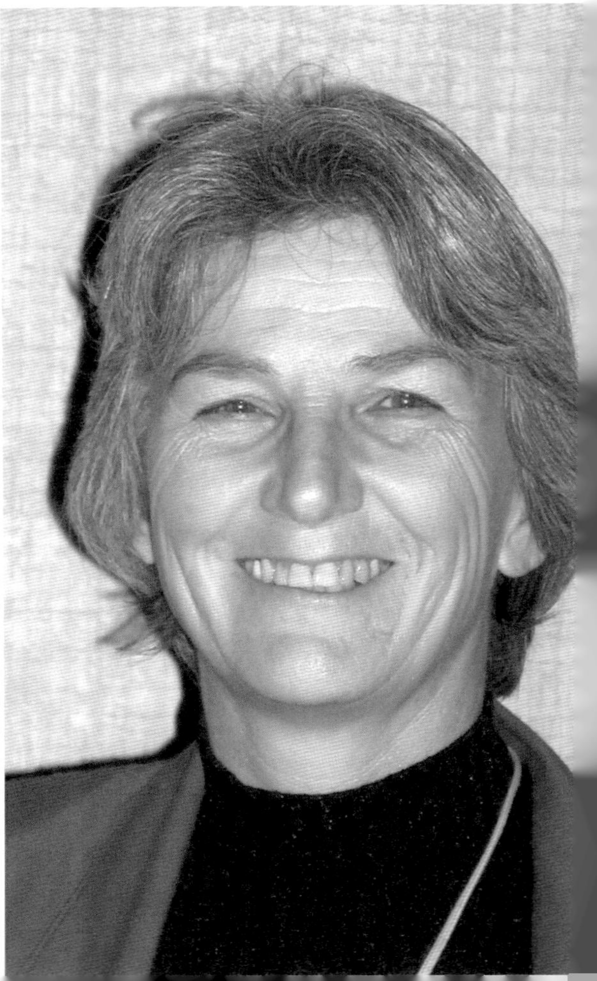

Sue Digre

Like her fellow council member Pete DeJarnatt, Sue Digre came into political office through her work with the Concerned Manor Residents and her strong views on preventing what she saw as excessive development. Her husband, Erick, a ranger with the San Francisco Watershed, was also a brave first responder who went to New York City after the September 11th attack and helped search through the rubble of the World Trade Center ruins. Digre also worked at PARCA (a nonprofit serving people with developmental disabilities and their families), and she was often viewed as a champion of developmentally disabled people. One of her children was born with Down syndrome and he often accompanied his mother to public events. She also was a force behind the Blue Star Mothers group and other veteran support organizations. She is the last remaining city council member whose legacy will be more than two terms since she was in her third term when the public voted to establish a two-term limit in 2012.

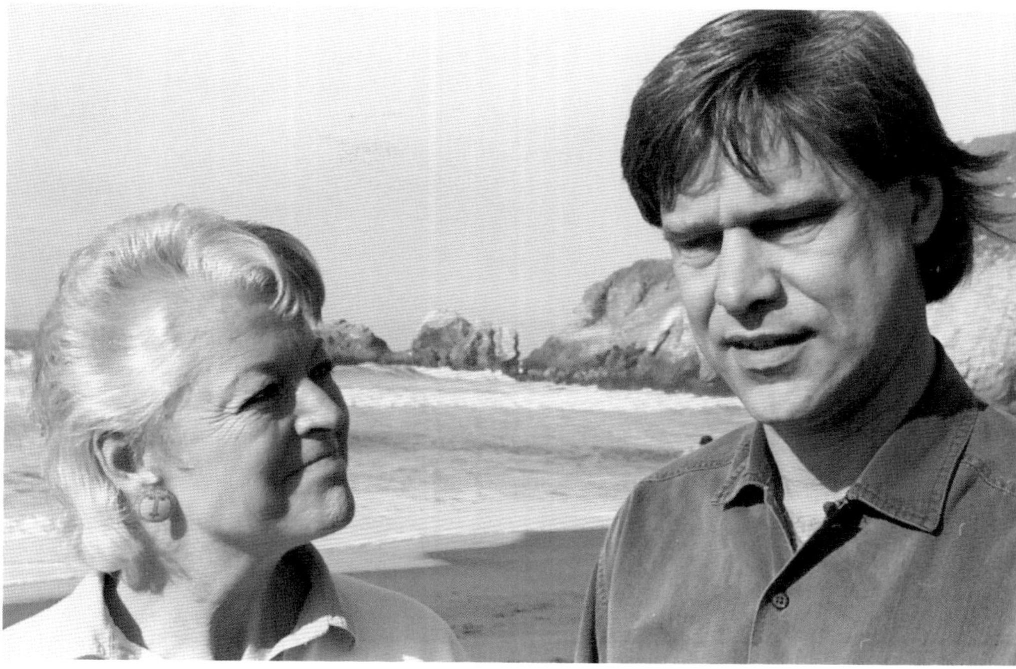

Peter Loeb

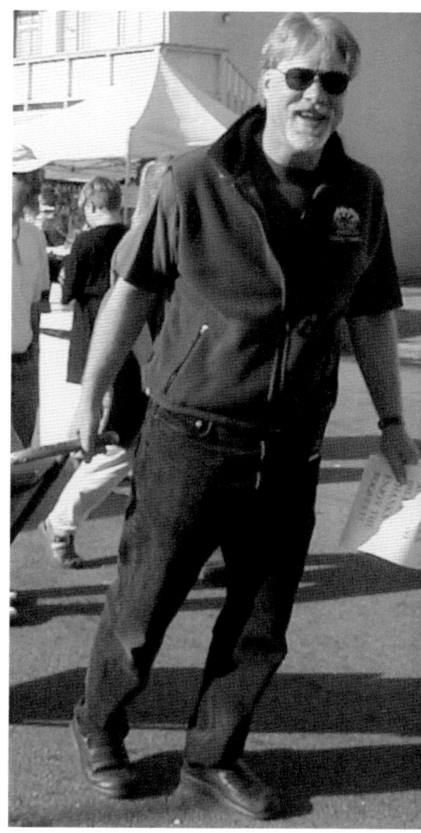

Peter Loeb moved to Pacifica in 1975 and almost immediately became part of the fabric of the city. "I've always been somewhat of an activist, and it didn't take long for me to become involved in Pacifica politics," he said. "I started to pay attention when proposed redevelopment of Rockaway would replace the house I lived in with a parking lot." He read the *Pacifica Tribune*, started attending meetings, and was instrumental in organizing the Friends of Pacifica political action group. "It dawned on us that we really couldn't make a difference unless we were on the city council," he said. That realization resulted in Loeb and two other leaders of the Friends group—Jeannette Warden and Chuck Curry—being elected to the council in 1982. Loeb served two terms and retired from the council in 1990, having also been mayor twice. "One of the finest moments I had as a new and very green mayor was the dedication of Sweeney Ridge as part of the Golden Gate National Recreation Area," he said. He was also greatly involved in the original creation of the Pacific Coast Fog Fest as a marketing magnet and event for Pacifica. The humorous name of the festival was a bone of contention for many, but it stuck through more than two decades of different organizational direction. Loeb has been a constant fan and leader of the Fog Fest, serving as president of the Fog Fest Organizing Group for five years. "The Fog Fest remains one of my favorite accomplishments," he said. "One I share with many other people including the dedicated FFOG board members." Since 1985, he has worked with Allen/Loeb Associates, a consulting firm providing program evaluation and other services primarily in the areas of substance abuse, mental health, and HIV. He and his life partner, Nancy Morrison, continue to be involved in local Pacifica issues.

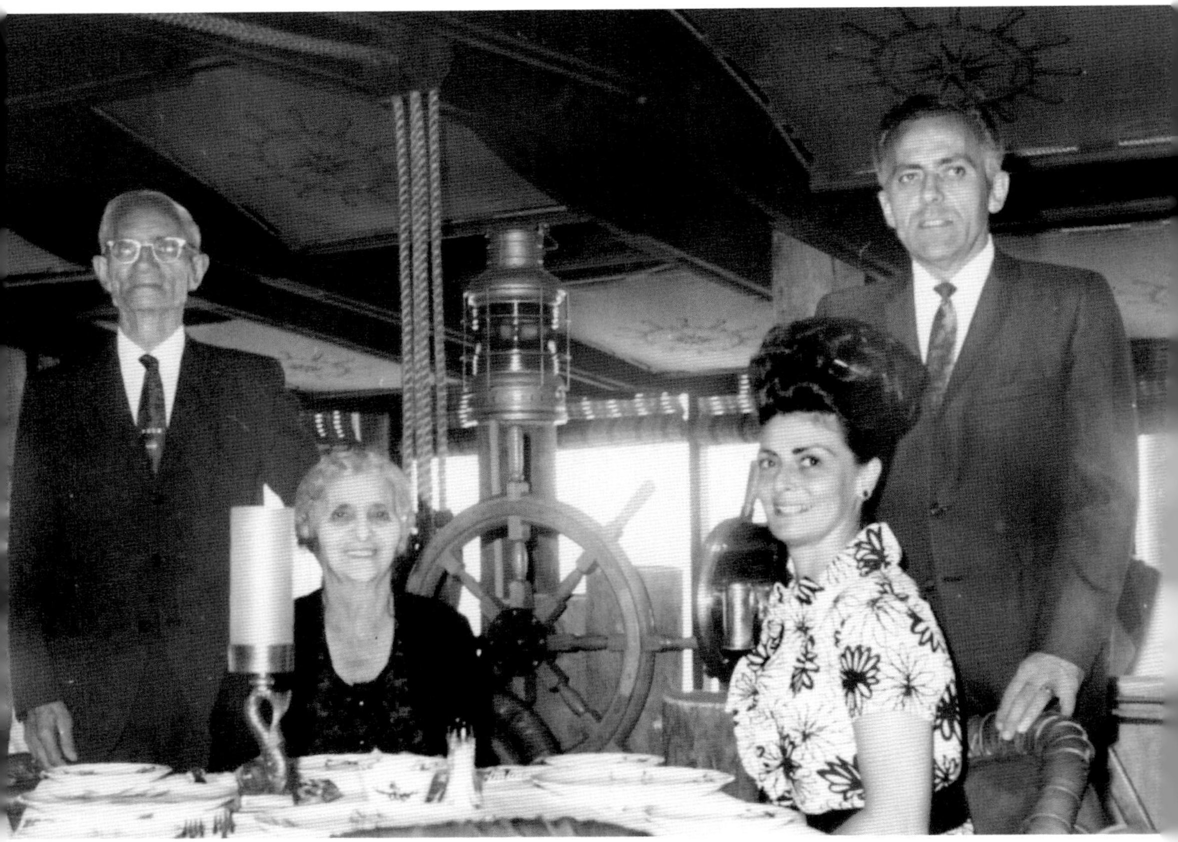

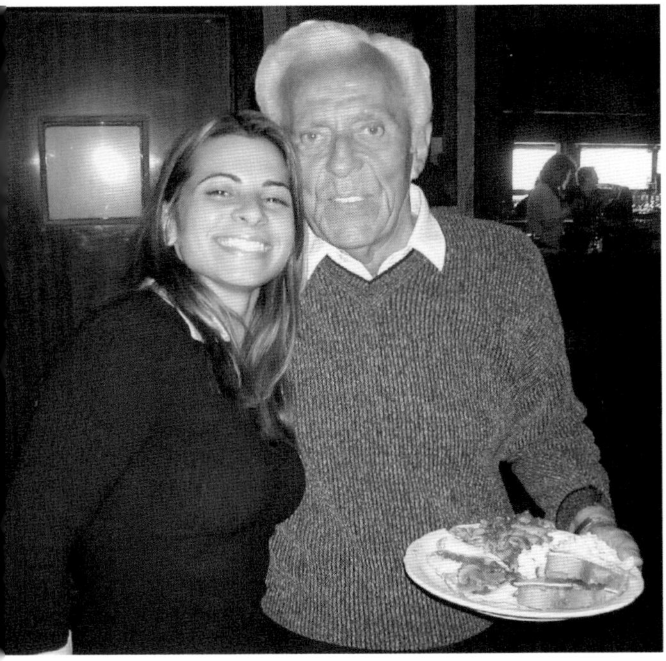

The Gust Family

The Gust family has dominated Pacifica's business and political environment for decades. In the photograph above, Nick and his wife, Lorraine, are on the right. Nick's parents, Charles and Anastasia, are on the left. The family's restaurant business has been in operation since 1927. Nick became a politician and served as mayor of Pacifica four times, even though he was opposed to the incorporation itself. He and Lorraine ran the family restaurant for decades, and, now in his 90s, he still can be found holding court there. His son Chuck and Chuck's daughter Lena continue to operate Nick's Restaurant and the Sea Breeze Motel. Nick Gust and his granddaughter Lena are pictured at the left.

Cal Hinton

A former fire chief who became a city council member, Cal Hinton owned a large parcel of property in the middle of Pacifica though his address was actually on Hinton Ranch Road. He ran for office multiple times, never giving up until he finally won a seat on the council. A contentious development issue, in which he backed a proposal to turn the Rockaway Quarry into a mixed-used project, led to him not winning a reelection bid in 2008, two years after fellow council members Barbara Carr and Maxine Gonsalves also lost their reelection bids because of their support for the Rockaway Quarry development proposal.

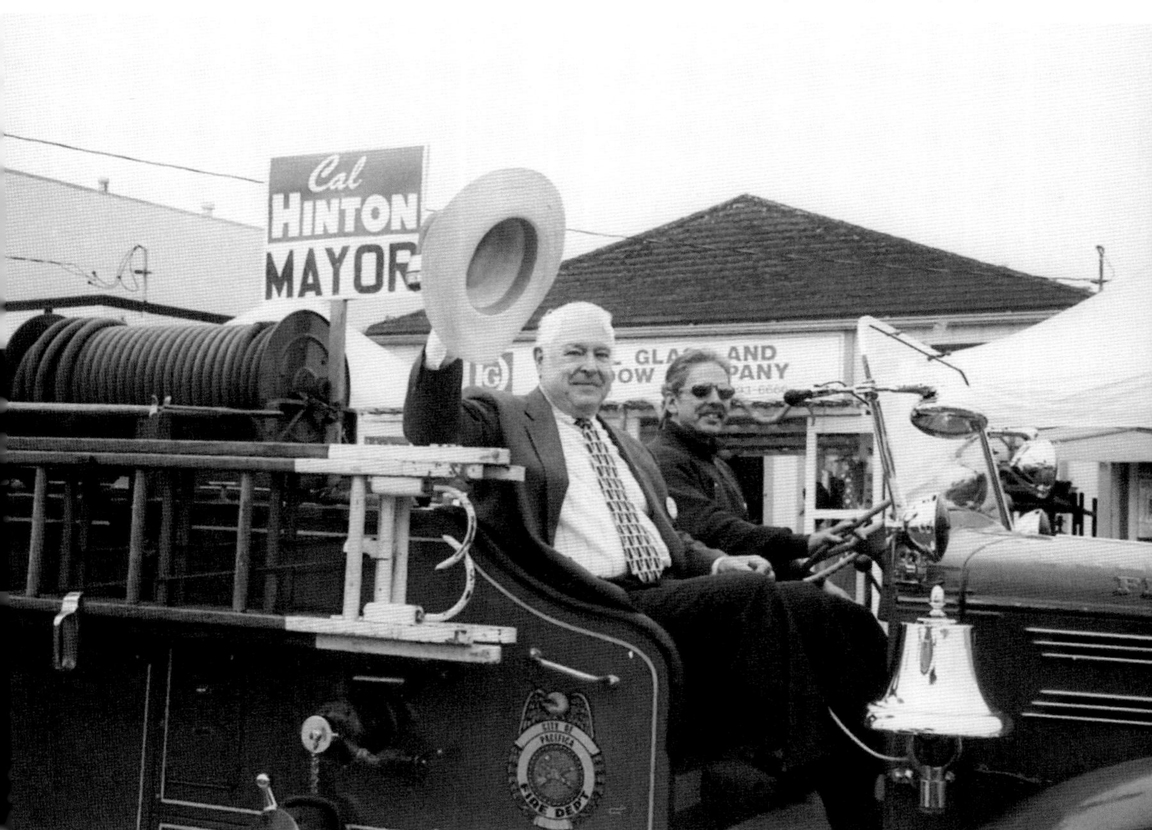

Grace McCarthy

She was a teacher who became one of the icons of Pacifica. Known as "Lady Grace," she was respected for her political acumen and devotion to Pacifica. Her husband, Carl, took thousands of people on personal journeys up to Sweeney Ridge Discovery Point, making the case for it to be established as an official historical site. Grace, meanwhile, was mayor of Pacifica three times and helped shape the distinct personality of the coastal town. While she was still alive, the city established the Grace McCarthy Vista Point on Sharp Park Road, looking over the area that stretches to the pier and the Pacific Ocean. In the photograph below, she is pictured at that location. She was fond of saying that as a young girl, she met Pancho Villa in Mexico, which offers a glimpse into her longevity. A powerful three-time mayor, she was often called "the heart of Pacifica."

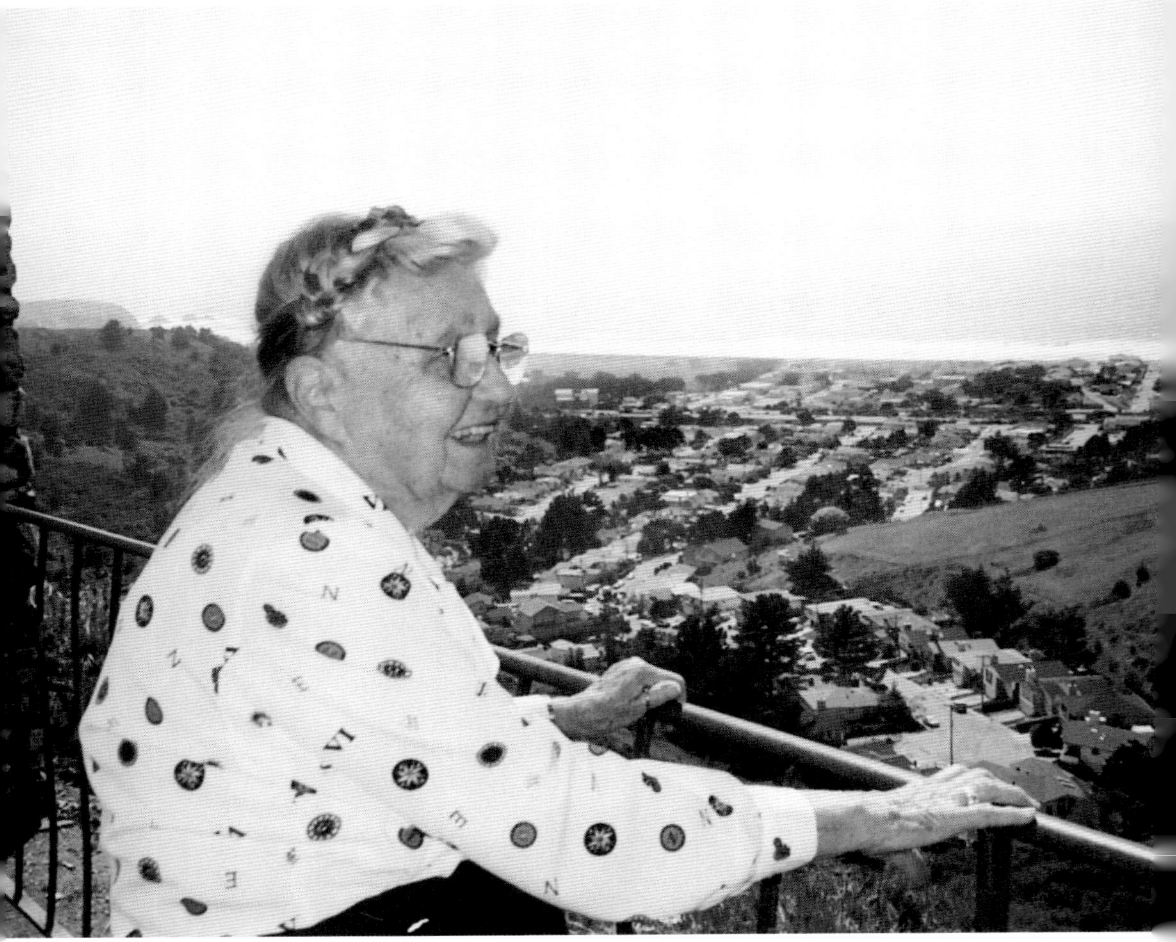

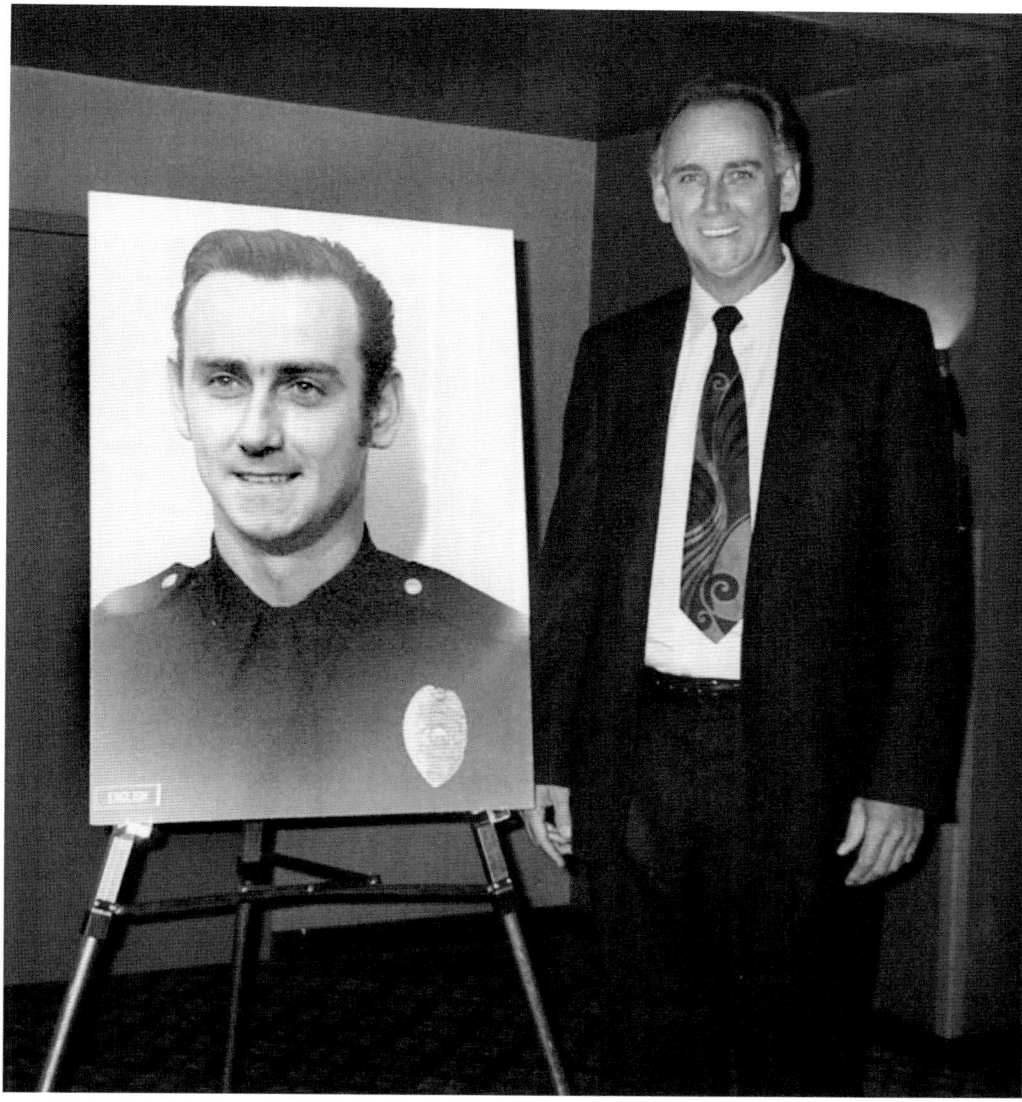

Charlie English

Charlie English is the only Pacifica police chief who also became the city manager. A native son who attended grade school in the building that eventually housed the police department, English joined the city's law enforcement arm in 1966 and made it all the way to top cop. "My new office over there is just about where I was sitting when I was in the third grade," he said. A charter member of the Kiwanis Club, an avid golfer, and also a lawyer, English was hired as the city manager in addition to his police job in 1994 due to budget concerns. Two years later, he retired from the police department but maintained his job as the city manager.

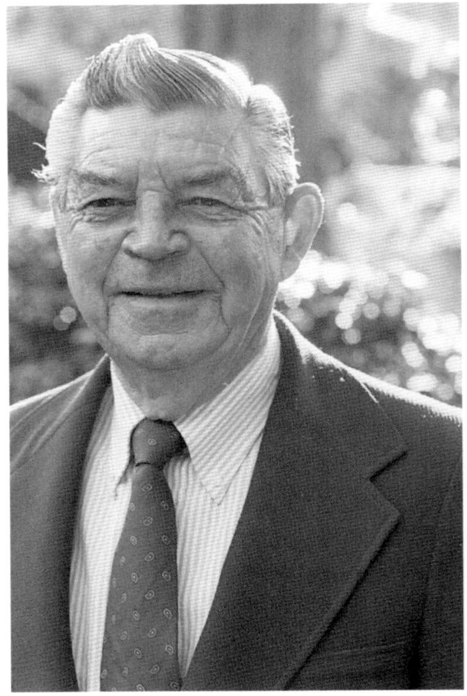

Russ Conroy

Folks in Pacifica voted for Russ Conroy more than any other politician in the city's history, even eclipsing Congressman Tom Lantos, who served for 30 years until his death in 2008. Conroy, on the other hand, was elected and reelected to the North Coast County Water District enough times to snag a spot on a list of longest-serving California elected officials. From 1955, two years before the City of Pacifica was actually incorporated, through 1998 when he retired, Russ Conroy's name was synonymous with the local water district. During his tenure, he also was the president of the board for 32 years, from 1960 until 1991, and again for a single term in 1995. After retiring, Conroy was honored by being named director emeritus by his fellow directors, giving him the honorary ability to continue attending meetings and giving advice. His expertise at offering advice may have stemmed from his career as a bartender at Nick's and Winter's Tavern. He once said, "It may sound funny, but during my many years behind the bar, I've learned to separate phonies from the real people."

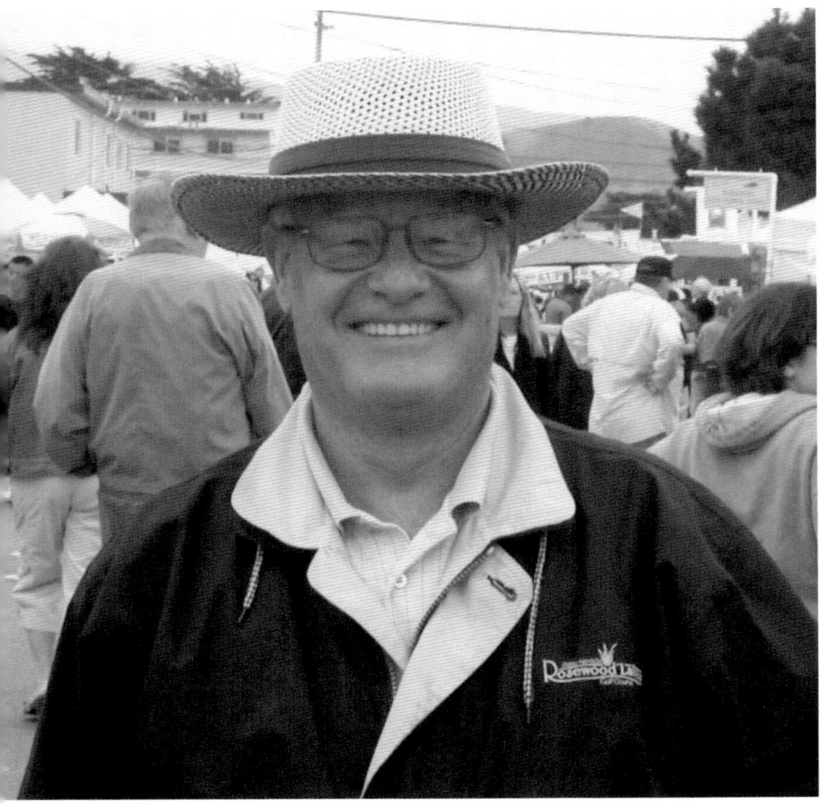

Fred Howard

Fred Howard was on the city council from 1978 to 1982 and again from 1986 to 1990. His experience also included a stint on the Pacifica Parks, Beaches and Recreation Commission, as well as director of the Pacifica Youth Service Bureau. He did not return to the council in 1990, coming in fourth for a race that had three seats. For years, he remained active and vocal about his views of Pacifica. He later was a leader in the Fog Fest Organizing Group and served as president of that popular event for several years. That experience led to his eventual job managing the events at the Moscone Center in San Francisco, a job that he willingly tells friends he loves.

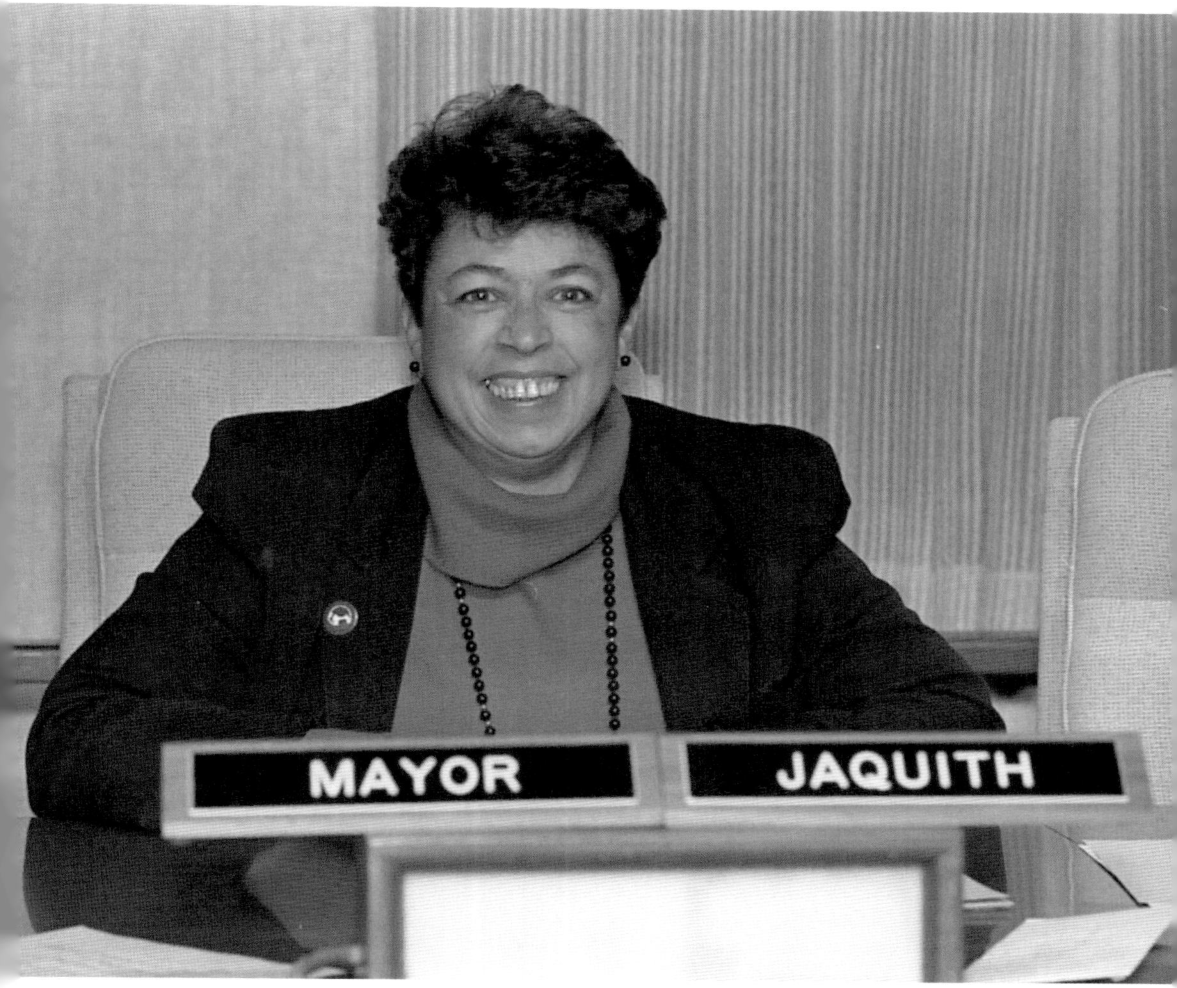

Ginny Jaquith

Ginny Jaquith was a parks and recreation department employee who went on to become a city council member and community activist. While being very popular as a politician, she still was recalled during the heated debate over the Lighting and Landscaping Tax proposed in 1992. Along with John Schneider, Michael Vasey, and Jon Galehouse, Jaquith was recalled, but she never lost a strong popularity with Pacificans in general. As a longtime advocate for the Pacific Coast Fog Fest and a supporter of the Pacifica Resource Center and the Pacificans Care nonprofit, not to mention her work with the Pacifica Rotary Club, Jaquith maintained a healthy connection to the inner workings of the city. Her reputation helped get her appointed to an empty seat on the city council in 2012 as an interim member and by all accounts she served the community well during that time.

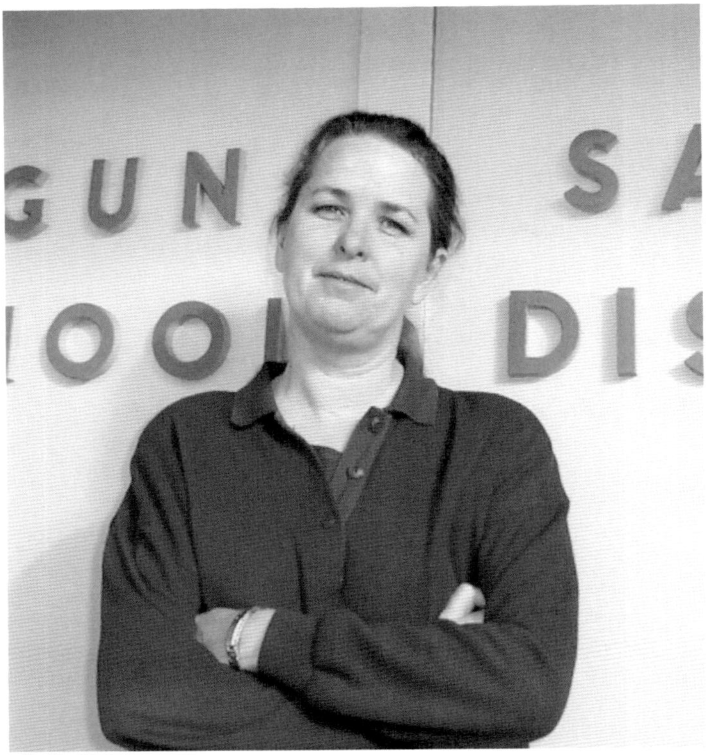

Julie Lancelle
Part of the all-woman city council in 1992, Julie Lancelle served on both the city council and the Laguna Salada Union School District. She did not run for reelection during the end of her first tenure on the city council and was subsequently appointed to a seat on the elementary school board. Later, she reenergized her interest and won a chance to go back to the city council. Active for nearly 20 years in elective politics, Lancelle decided not to run for reelection although she continues to stay involved as an active citizen on certain local projects.

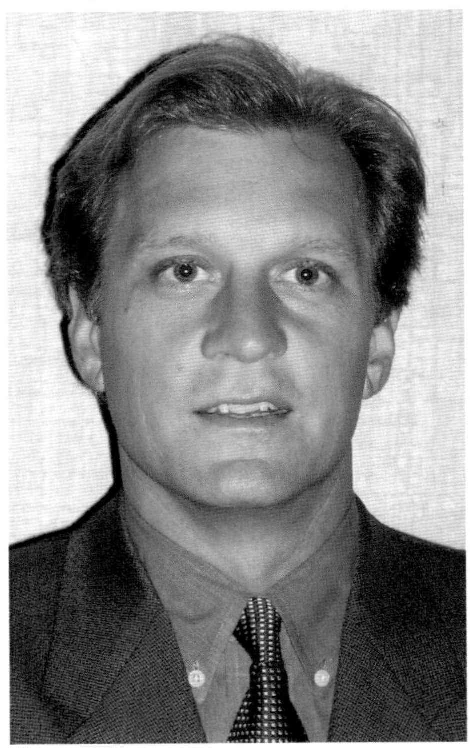

Jim Vreeland
A former planning commissioner who won a seat on the city council, James "Jim" Vreeland was elected three times and served as mayor three times, too. An accomplished surfer whose job was with the Environmental Protection Agency, Vreeland was an immensely popular councilmember, judging by the volume of votes he earned. Health issues caused him to resign from the city council in 2012.

CHAPTER TWO

Pacifica Arts and Music

As a bedroom community on the outskirts of San Francisco, Pacifica has always been known as a home for artists of all persuasions. The city created the Sanchez Art Center as a home for artists, with studios leased to local artists who display their work at regular gallery viewings. The art center is also home to the Mildred Owen Performing Arts Center, named for another legendary local profiled in this book. Artists and musicians are a dominant part of the community fabric of Pacifica, and dozens of individuals have made lasting impressions through the years.

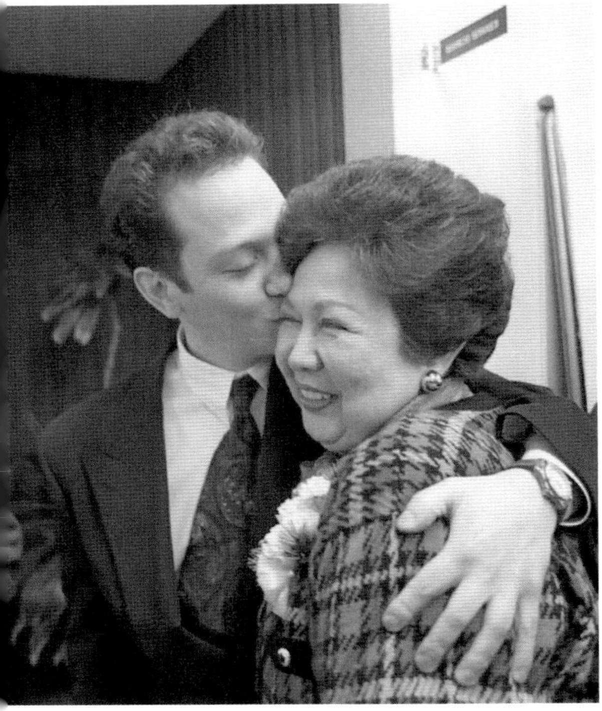

Rob Schneider

Hollywood funnyman Rob Schneider, who grew up in Pacifica and graduated from high school at Terra Nova, has given back to the community through the creation of the Rob Schneider Music Foundation. The stand-up comedian was a regular cast member on *Saturday Night Live* throughout the 1990s, eventually moving on to become a movie star in films such as *The Hot Chick* and *Deuce Bigalow, Male Gigolo*. He also has appeared in many of his buddy Adam Sandler's movie hits, such as *Grown Ups* and *Fifty First Dates*. But it is his continuing connection to Pacifica through his music foundation that has kept him involved in his hometown and makes him truly legendary. More than a million dollars has been funneled to Pacifica public schools in 10 years, with the Rob Schneider Music Foundation paying the salaries of two music teachers and jump-starting the dormant band program at the middle-school level. This has reinvigorated the high school marching band programs since the middle schools act as feeder schools for the high schools. Rob Schneider's mother, Pilar, was a longtime school board member, his brother John Schneider was a city council member in the early 1990s, and his sister April has followed in the footsteps of their late father, Marvin, who was a prominent realtor in town. Another brother is a cartoonist in San Francisco. While many celebrities give back through their involvement in national and international charities, Rob Schneider's dedication to a hometown need makes him very special to the heart of Pacifica. As a high school student, Rob played the trombone, and he saw the constant cutting of music and art programs as an educational emergency that he could address. Bringing his star power back home to Pacifica allowed him to do just that.

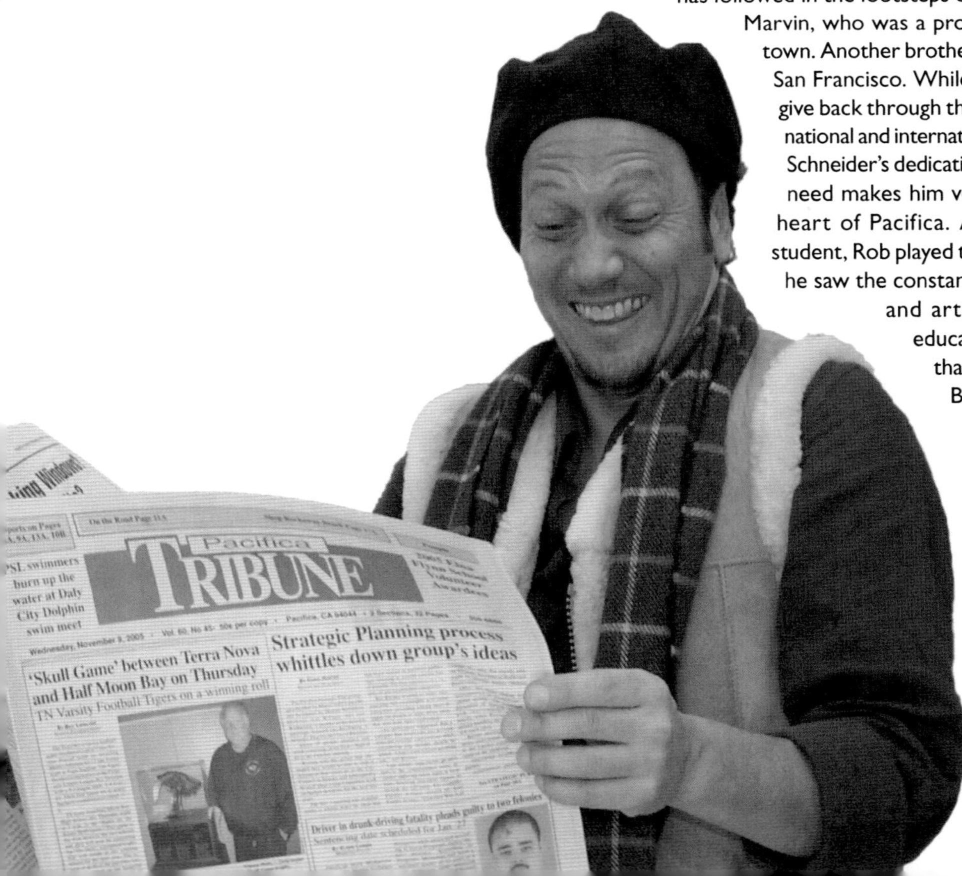

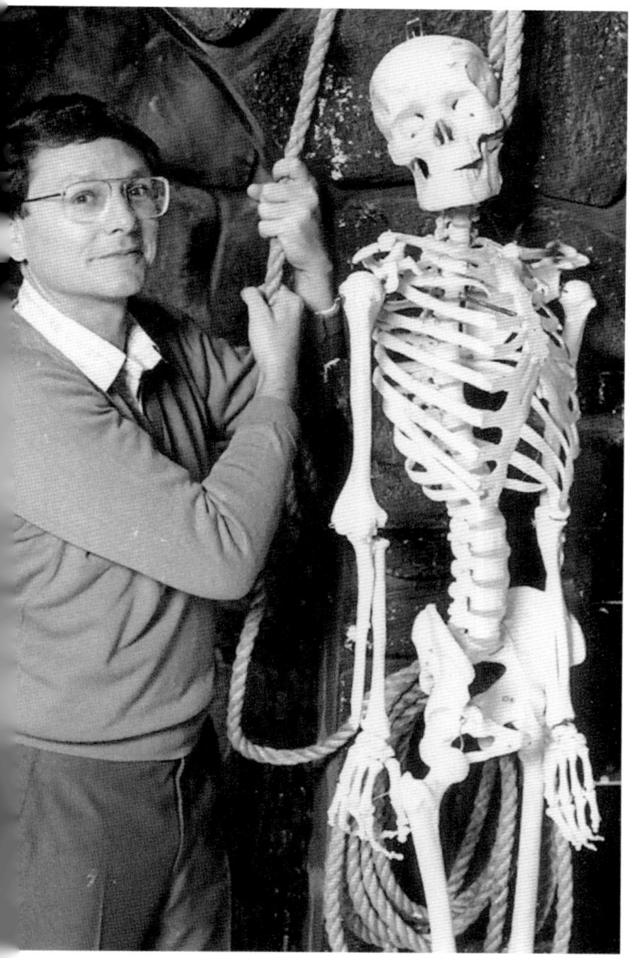

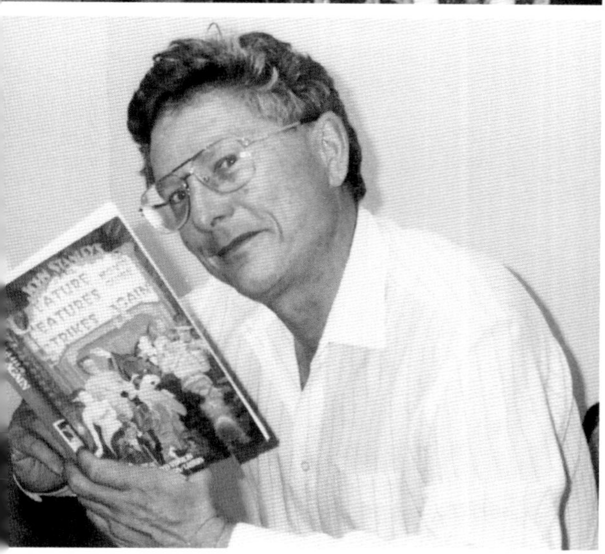

John Stanley

For a long time, John Stanley enjoyed scaring people all over the Bay Area. As the host of the immensely popular *Creature Features* television show from 1979 to 1985, Stanley met and interviewed many "famous monsters of film land" while presenting spooky movies to adoring audiences. He also worked for the *San Francisco Chronicle* as an entertainment writer and editor, something he still does on a freelance basis to this day. A prolific writer, Stanley turned his love of movies and his horror background into several books and movie compendiums. He wrote novels, made his own horror movie, and sold more than 2,000 customized crossword puzzles. A list of celebrities he has interviewed through the years would encompass most of Hollywood, and his deep love of the entertainment business is clear in everything he writes. In fact, one can purchase collections of John Stanley's taped interviews and his personal recollections of times spent with Clint Eastwood, Chuck Norris, James Stewart, and dozens of other stars. A longtime Pacifica resident, Stanley has a movie collection that encompasses an entire wall in his home. A big supporter of the local public access community television station PCTV, John is often seen helping out on various projects to raise awareness on Pacifica Community Television. That is remarkable considering his own schedule continues to be busy. In 2013, he was marketing his book *The Gang That Shot Up Hollywood* and republishing a book he wrote about Humphrey Bogart and Peter Lorre solving a 1948 Hollywood murder. For many years, he was also a very popular Elderhostel teacher, giving film histories to eager, traveling seniors. "My Elderhostel/Road Scholar work has really slowed these past two years and I'm trying to get some other projects rolling," he said. Few Pacificans have maintained such a hectic pace of literary production as John Stanley. (Courtesy of John Stanley.)

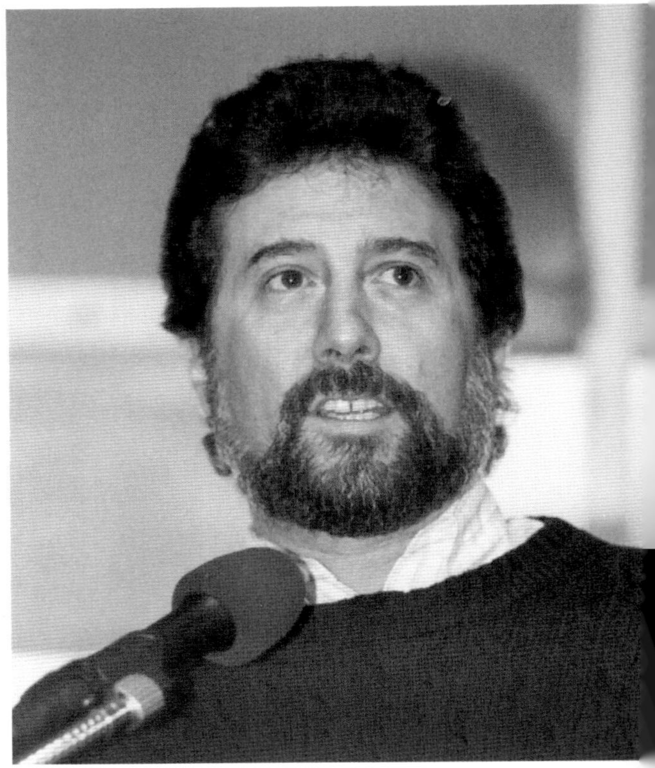

Dave Sholin

Dave Sholin was the last journalist to interview John Lennon; the Beatles member was murdered five hours after sitting for an interview with Sholin in New York City on December 8, 1980. Sholin has had an extraordinary career in the music business, working for several radio stations and becoming the national music director for RKO Radio. He and others who worked at the *Gavin Report* eventually bought the trade publication and rebranded it *Gavin* magazine. In 1995, he was inducted into the Rock 'n' Roll Hall of Fame radio section and in 2008, he was tapped to be in the Bay Area Radio Hall of Fame. Sholin's classic radio voice is instantly recognizable and he has often been asked to moderate political campaign panels.

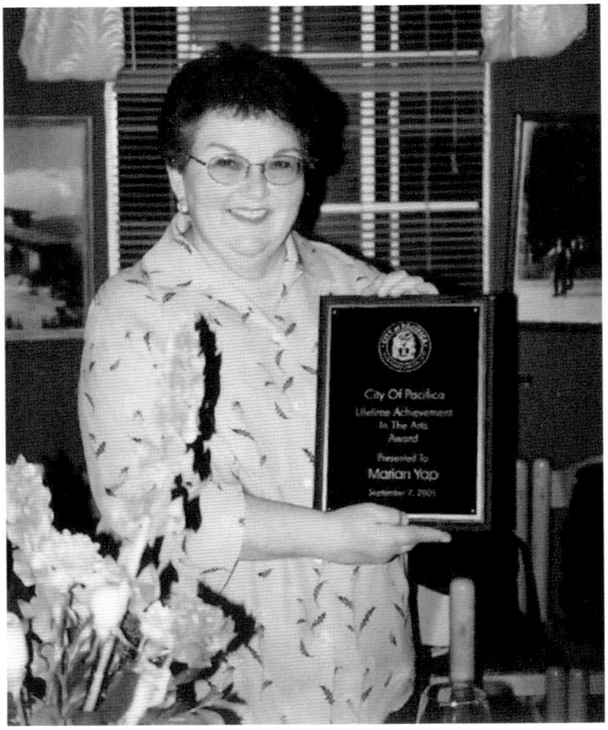

Marian Yap

A longtime artist who has been involved in the Pacifica art scene as well as the broader San Mateo County art scene, Marian Yap received a Lifetime Achievement in the Arts Award from the City of Pacifica for her longtime dedication to the arts. "Whether I am doing an abstract, a figurative image or a landscape, I am always amazed at the versatility of pastels, the lasting brilliance of the colors and the variation of possible techniques and tools," she explains about her art on her online blog. Yap is currently the president of the Peninsula Chapter of the Women's Caucus for the Arts and a frequent exhibitor at the Coastal Art League Gallery in Half Moon Bay.

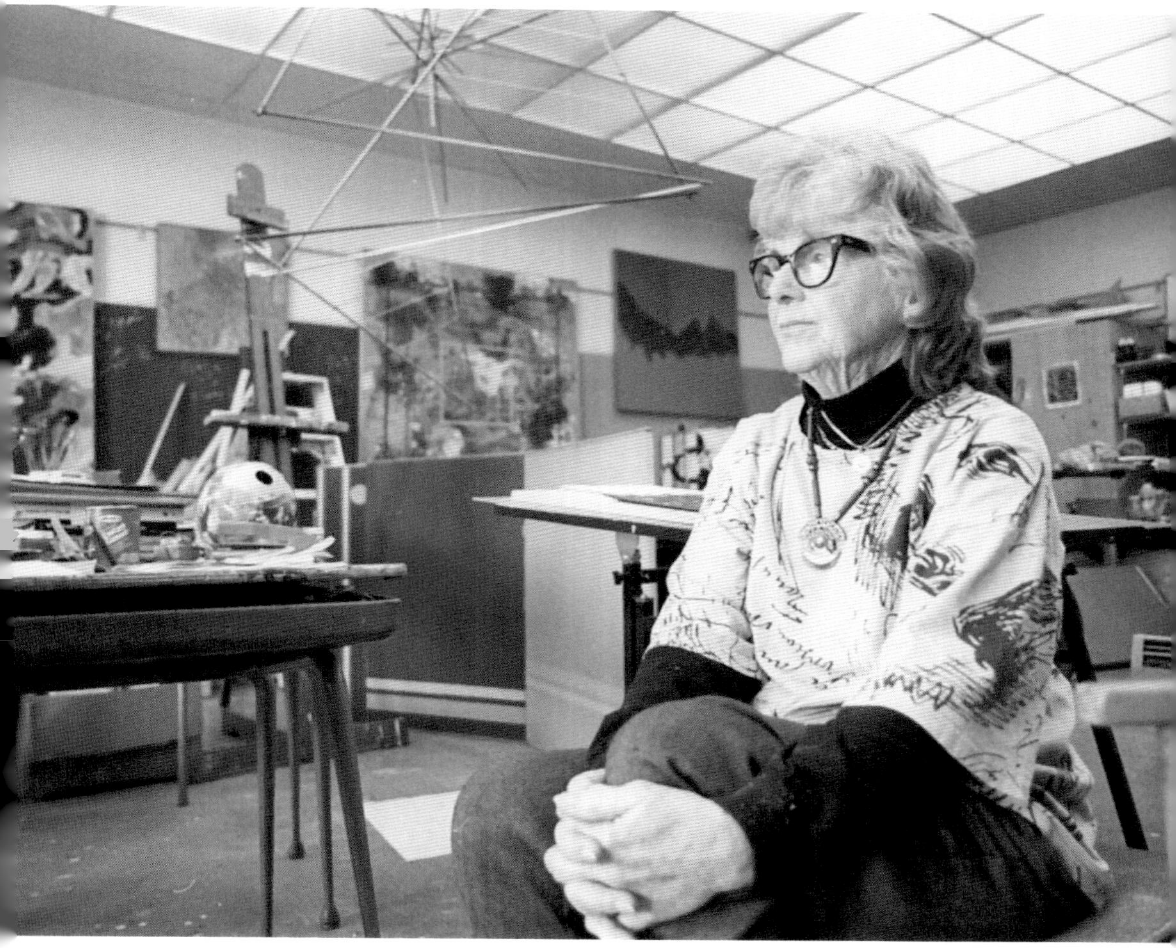

Mary Harris
There is no one quite like Mary Harris. A talented artist and art teacher, Harris is also a political rebel who advocates the World Federalist Movement. She lives in the beautiful—but hard to reach—Shelter Cove area of Pacifica. Her studio in the Sanchez Art Center is one an original, and she is a constant presence at art shows and events. Now in her 90s, she is a legend to the many Pacificans who know her, whether in the environmental, political, or art realms. For everyone, she is an inspiration to keep on moving forward, physically, artistically, and intellectually.

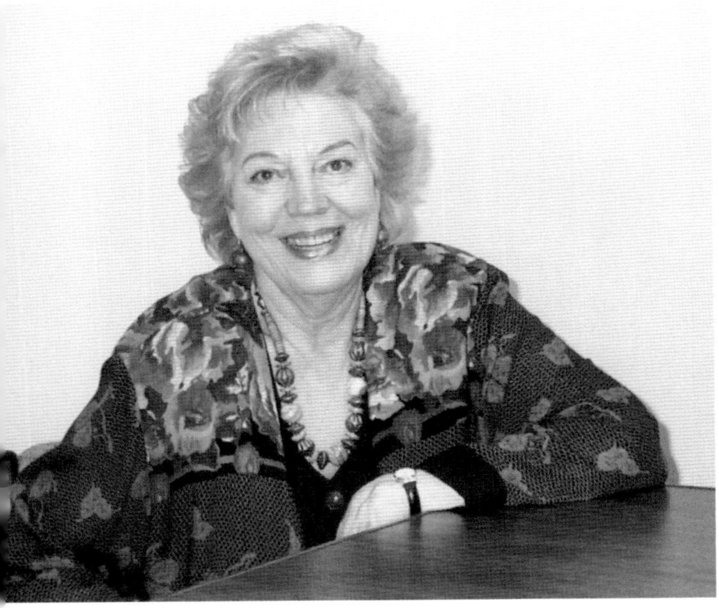

Mildred Owen

No one was more instrumental in the development and promotion of the arts in Pacifica than Mildred Owen. A polished singer, Owen was a much sought-after singing teacher at the college and professional levels, training generations of singers. Her true passion was providing outlets for other performers to entertain Pacificans through the Pacifica Arts and Heritage Council, which evolved into the Pacifica Performances group, which she guided for many years. After her death, the arts community named after her the performance space at the Sanchez Center for the Arts, calling it the Mildred Owen Concert Hall.

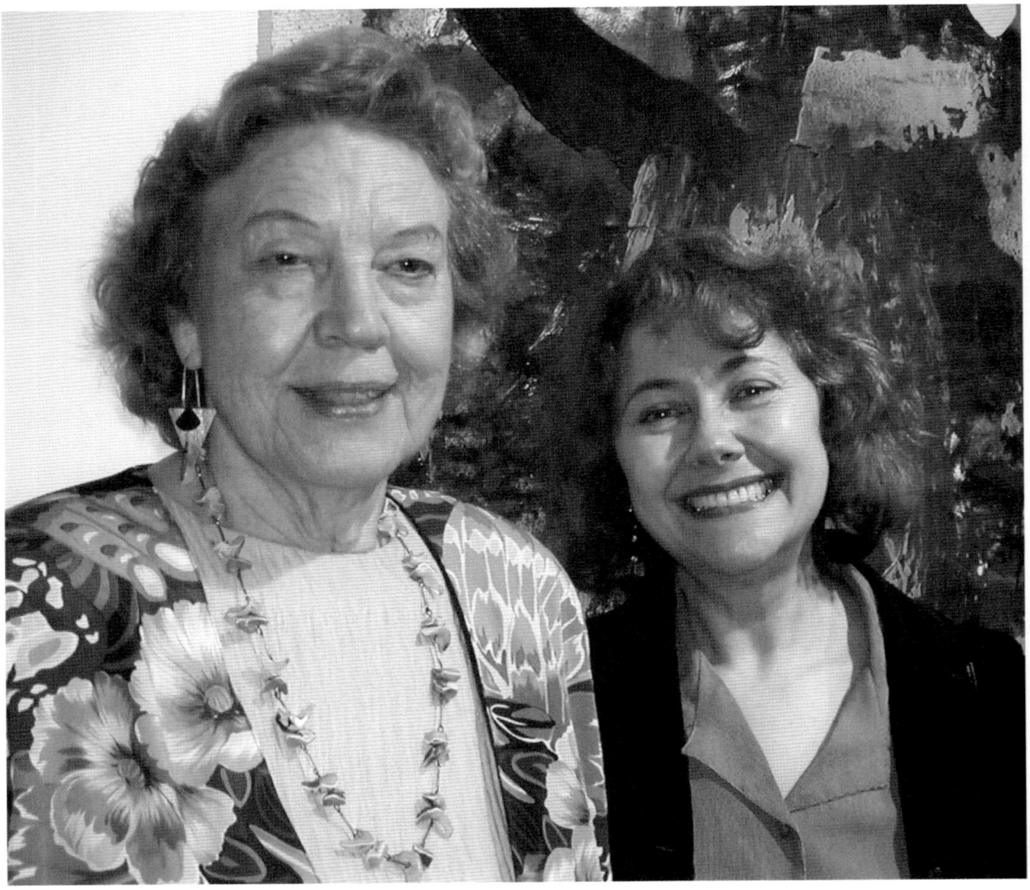

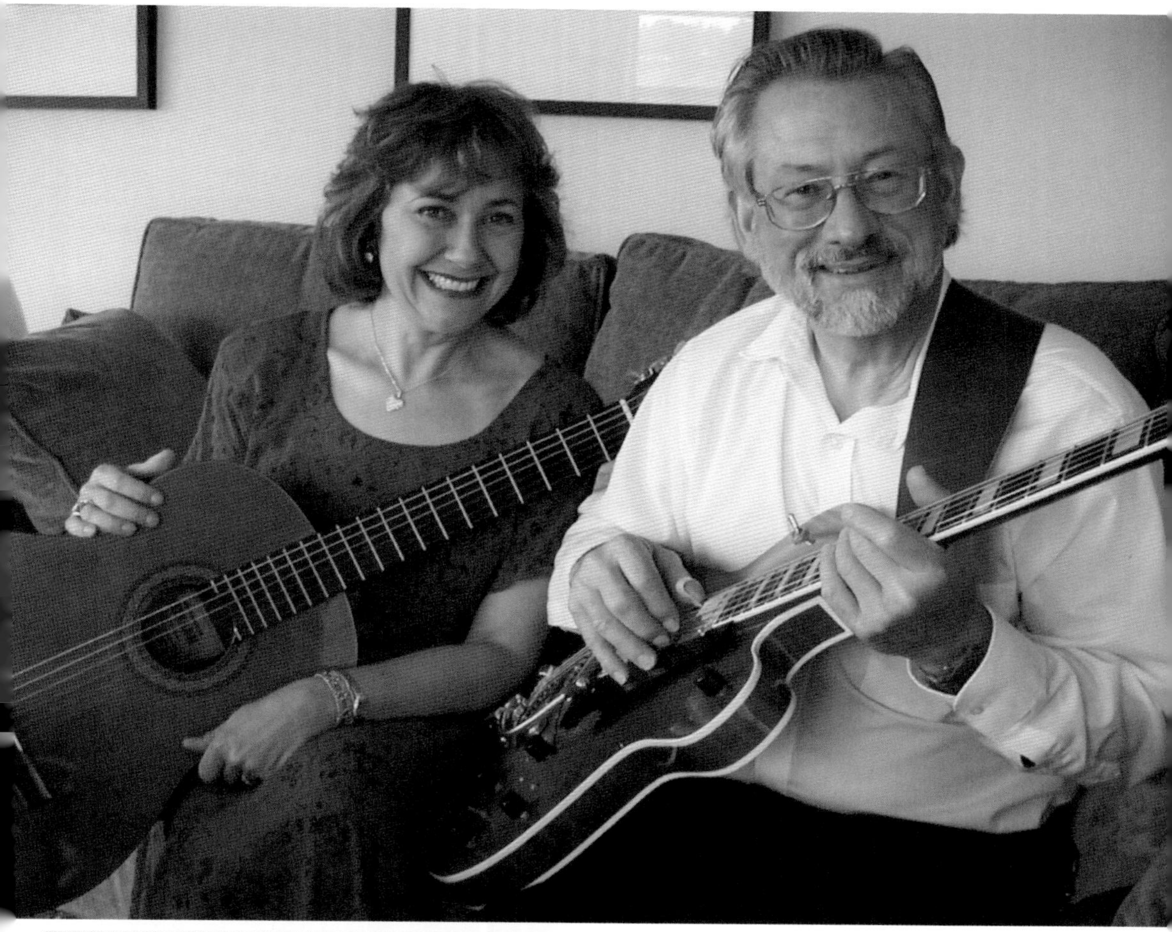

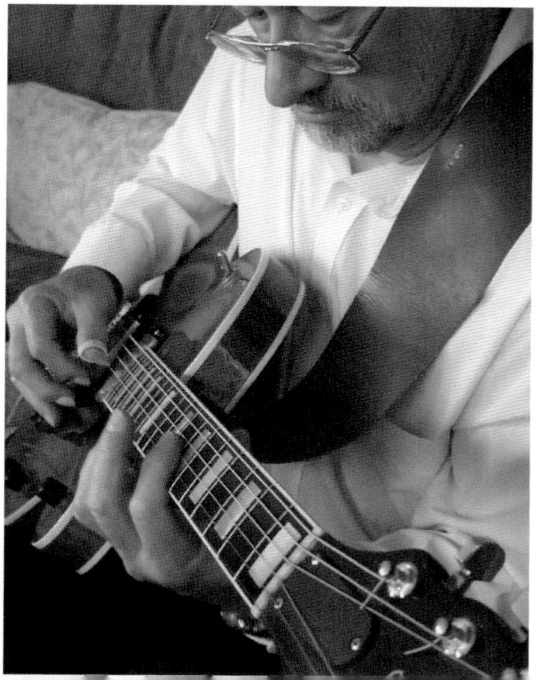

Jim and Morning Nichols

Jim Nichols is perhaps one of the greatest living proponents of the Chet Atkins finger picking style of guitar playing. An international star who attends music conferences around the world, Nichols has recorded multiple CDs and has performed at countless venues. His wife, Morning Nichols, is a singer whose reputation equals her husband's in popularity. Together, they perform regularly in Pacifica, San Francisco, and other places. Morning is also the current artistic director of the Pacifica Performances concert series, booking interesting acts year-long at the Mildred Owen Concert Hall.

Lynn Ruth Miller

It is not often that a stripper is considered an inspirational figure, but Lynn Ruth Miller is certainly that. As a senior citizen, Miller became inspired to explore her artistic interests long after most people are retired and watching television every night. She exploded in creative output, writing novels, painting, performing, and developing an internationally known comedy act. She began traveling to the Edinburgh Fringe Festival in Scotland and became a mainstay there. Doing the "Stripping Granny" act at comedy clubs throughout the Bay Area, she developed a reputation that evolved into somewhat of a comedy legend. Younger performers were inspired by her fearlessness and older peers decided to seek out their own bliss—if Lynn Ruth Miller could do what she loved, perhaps they could, too. Her early years were wounded by difficult relationships and depression, but as an older woman, she took life by the hand and guided it in the direction she sought.

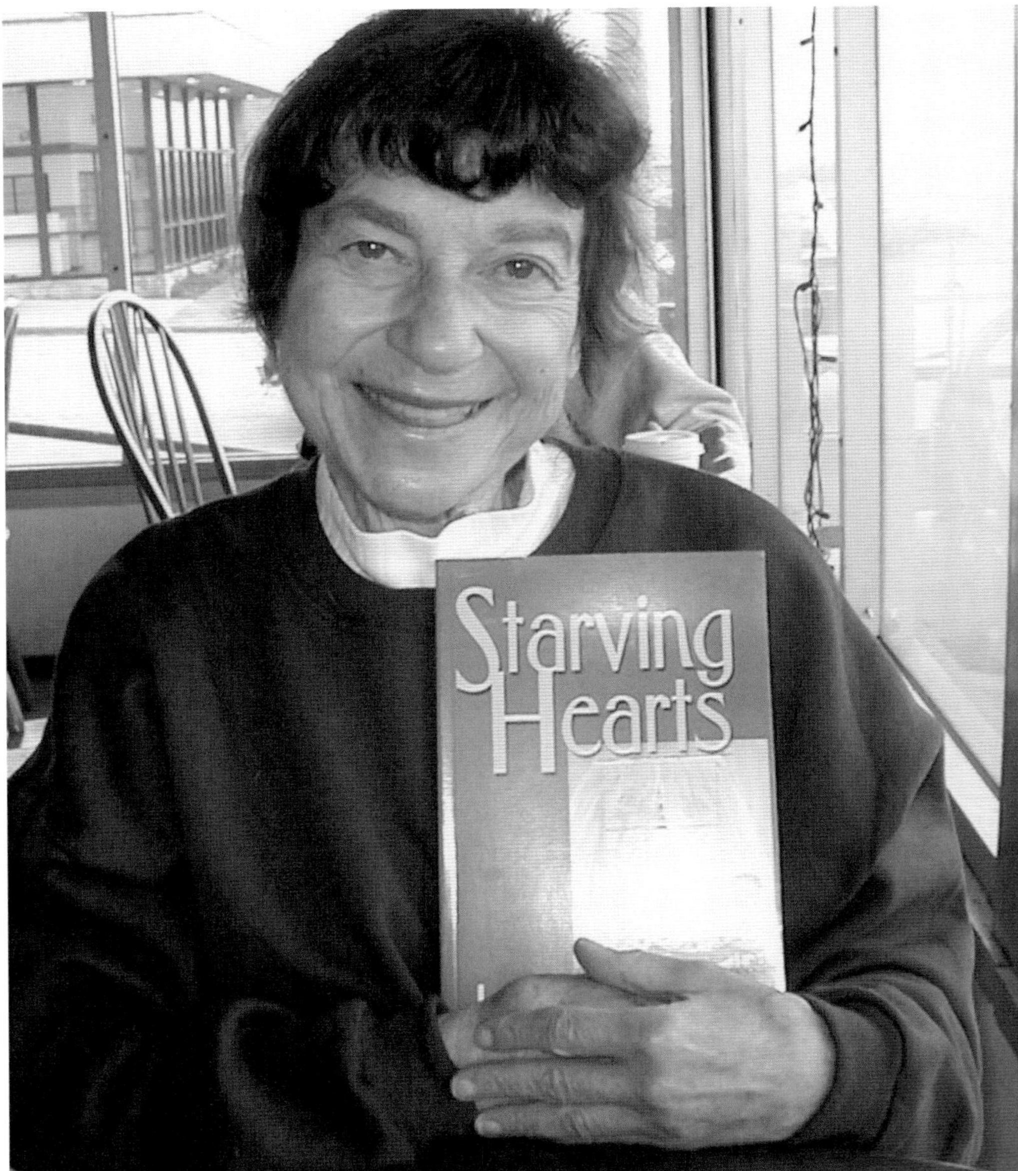

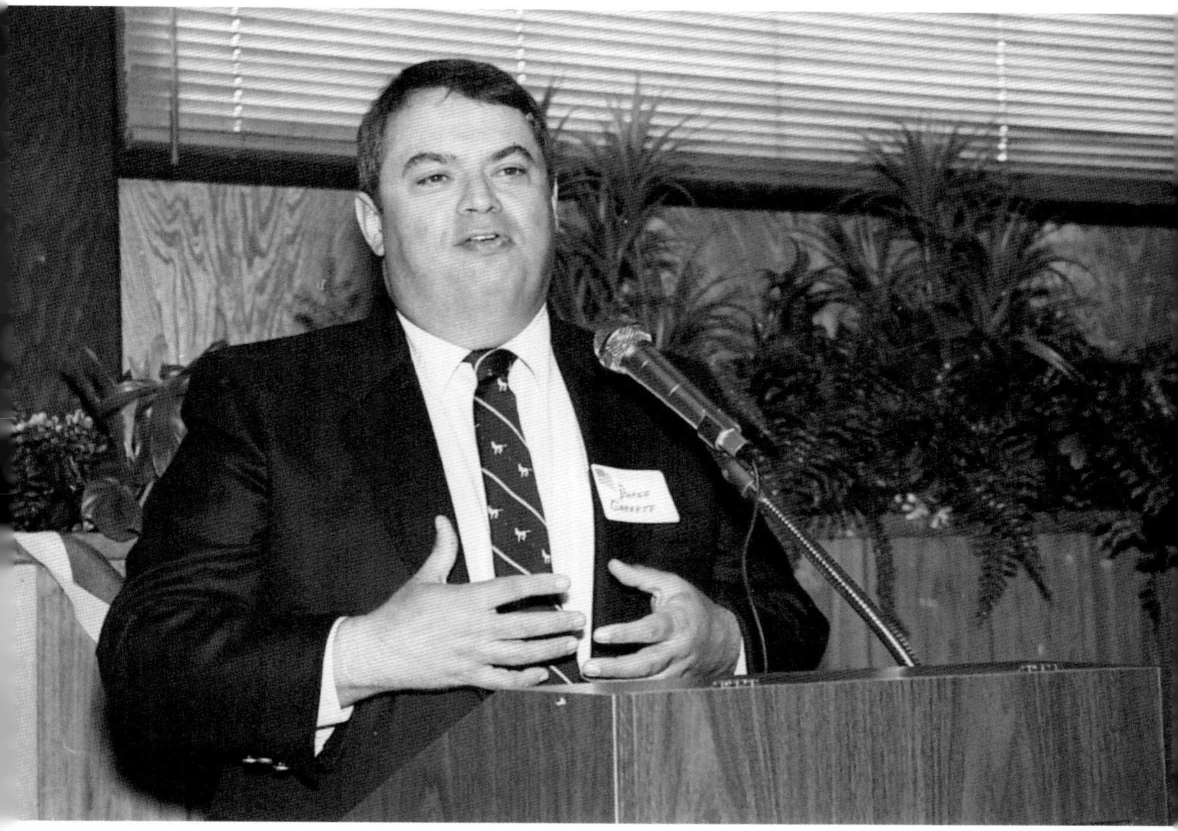

Duane Garrett
After popular radio talk show host Duane Garrett threw himself off the Golden Gate Bridge in the summer of 1995, apparently overwhelmed with financial problems stemming from a sports memorabilia business, Vice Pres. Al Gore called the radio station and spoke movingly about his longtime friend. A Pacifican who grew up living on Gypsy Hill overlooking the Pacific Ocean, Garrett became a lawyer and went on to work for the North Coast County Water District as its staff counsel. He was a staunch Democrat who moved into talk radio and became a powerful liberal voice on the mostly conservative airwaves. A political campaign activist with a gift for fundraising, Garrett worked on dozens of campaigns, including those of Walter Mondale, Bruce Babbitt, and Dianne Feinstein, and he was eventually a senior advisor to Vice Pres. Al Gore. A bear of a man with a vast appetite for just about everything, Garrett was an art collector, investor, and sports fanatic. His unexpected death at 49 stunned the San Francisco Bay Area because, like so many other suicides, it seemed so out-of-character for the beloved, brilliant, and often inspiring personality heard on the radio. Then California senator Dianne Feinstein called Garrett "larger than life" in a statement released after his death. "Duane was very special in my life," she said. "There are some people who are a 'one of'—God makes one of them and then throws away the mold. Duane Garrett was one of those. He enriched the bright tapestry of San Francisco in so many ways."

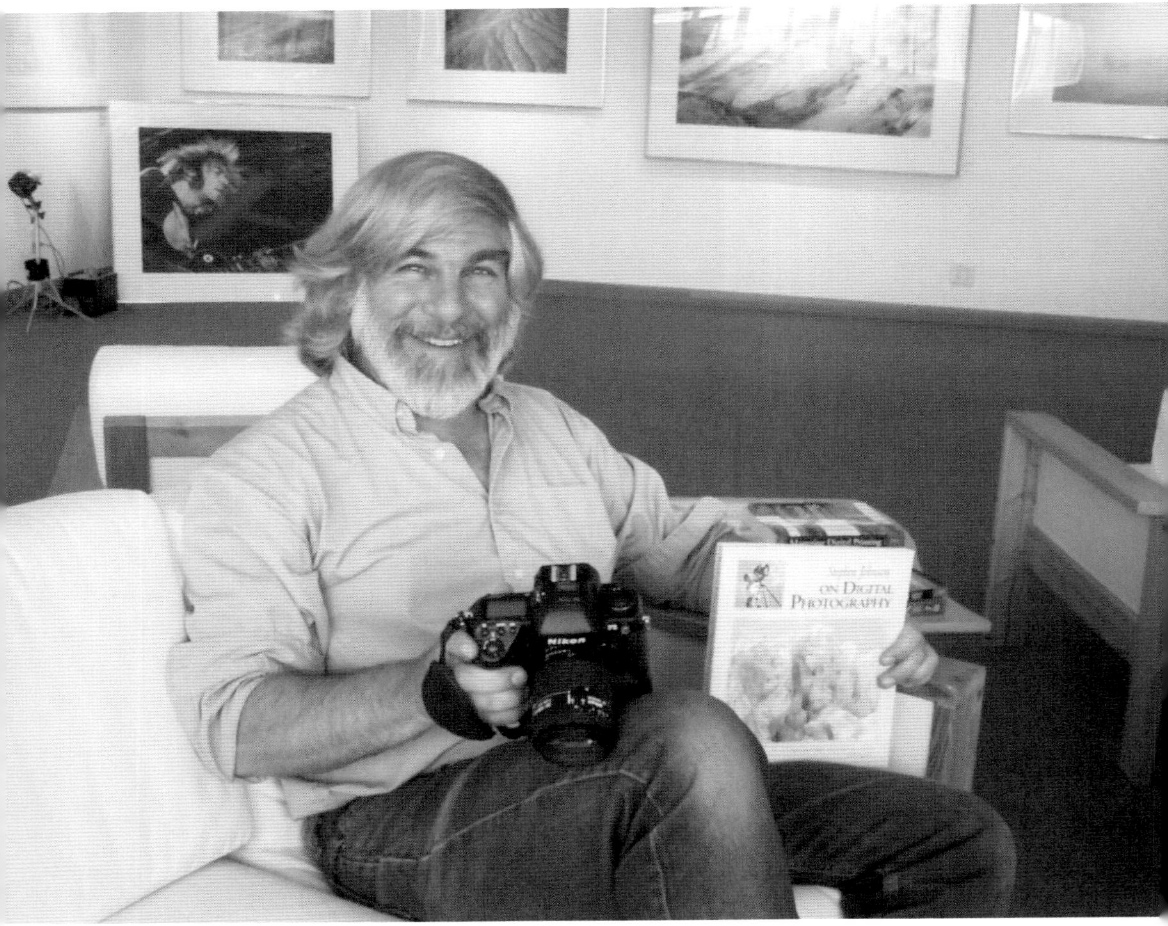

Stephen Johnson

Digital photographer Stephen Johnson could easily be called a pioneer in the landscape photography business, but he is also a tech wizard who championed digital photography before everyone else in the world threw away their film cameras. With a studio in Pacifica, Johnson holds classes and offers art gallery shows of his work. He has written textbooks for photographers and is in demand internationally as a lecturer and teacher. The amazing digital detail that goes into his high-definition landscape photographs captures images so precise that they can be enlarged on a wall and seem like a window on nature itself. A photograph of Mount Saint Helens gives the illusion that you could use a binocular to see across the volcanic crater. He is in demand as a technology tester as much as an artist and maintains an up-to-the-minute grasp of the newest digital equipment and methodology. In fact, he is one of the people responsible for pushing the limits of the photographic abilities of computers.

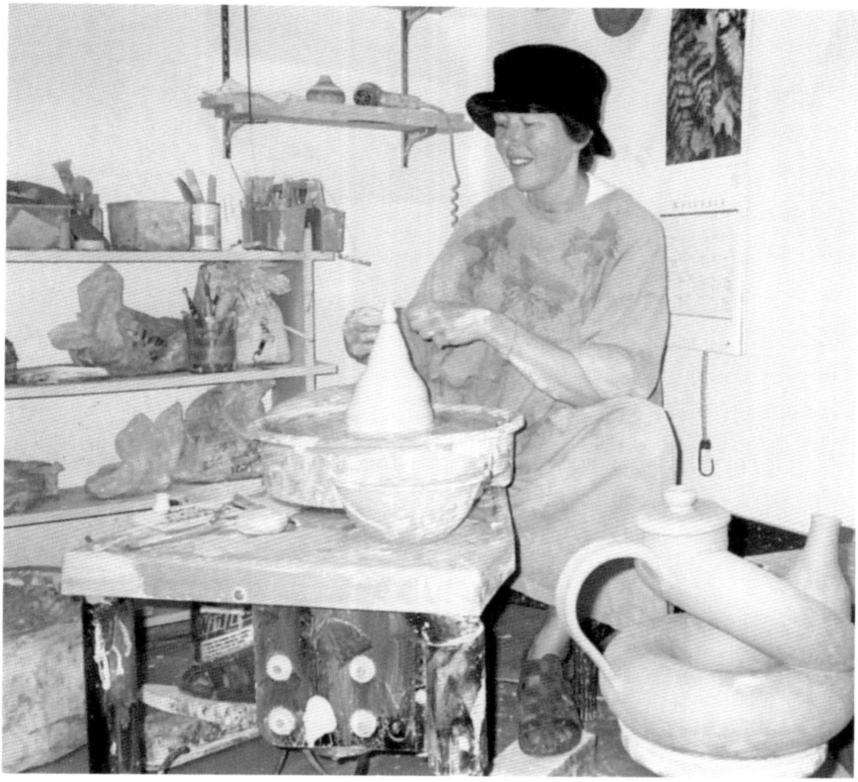

Stephen Johnson and Karina Berrner

Generations of students in Pacifica were fortunate to have Steve Johnson inspire them as their teacher. A longtime member of the alternative school, later named Ocean Shore School, Johnson also taught in the home school program and, after his retirement, he continued to teach at Sunset Ridge. His soft-spoken sincerity and deep caring for his students kept many of them as lifelong friends as they grew older. In addition to his teaching career, Johnson maintained a fascinating involvement in various historical re-enactment festivals, from the Renaissance Festival to the Dickens Faire. His expertise in calligraphy also was in high demand, both as an instructor and an artist. Johnson faced the tragic adversity of his wife's, Karina Berrner's, breast cancer with strength and brave support. A dynamic artist herself, Berrner documented her medical struggle, using various alternative treatments, writing a book about her battle, and inspiring those around her. Ultimately, she died and Johnson became a widower raising their young daughter, Sienna, by himself. Few who know Johnson, either as a friend or a teacher, doubt that his subtle impact on the community reaches far and wide.

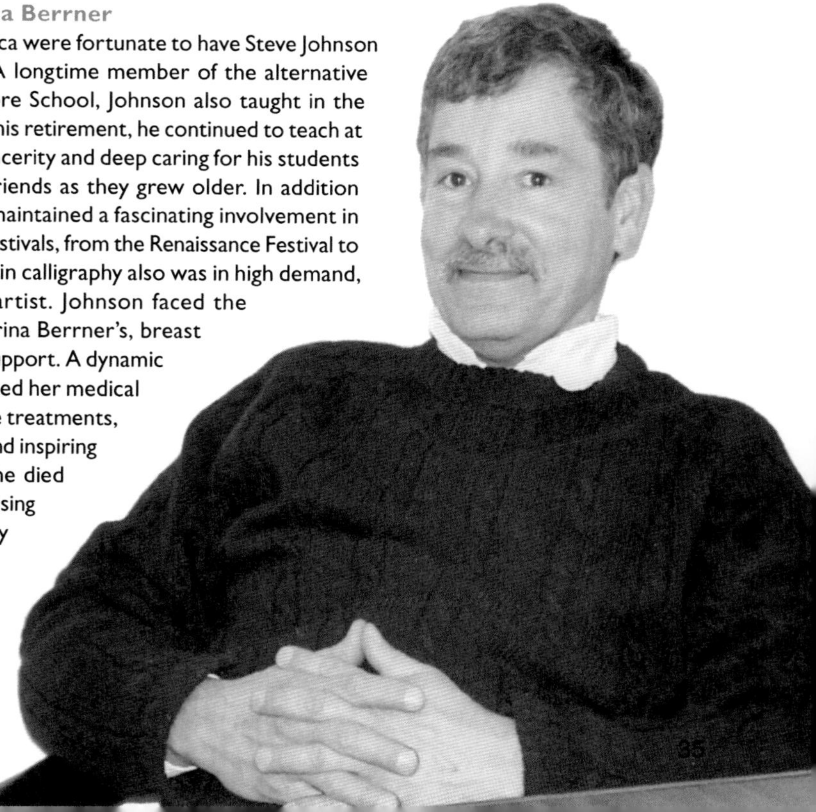

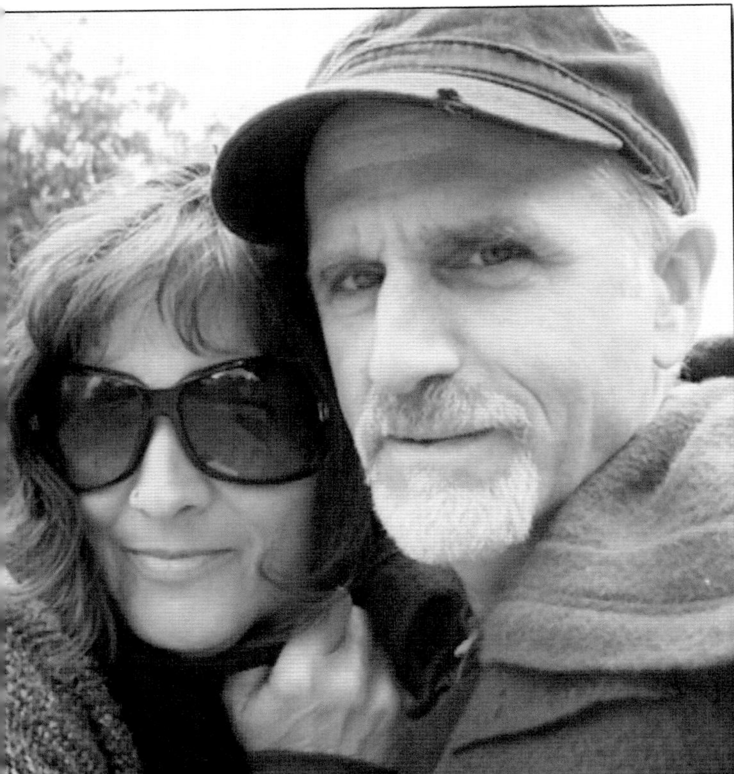

Andrew Leone and Nancy Hall
Andrew Leone and Nancy Hall are Pacifica artists and activists who have definitely made their mark on the community. Leone is a founding member of the Sanchez Art Center and maintains a studio there. Hall is a songwriter and performer who has toured with Neil Young, who incidentally, attended the Leone-Hall wedding in the San Pedro Valley County Park. From demonstrating against the cutting of eucalyptus trees to adamantly arguing against development in the Rockaway Quarry, they are widely known for their political beliefs as much as for their artistic endeavors. Hall's annual holiday concerts with her group, the Curios, are sold-out events at the Mildred Owen Concert Hall.

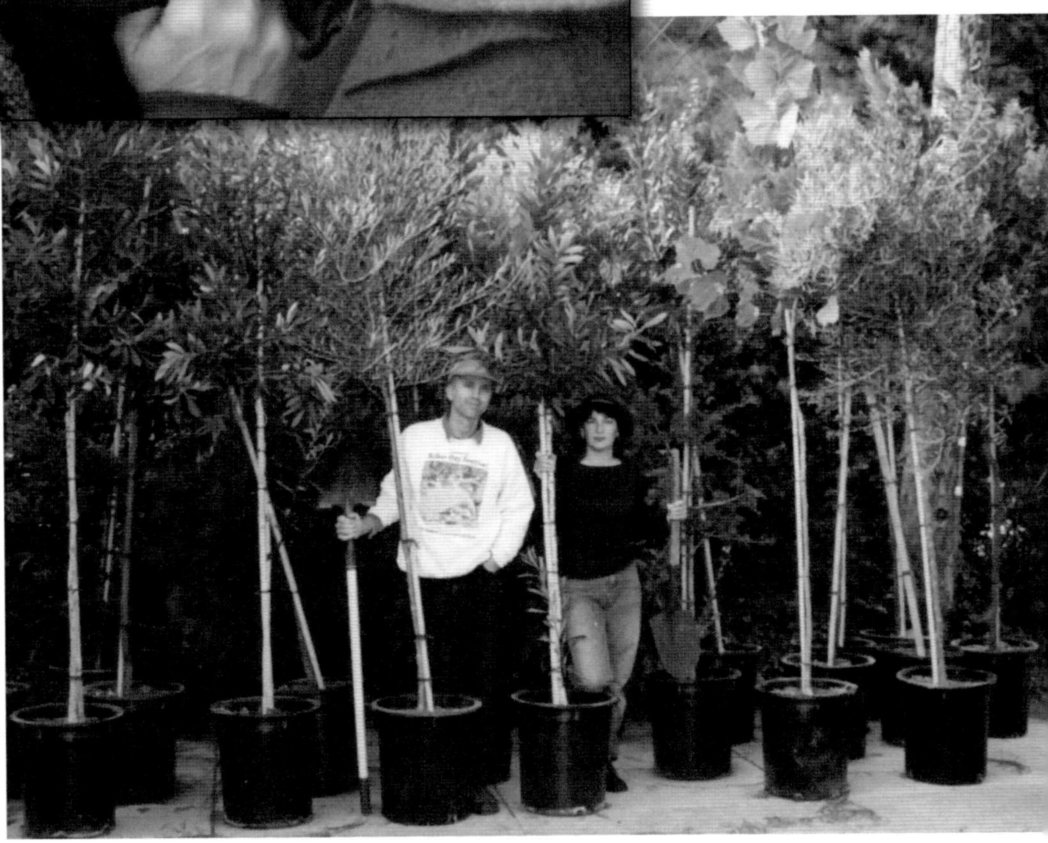

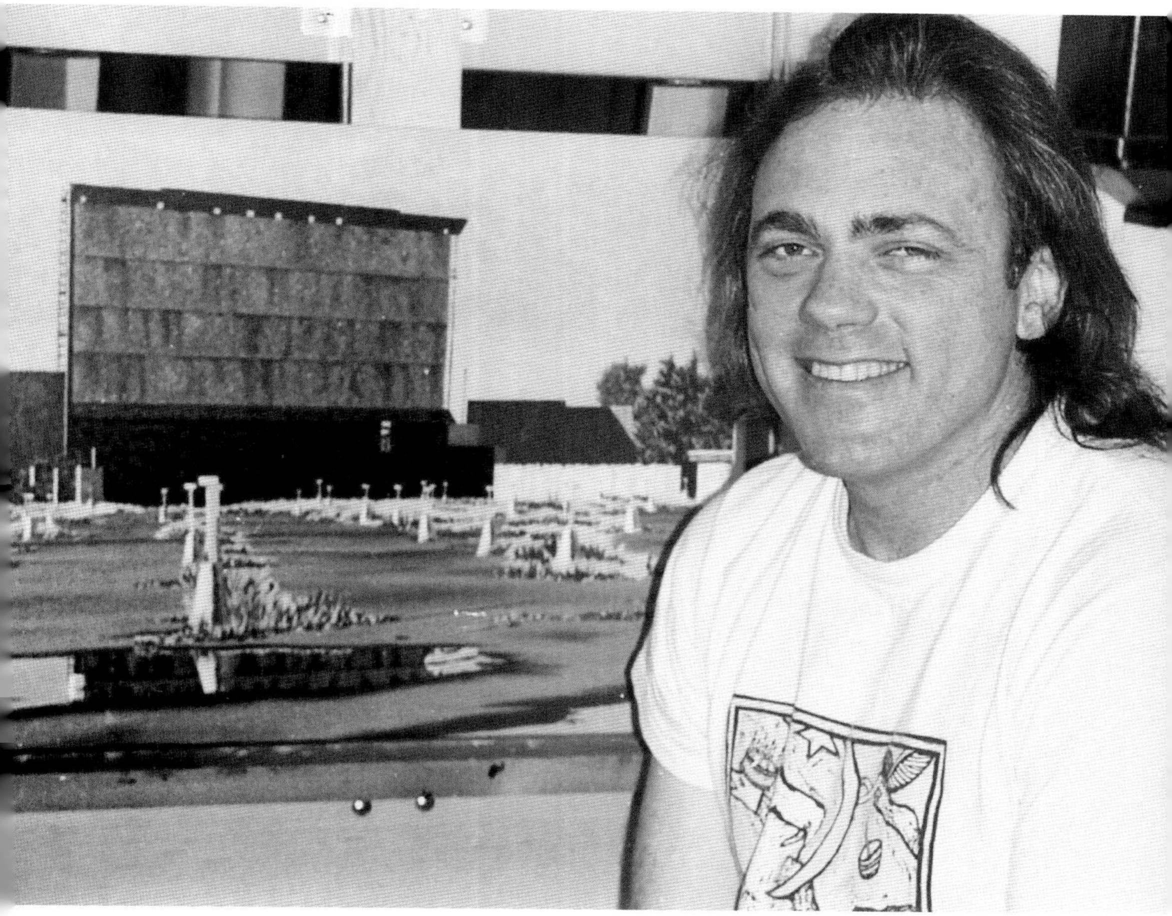

James Torlakson

A brilliant artist whose ability to capture realism on canvas made him nationally famous during the 1980s, James Torlakson is also an art teacher at City College of San Francisco and was a dedicated surfer for many years. His paintings of fireworks booths, crashed trucks, old buildings, and landscapes bring a sense of wonder to viewers. A personal tragedy shadowed his life when his daughter killed herself by walking into a BART tunnel. Torlakson mounted a personal campaign against antidepressants, which he believed contributed to the death of his daughter. He created grim paintings and lobbied against drug companies and tried to bring attention to the dangers of certain medications. His view has gained much public and professional acceptance in recent years and warnings to the public that some antidepressants can induce suicidal thoughts in people are standard instead of strange.

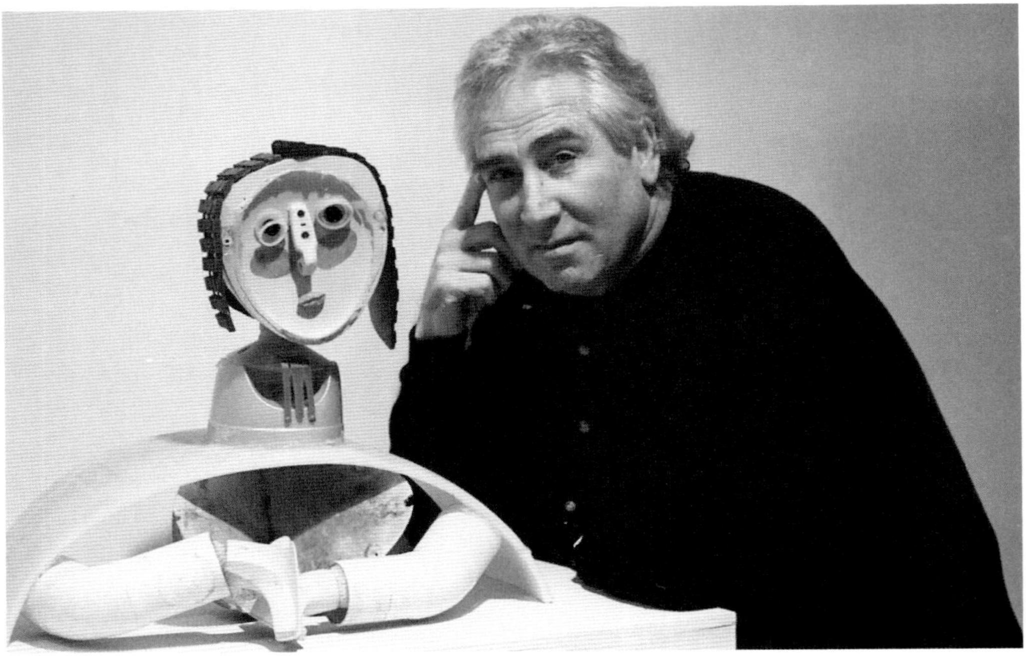

Jerry Barrish

Jerry Barrish's original claim to fame was as a 1960s bail bondsman in San Francisco. Countless articles have been written about the many counter-culture celebrities from San Francisco who availed themselves of the supportive Barrish. He then turned himself into an internationally famous sculptor using "found" items. Barrish is fond of saying that he started picking up litter on the beach and creating art out of it. Ultimately, his sculptures of musicians, animals, people, and countless other subjects, made out of odd bits of discarded plastic and other items wound up in museums and art galleries instead of garbage dumps. Living on the beach in Pedro Point and maintaining a studio in San Francisco, Jerry Barrish is both inspirational for his dedication to creating a mark in the modern art world for himself, as well as his support of the local Pacifica art scene throughout the years.

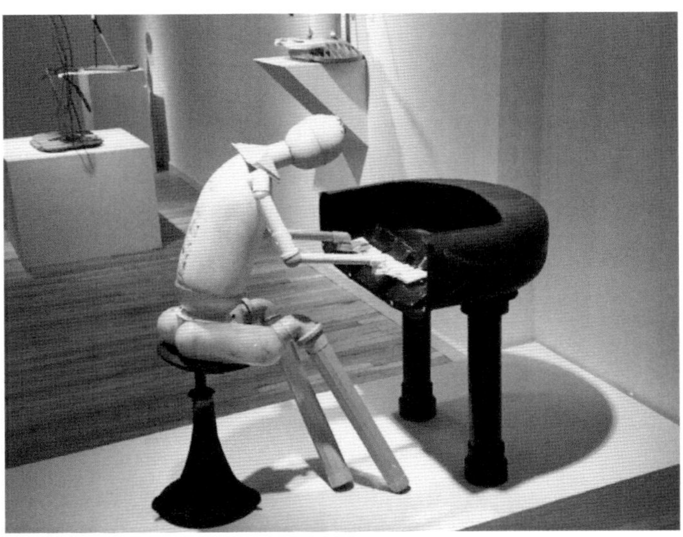

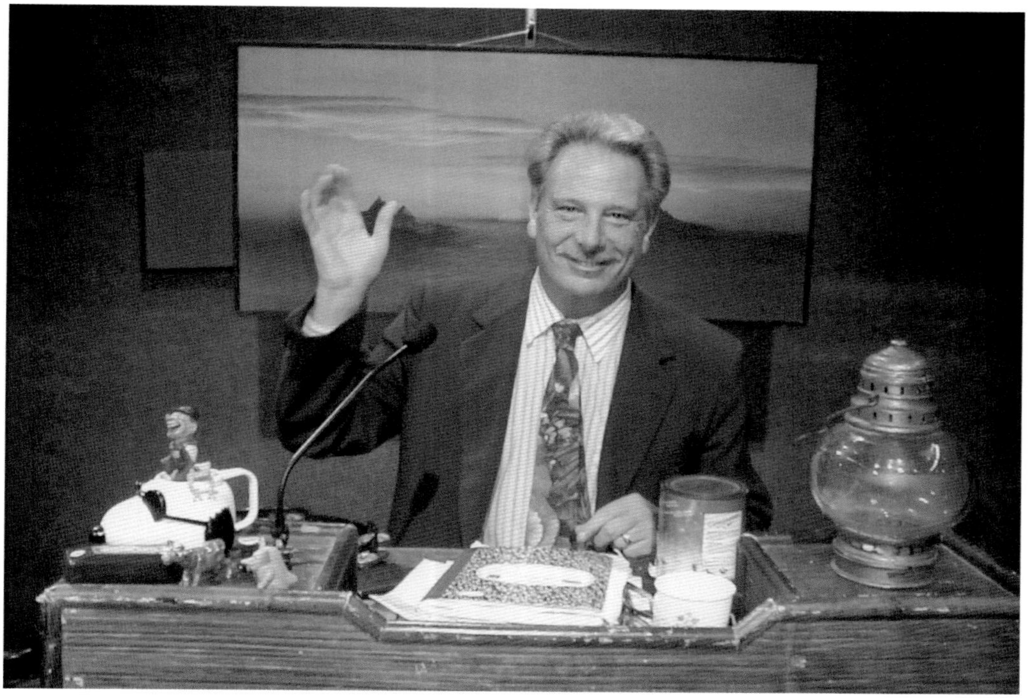

Bruce Latimer
There is probably no one on the planet who loves having his own entertainment and talk show more than Bruce Latimer. For more than 800 shows, spanning nearly three decades, Latimer brought his droll and sometimes old-fashioned humor to the *Bruce Latimer Show* on Pacifica Community Television, the cable access television station in Pacifica. He would bring on a wide range of entertainers, introducing a spectrum of performances ranging from Rambling Jack Elliot to a high school jazz band. Latimer's personal enthusiasm never waned, and he developed an almost cult-like following in the years his show was on television. By day, he managed a local cemetery, but when the lights came up on the *Bruce Latimer Show*, he was as lively as any talk show host.

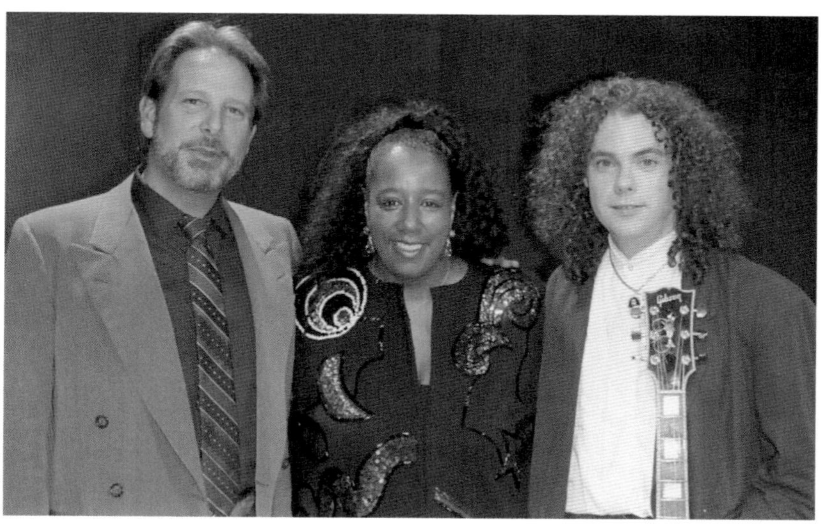

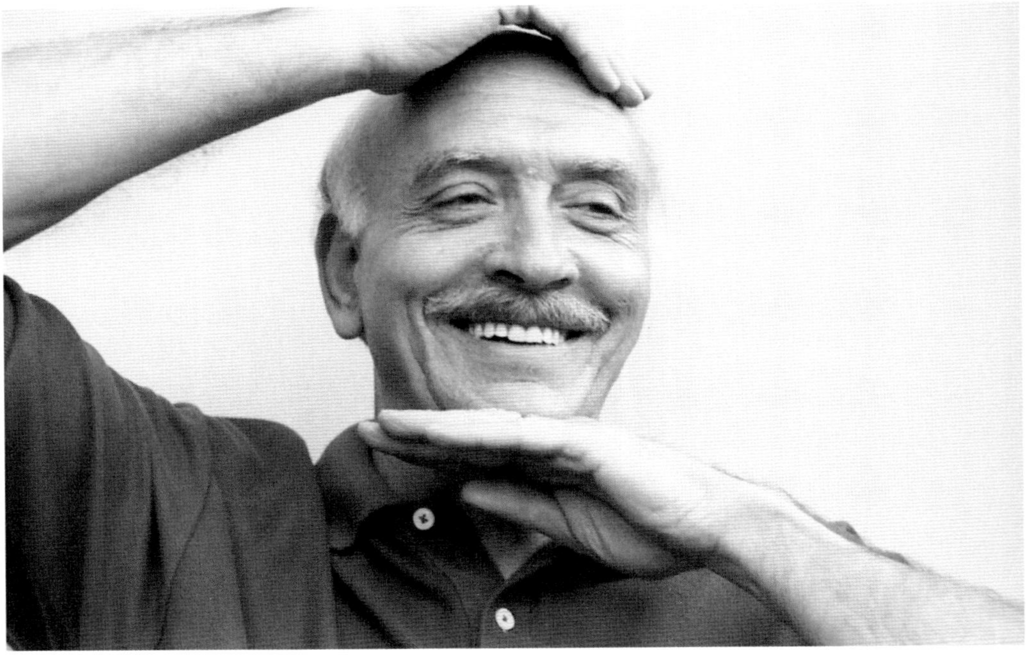

Roger Genereux

While he acted in and directed shows for the local community theater, Roger Genereux also ran his own theatrical group called *Asylum* for more than two decades, wrapping it up in 2013. He helped manage the business side of the Pacifica Spindrift Players, served on the board of directors, and was one of the stalwart standard bearers for that artistic community. Most people in Pacifica who attended the local productions recognize him instantly as the haunted Marley from the many productions of *A Christmas Carol* or variations on that theme. His improvisational comedy group was a performance home for many talented players, and it was a bittersweet evening when *Asylum* held its final show.

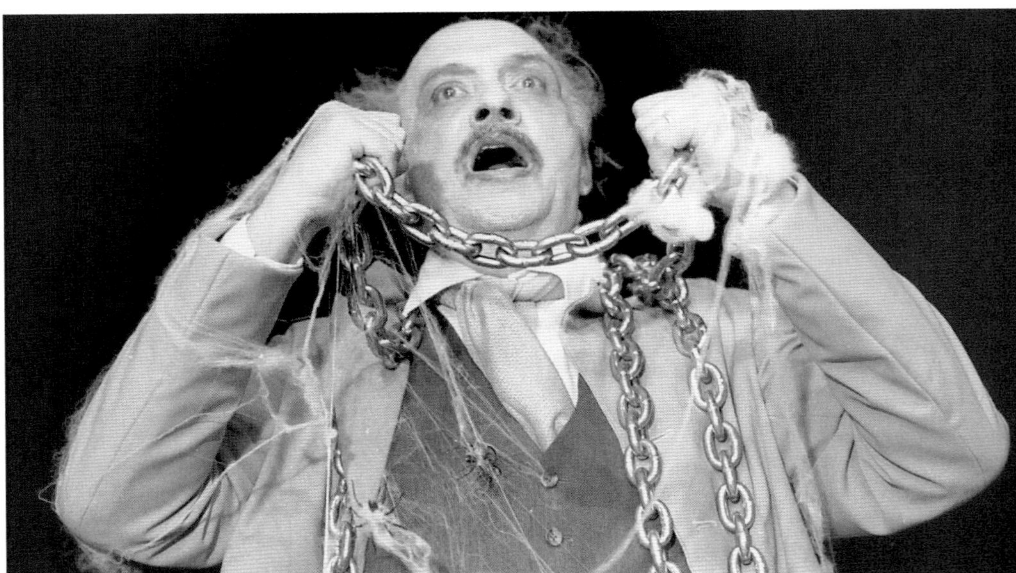

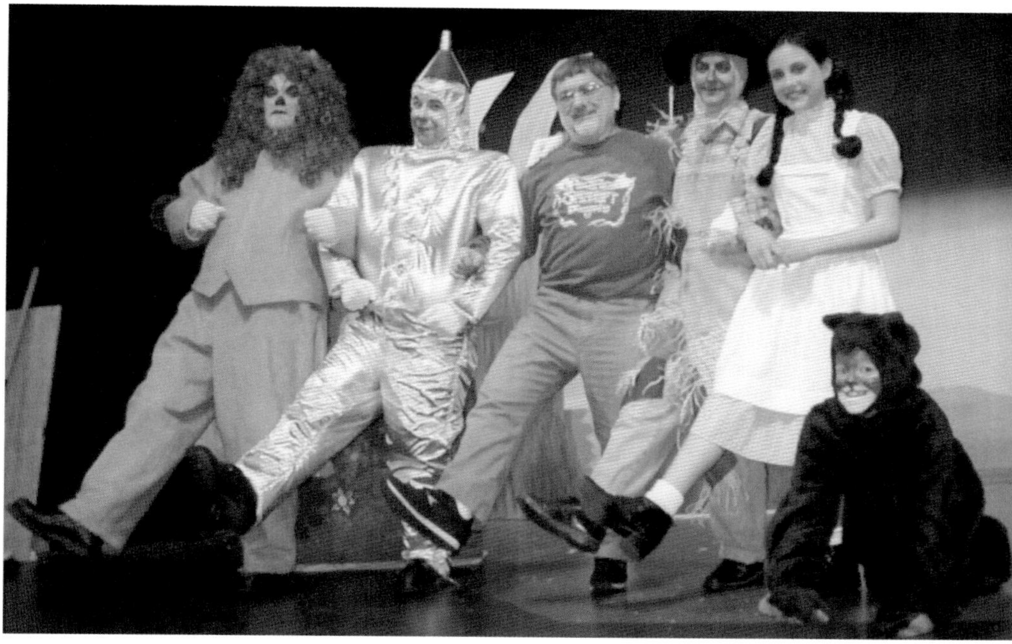

John Pantoleon

John Pantoleon spent decades working with the Pacifica Spindrift Players as an actor, a board member, and practically a patron saint. He performed as Tevye multiple times in *A Fiddler on the Roof* and directed countless children's productions in schools around Pacifica. Some of his young students grew up to appear in high school plays and then study drama in college. His wife, Kathy, was an equally talented performer who appeared in many productions through the years. In these photographs, he is seen with the cast of a production of *The Wizard of Oz* (above) and at a ceremony with his wife, Kathy, as he receives a Lifetime Achievement Award in the Arts from the City of Pacifica (below).

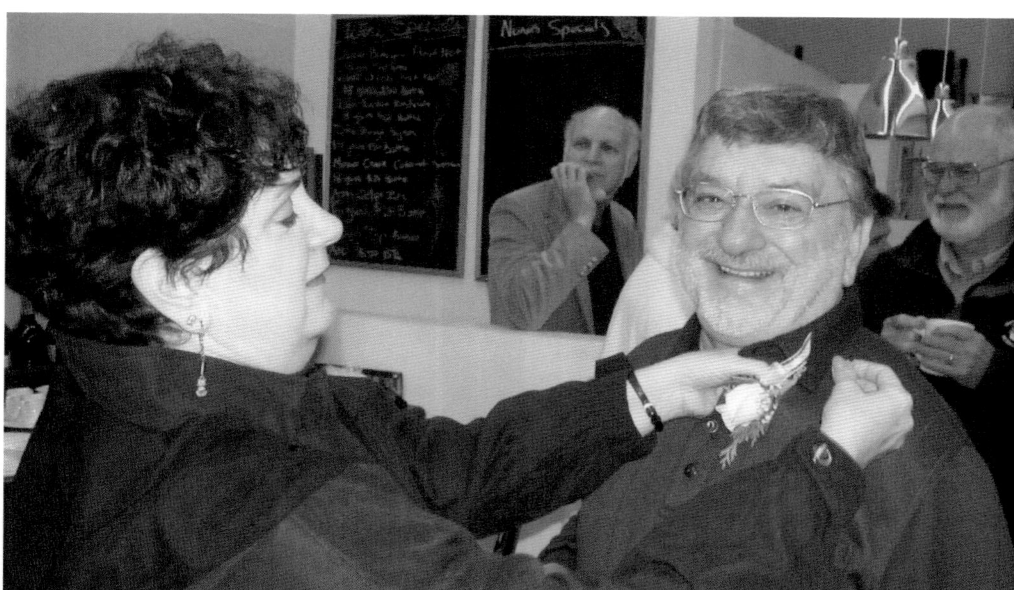

Michael Rothenberg

A poet, writer, artist, businessman, and local environmental activist, Michael Rothenberg was also the cofounder of the Shelldance Nursery, which specializes in orchids. Perhaps his most notable contribution to Pacifica was his long battle against any development on Mori Point, the majestic property on the ocean that eventually became a part of the Golden Gate National Recreation Area. Rothenberg moved to Pacifica in 1976 and quickly established a high profile for himself in the arts and activism of the community. He never ran for public office, but he was deeply involved in the local political scene, supporting the candidates who agreed with his vision of maintaining the open space area on the coast. A prolific painter and writer, he also cultivated a relationship with the Beat poet Philip Whalen and edited a well-received collection of his poems. Together with his then-wife Nancy Davis, also an artist, he created Big Bridge Press, a fine arts literary press. He continues to write and publish poetry and is the editor of the Big Bridge webzine of poetry. In 2011, he and Terri Carrion created *100 Thousand Poets for Change,* promoting a global poetry movement.

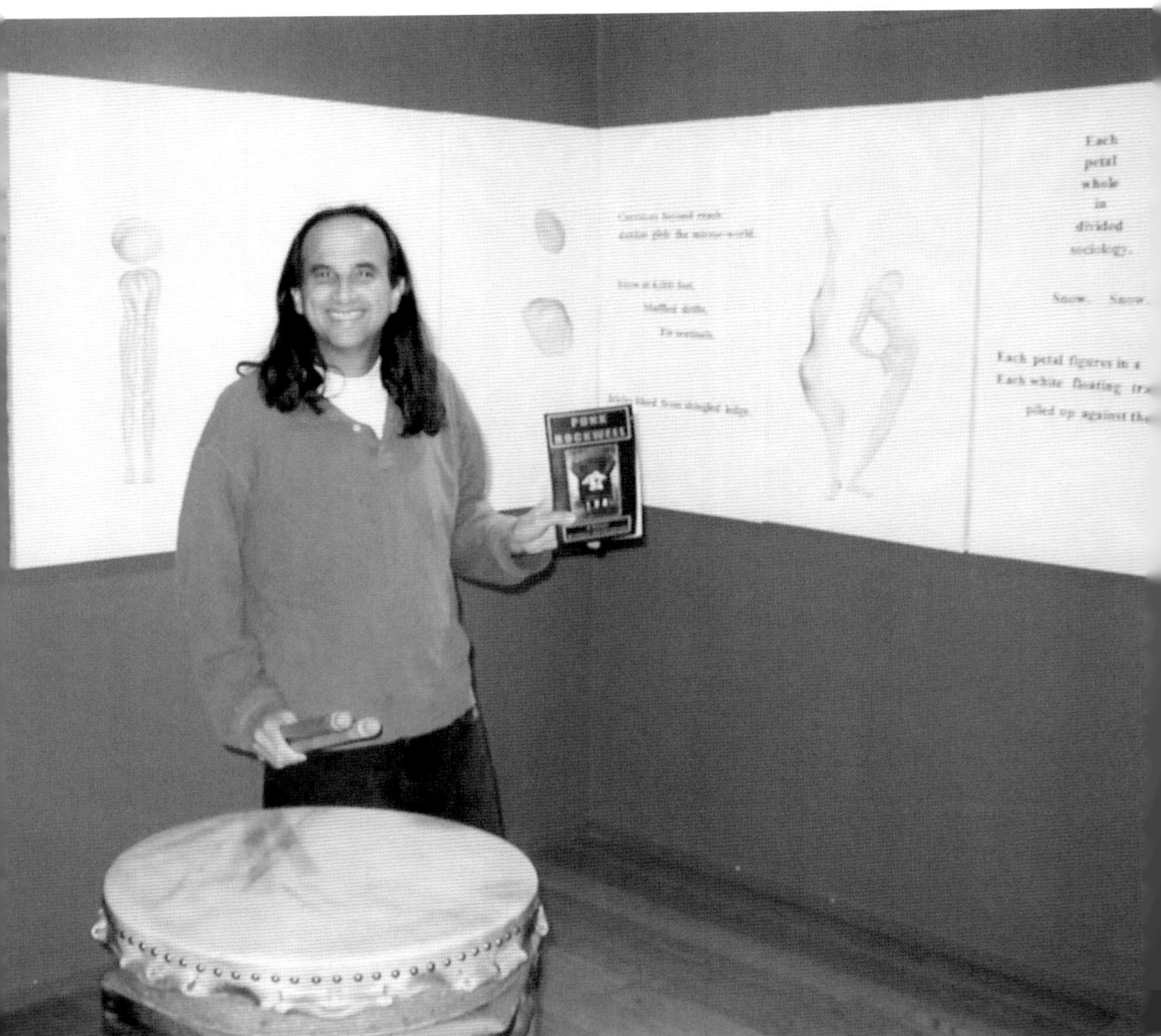

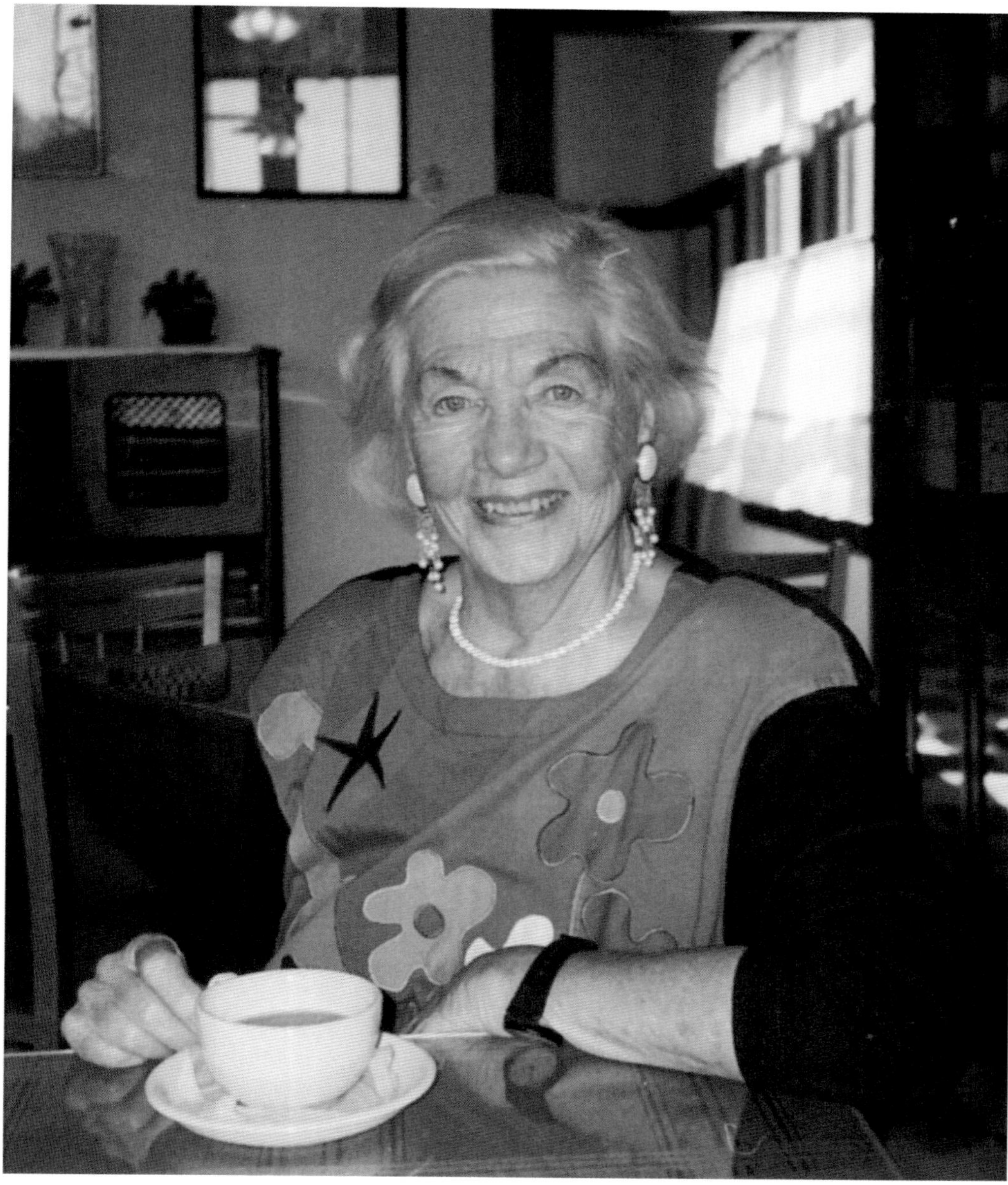

Roberta Ewald

A former travel agency owner, Ewald went on trips throughout the world and came back to Pacifica to paint her memories. She also founded the Keyboard Productions organization, which produced original musicals through the years. A strong supporter of the arts environment in Pacifica, her constant encouragement of all things artistic helped many local artists gain confidence and enjoy their talents. One of her most memorable productions was the *Coastside Bowl,* which lampooned the history of Pacifica. Her son Grant Ewald is a professional musician and bandleader who has performed regularly at Nick's in Rockaway Beach and a wide variety of other venues.

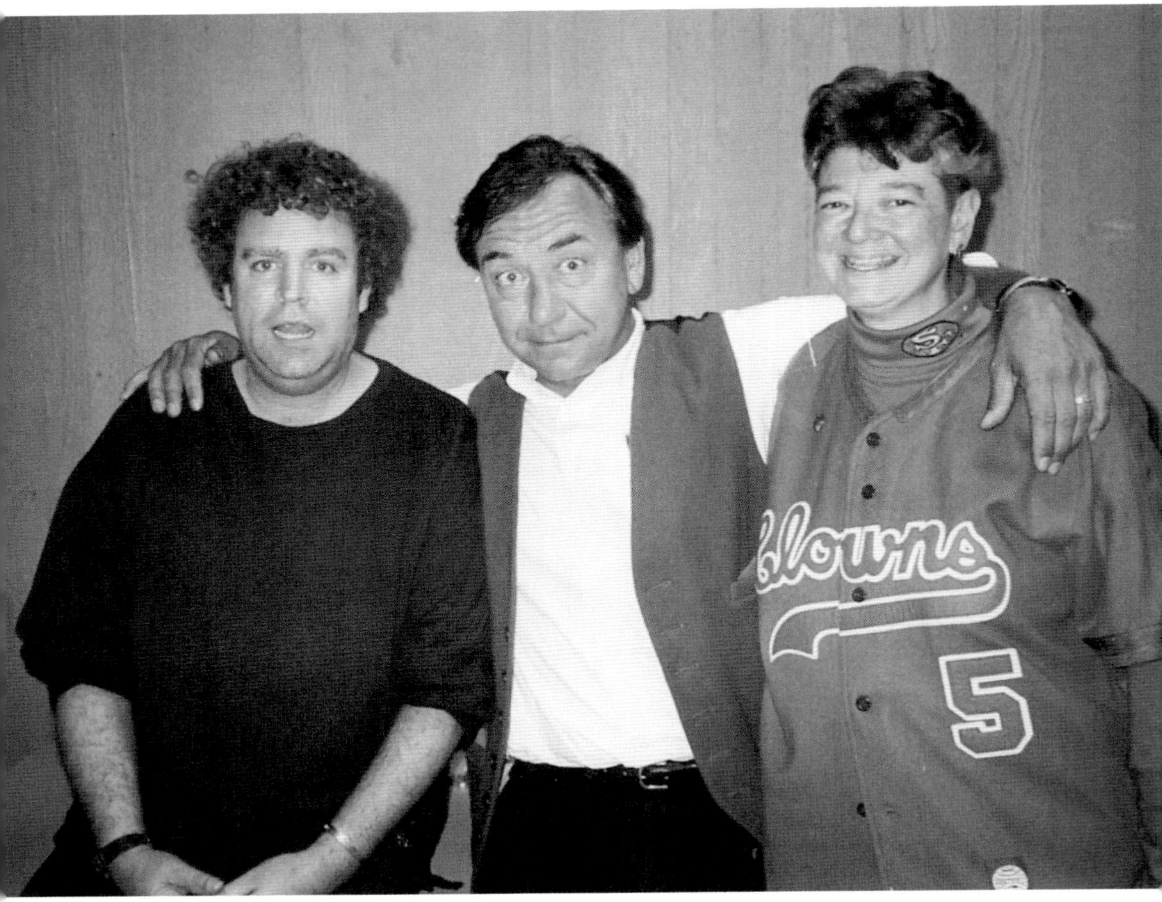

Deb and Mike
Debi Durst grew up in Pacifica and was always known for her sharp sense of humor. She is a popular comedienne and teams up with Michael Dossier, also a Pacifican, for the comedy improvisation duo known as, obviously, Deb and Mike. She is married to the political satirist Will Durst (in the center of this photograph), who is viewed as an honorary Pacifican. Debi Durst is very active in the local community theater company, Pacifica Spindrift Players, appearing in several productions a year when she is not touring or traveling with her husband.

44

Emmanuel Williams
A poet who specializes in inspiring students to learn about and practice poetry, Emmanuel Williams has developed a reputation for thoughtful encouragement of other poets. He has widely published his own poetry and continues to write. He is perhaps one of the last remaining poets who really loves riddles.

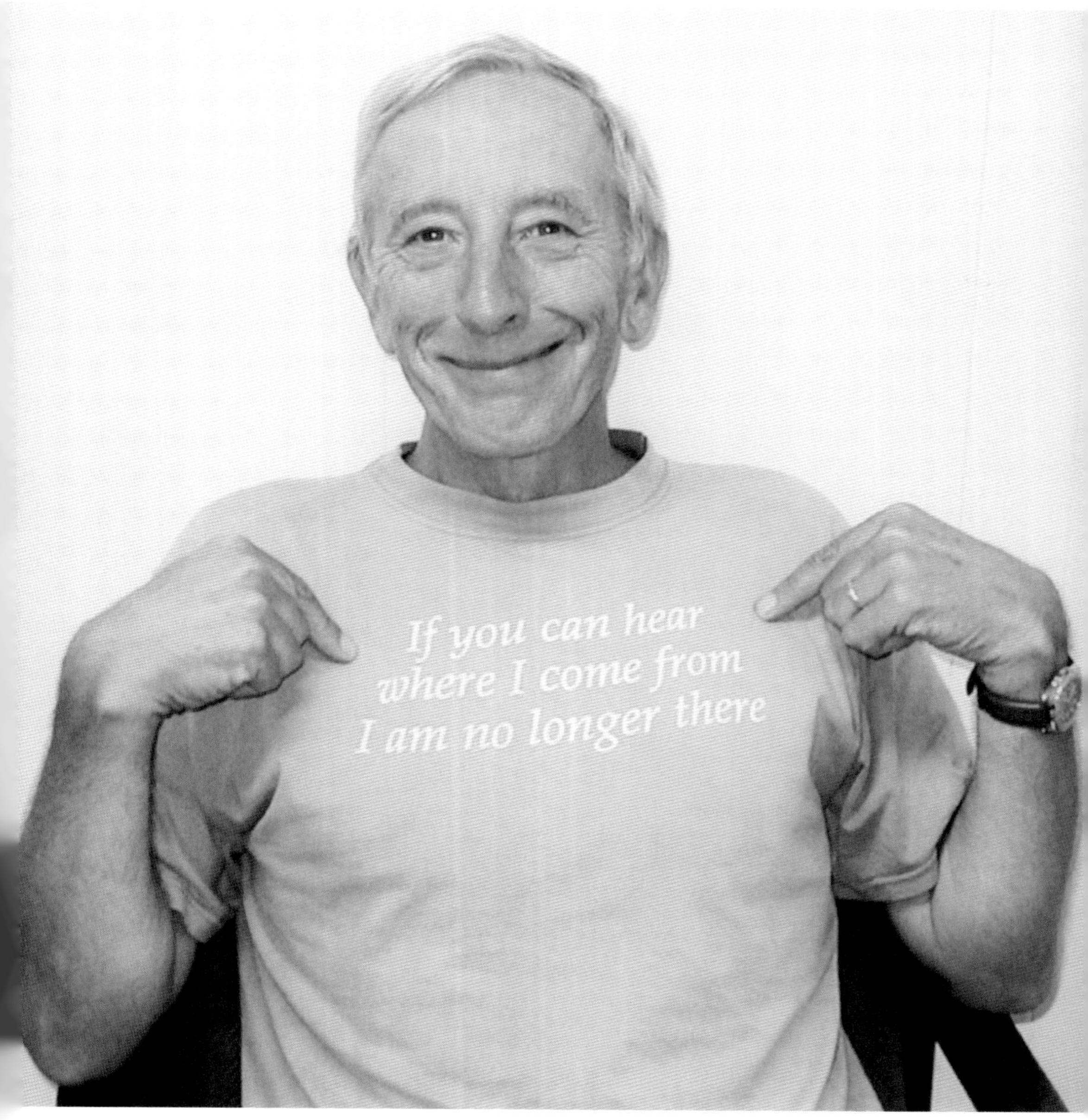

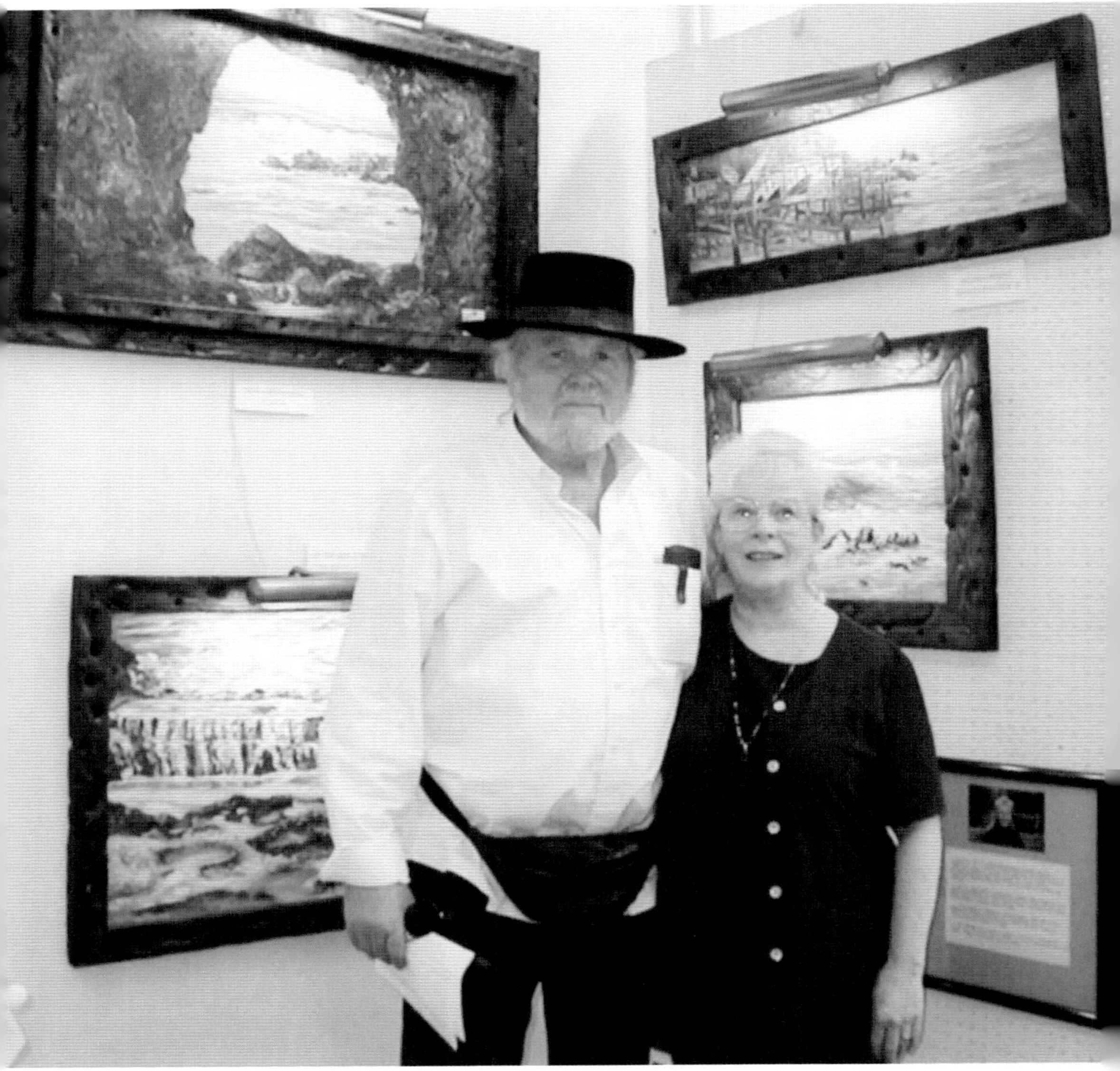

Tom Jackson and Jackie DiCello

This artist couple of Tom Jackson and Jackie DiCello combine to make a formidable cultural team. Cartoonist Jackson specialized for years in humor based on hospital and medical experiences while DiCello paints wildlife and natural scenes. She is an in-demand art teacher, and Jackson is a raconteur and prolific writer of letters to the editor. Both are regular winners at the San Mateo County Fair art contests

CHAPTER THREE

Pacifica Educators

At one time, Pacifica's elementary school system consisted of 11,000 students in 15 schools, with each school considered a neighborhood school within walking distance of every family in town. While the population stayed static, the youth population has shrunk and the Pacifica School District contracted to 3,000 students in seven schools. The high schools in town draw students from Daly City and Brisbane, as they are part of a larger regional district. Nonetheless, the educators and administrators of Pacifica's school community have played an important role in the history and vision of the city. Tax measures have been supported so facilities have been modernized at all levels. The political leaders of the city have always been intertwined with the educational leaders and there are always some candidates who use school board experience as a foundation for city council runs. Throughout the years, many individuals have stood out as truly legendary, for example, the public pool at Oceana High School is named for Jean Brink, a longtime board member on the Jefferson Union High School District whose personal impact was wide-ranging. Youth athletic director Ingrid B. Lacy, whose name identifies the Pacifica School District's vanguard middle school, is another legend in town whose story is also included in this book.

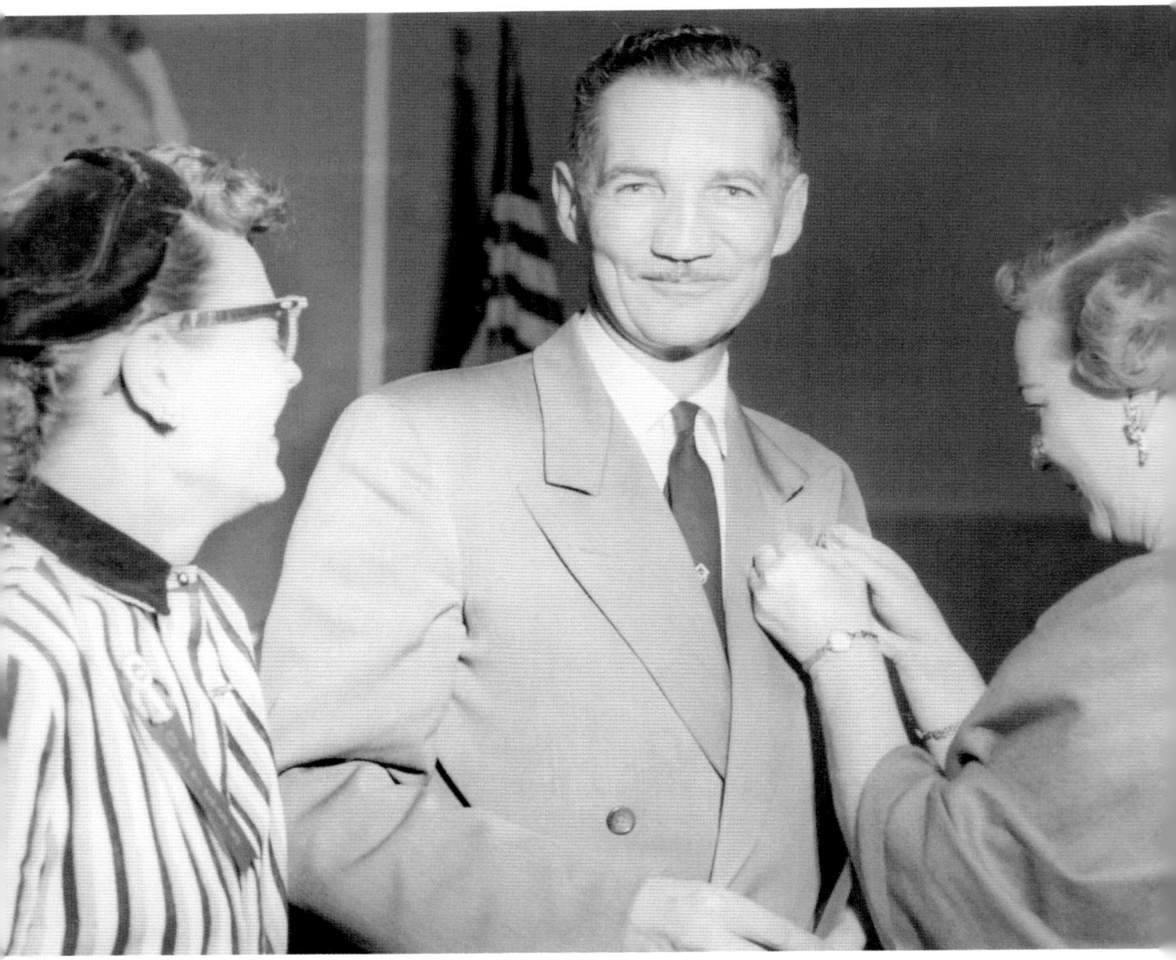

Fred Lucas
Although not the very first superintendent of the Laguna Salada Union School District, Fred Lucas came aboard shortly after its creation and went on to be a very important part of the personality of Pacifica itself. A cheerleader for the incorporation of the city, he viewed the school district as an important framework and support system for the families moving to the booming area in the 1950s. He encouraged parents to be active in the schools, and they eventually shifted that activism to community building. Some have suggested that Fred Lucas helped spawn the historic reality of school teachers and parents becoming instrumental in Pacifica's creation. A charismatic and handsome man, with Clark Gable looks, Lucas was also popular and a successful educator and administrator.

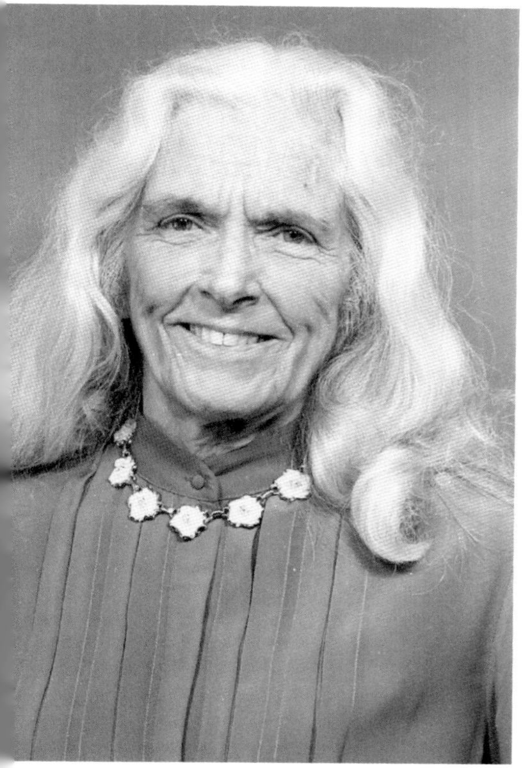

Ruth Boudinot

One of those amazing women who shaped the early community of Pacifica, Ruth Boudinot earned her reputation as an active political presence as a board member on the Laguna Salada Union School District and, following along with her children's educational growth, a member of the Jefferson Union High School District. A smart, savvy board member with a reportedly dry sense of humor and way of looking at issues, Ruth Boudinot began her work as a member of the PTA and then found her passion as an elected school board member. The school library at Oceana High School is named in her honor, and she was on the Jefferson Union High School District when it negotiated an innovative partnership with the City of Pacifica to establish an indoor swimming pool at Oceana shared by the two government agencies. People who knew Ruth Boudinot always comment on her intelligence, compassion, and fierce dedication to the schools in the community.

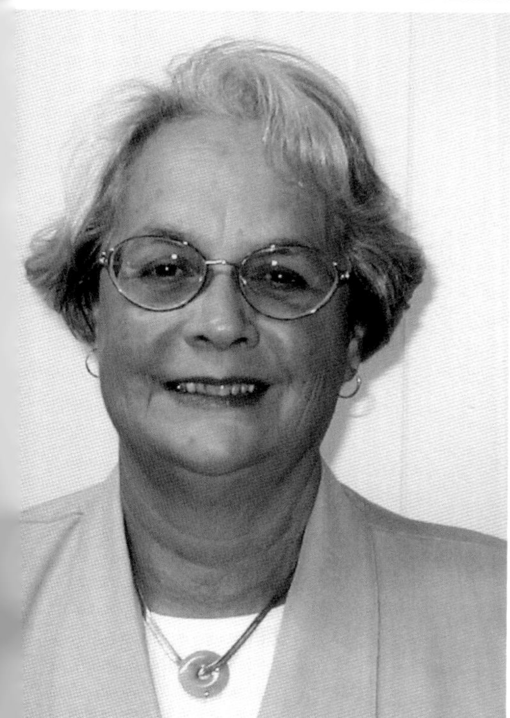

Jean Brink

A longtime member of the Jefferson Union School District, Jean Brink served for two decades, from 1988 to 2008. Perhaps her most lasting legacy is the district's indoor swimming pool at Oceana High School, which was named the "Jean Brink Pool" in her honor upon her retirement. A master swimmer herself, this was a very appropriate tribute to the popular board member. Active as a volunteer in many community organizations, especially her beloved Pacifica Sea Lions Swim Team and the colorful tile mural which is on the wall of the Brink Pool building, Brink also was an active member of the Fog Fest volunteer committee. A tragic moment in her family's life occurred when her husband John, a world-class sailor, was shot in the neck during an altercation over a parking space in front of the Brink house. The bullet severed John's neck artery and caused him to have a stroke, which paralyzed his right side. Not one to give up, John Brink eventually recovered enough to ride a motorcycle around town, weighted down with a sidecar on one side and mechanically altered to allow him to control and steer it with one arm and leg.

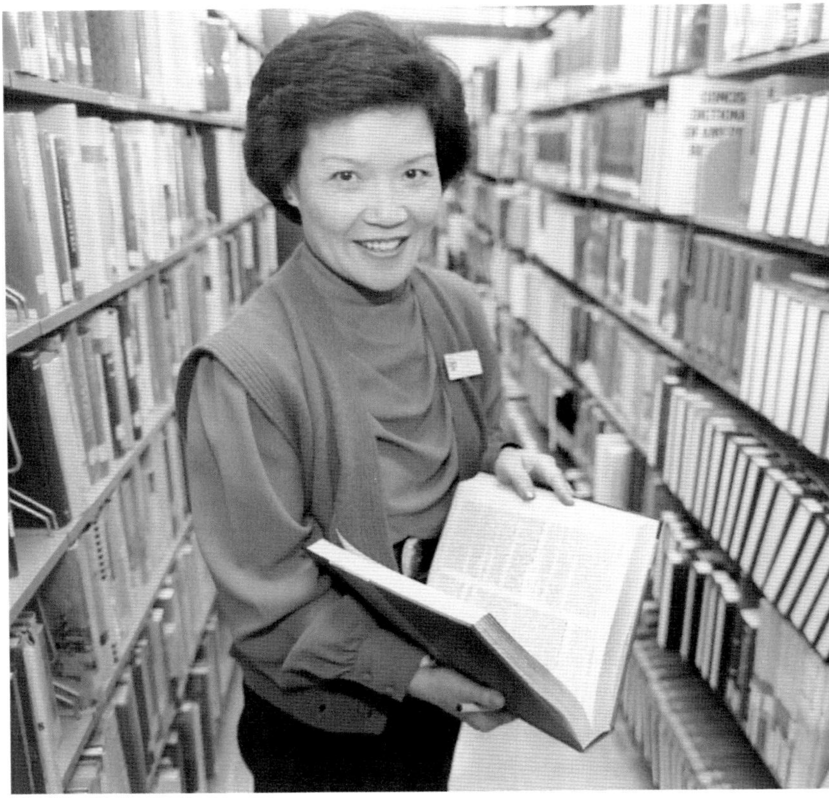

Elizabeth Sor

If Pacifica ever actually builds a new state-of-the-art library to replace its two small neighborhood libraries, there is no one who will be happier than Elizabeth Sor, who retired in 2005 after more than 20 years managing the city's libraries. She began work in Pacifica in 1978, after 10 years as the Millbrae Library children's librarian, as well as work in Foster City and Brisbane. Prior to coming to the United States, she worked as a journalist in Taiwan, which gave her a sympathetic connection to other writers. She was promoted to the head librarian for Pacifica in 1981. An active presence in the community, Sor was a popular and helpful librarian. Everyone who came into either small library was greeted with a smile and an offer of help. Countless students were assisted with research advice and readers were given great suggestions. She began a children's reading program on Pacifica Community Television called *Whales of Tales* and wrote a regular library column for the *Pacifica Tribune*. "I fell in love with the city when I was assigned to work in Pacifica in 1978," she said in a *Pacifica Tribune* interview when she retired. "Those were some wonderful, memorable years! Everyday, I looked forward to driving the beautiful scenic Sharp Park Road to the breathtaking Mori Point ocean view near where Pacifica Library is located. It was my home away from home for over 25 years! I appreciated the city leaders, library supporters, and the media, for all the effort to keep the two libraries afloat through the years." She actively campaigned for a library consolidation of the Sanchez and Pacifica libraries into a single, more effective facility, and spent an enormous amount of time in community meetings working towards that goal. After her retirement, she continued to volunteer at the Millbrae Library, eyeing Pacifica with only one regret: "In an ideal world, Pacifica should have at least two fully functional facilities, open long hours. Realistically though, I shared the vision with many library supporters for building a state-of-the-art library that would enable the city and library to effectively and efficiently utilize the limited resources to serve the entire community as a long-term solution. It did not happen while I was manager then. I am happy to know that library supporters continue to work on the project after all these years! When you build it, they will come!"

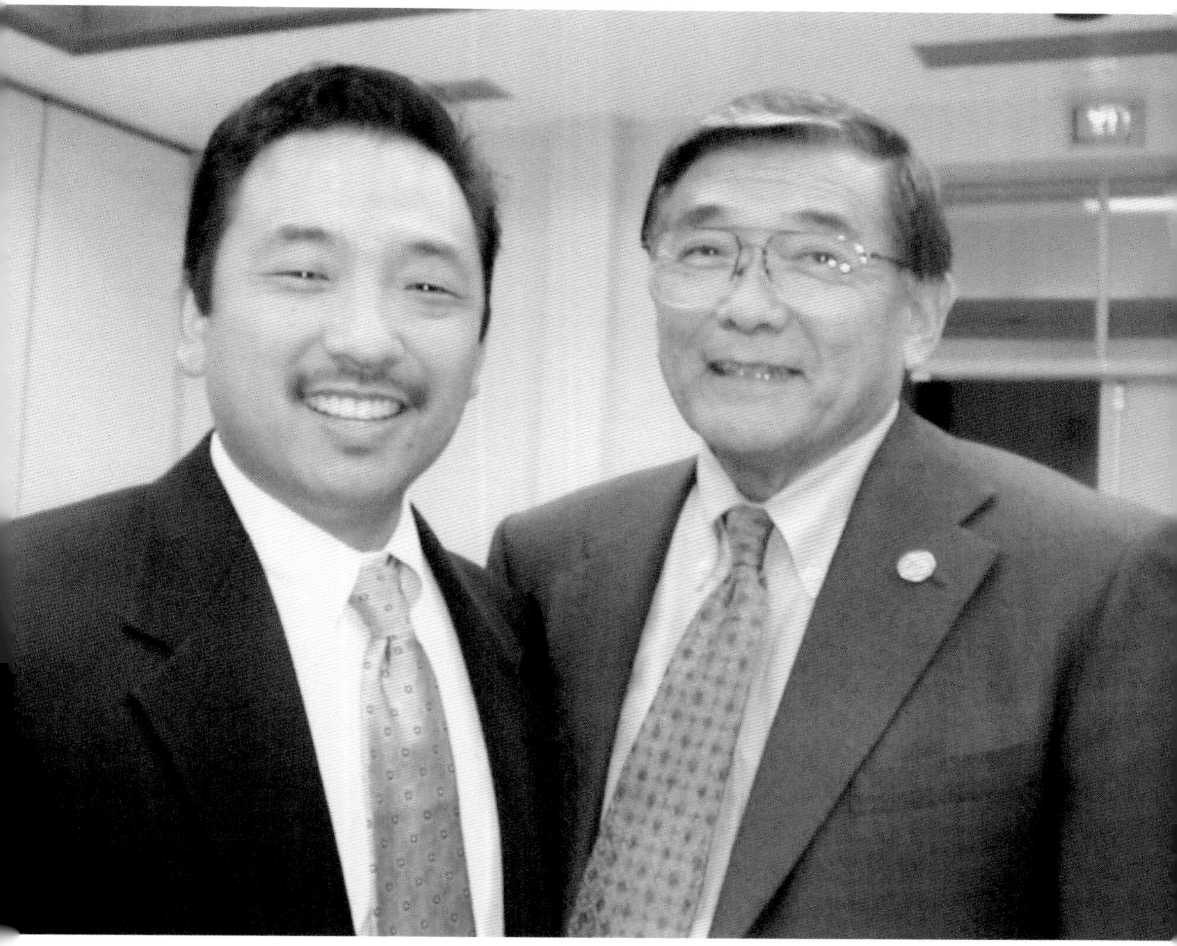

David Mineta

David Mineta (left), the son of Norman Mineta (right), a popular politician from San Jose who became a cabinet member in the administrations of both Pres. George W. Bush and Pres. Barack Obama and who has the San Jose International Airport named after him, was a popular member of the Jefferson Union High School District Board of Trustees for nine years. He is now working in Washington D.C. Formerly the director of the Asian American Recovery Services, David Mineta was tapped to be the Deputy Director of Demand Reduction for the Office of National Drug Control Policy by President Obama and was confirmed by the US Senate in 2010. His new job required him to resign from the school district board. In his new job, Mineta promotes drug prevention and drug treatment programs, as well overseeing the agency's newly created focus on programs for individuals in recovery from addiction.

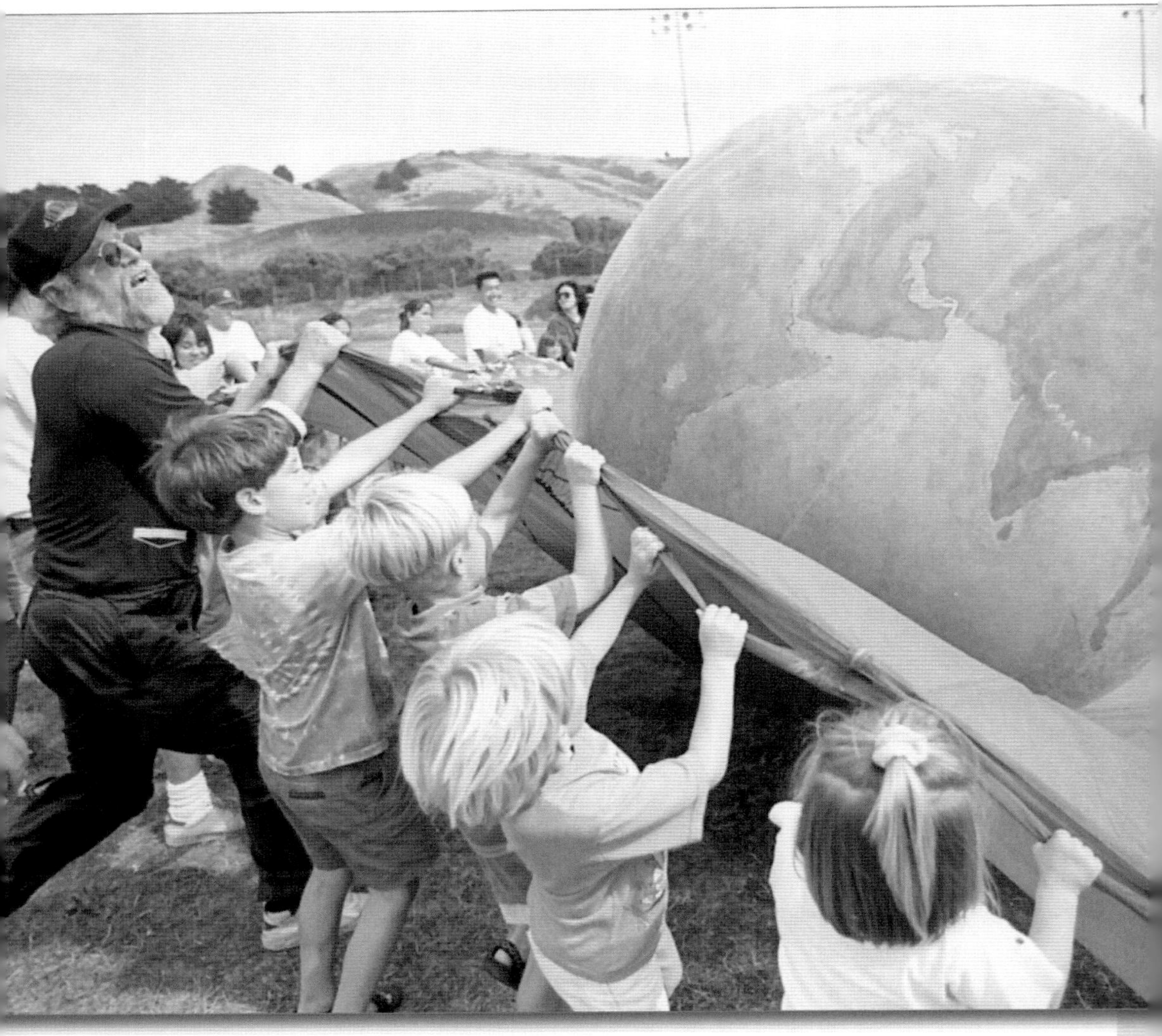

Dr. Bill Michaelis at the Family Fun Fest (ABOVE)
Dr. Bill Michaelis created the annual Family Fun Fest, which is a noncompetitive activity day during the Pacific Coast Fog Fest in Pacifica. His dedication to play combines fun and academic exploration. Generations of local children and families have enjoyed the Fun Fest for more than 25 years. This parachute game is one of the more popular events.

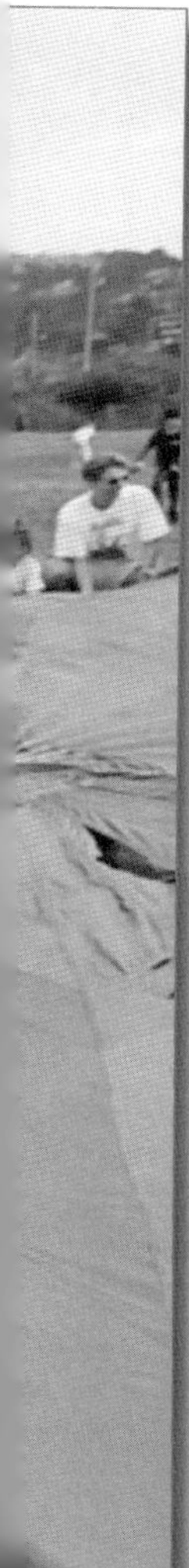

Dr. Bill Michaelis (BELOW)

Who makes a living teaching people how to play? In Pacifica, that would be Dr. Bill Michaelis, who teaches at San Francisco State University and travels the globe offering workshops on how to play. For two decades, his Family Fun Fest has been a counterpoint to the annual Pacific Coast Fog Fest, providing a family-friendly opportunity for people to paint a car, walk on stilts, climb a globe, and interact with others in a noncompetitive, playful environment. He is also a local activist, supporting the Pacifica Resource Center and being involved in a long list of Pacifica political debates. "I love this pirate town," he said. "After all it is part of the Barbary Coast. It's never boring with the widest range of caring talented opinionated folks, people who volunteer to help make this low-wealth city a vibrant beautiful family community. There are dedicated teachers who helped my kids get a good education. The city gets incredible mileage from a hard-working city staff. And of course there are a handful of folks who regularly exhibit snarky and rigid behaviors, who are not positive problem solvers. But I guess that goes with the territory (*aaaarrrrrrr* . . . as a pirate would say). But overall, Pacifica is a place I am proud to call home and to show off to visitors. I will always try to do my small part to help keep it a good place." Michaelis is a professor emeritus at San Francisco State University and has written, taught, and consulted throughout the world. With Ezra Holland, he owns and operates the organization known as Children Together, which presents play opportunities for conferences, schools, and other events.

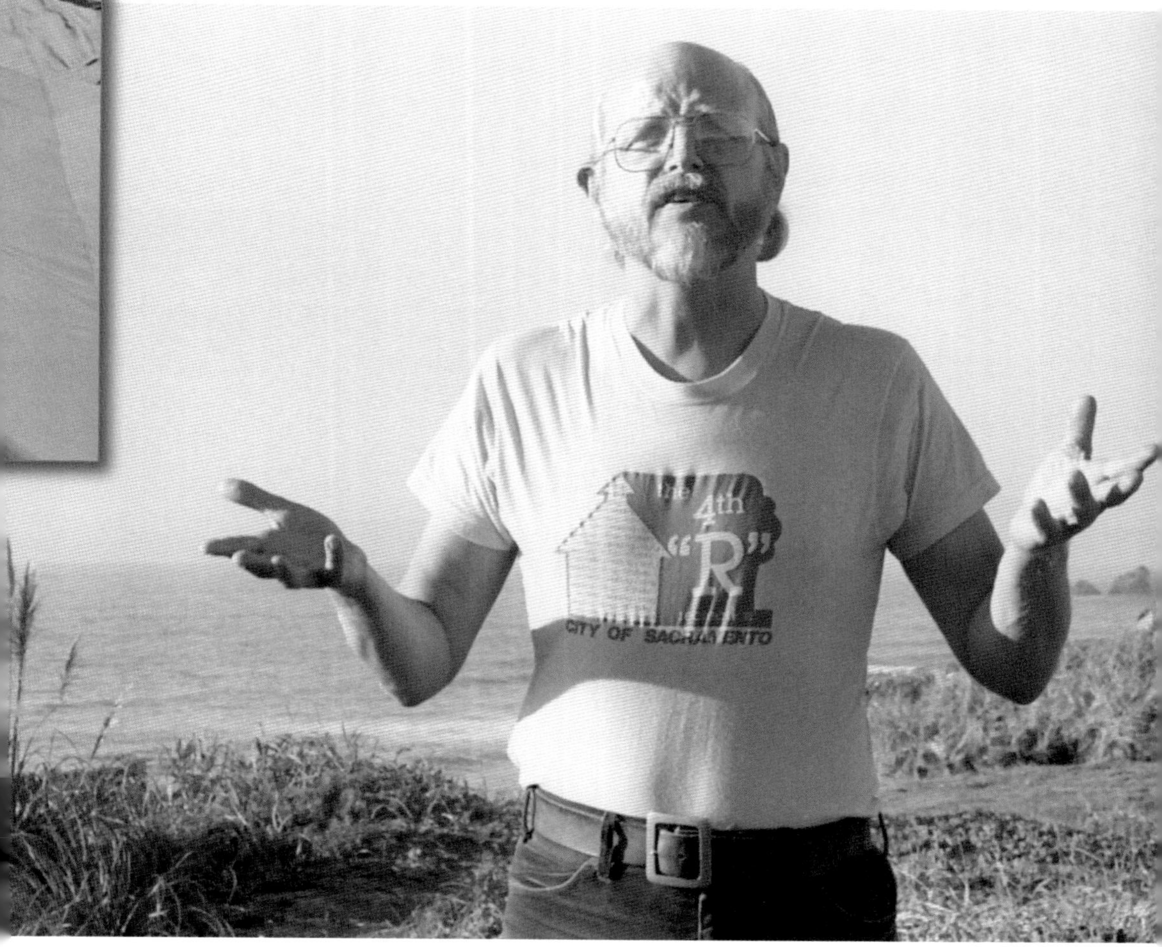

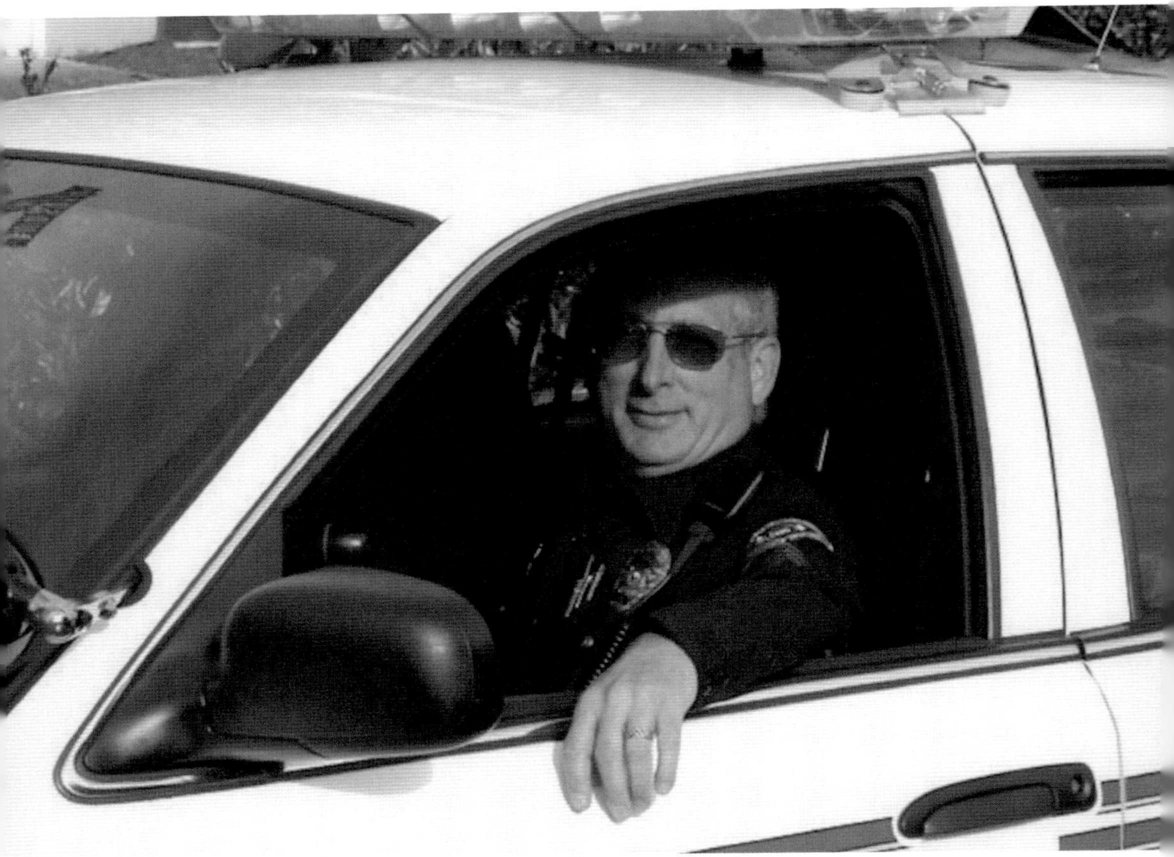

Eric Ruchames

A police officer with the Pacifica Police Department, Eric Ruchames specialized in hostage negotiations. It is possible that skill came in handy when he was elected to the Laguna Salada Union School District Board of Trustees, because there always seemed to be a crisis during the 1990s. Ruchames developed a reputation as a savvy leader with a wise ability to compromise when needed. His dedication to his community was evident by his public safety service and his election to the school board. After he retired from the police department, he became active in the campaign to build a new Pacifica public library, a task that had eluded other community activists for decades. Then, when school board member Michael O'Neill was elected to the city council in 2012, Ruchames was appointed to become a member once again and help out the school district.

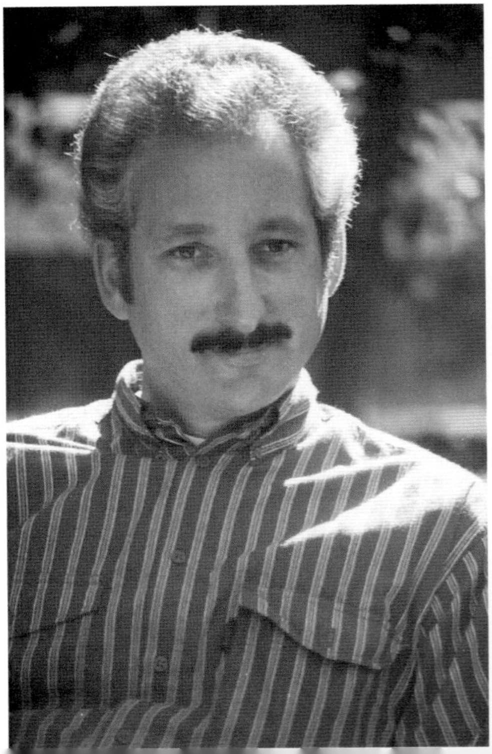

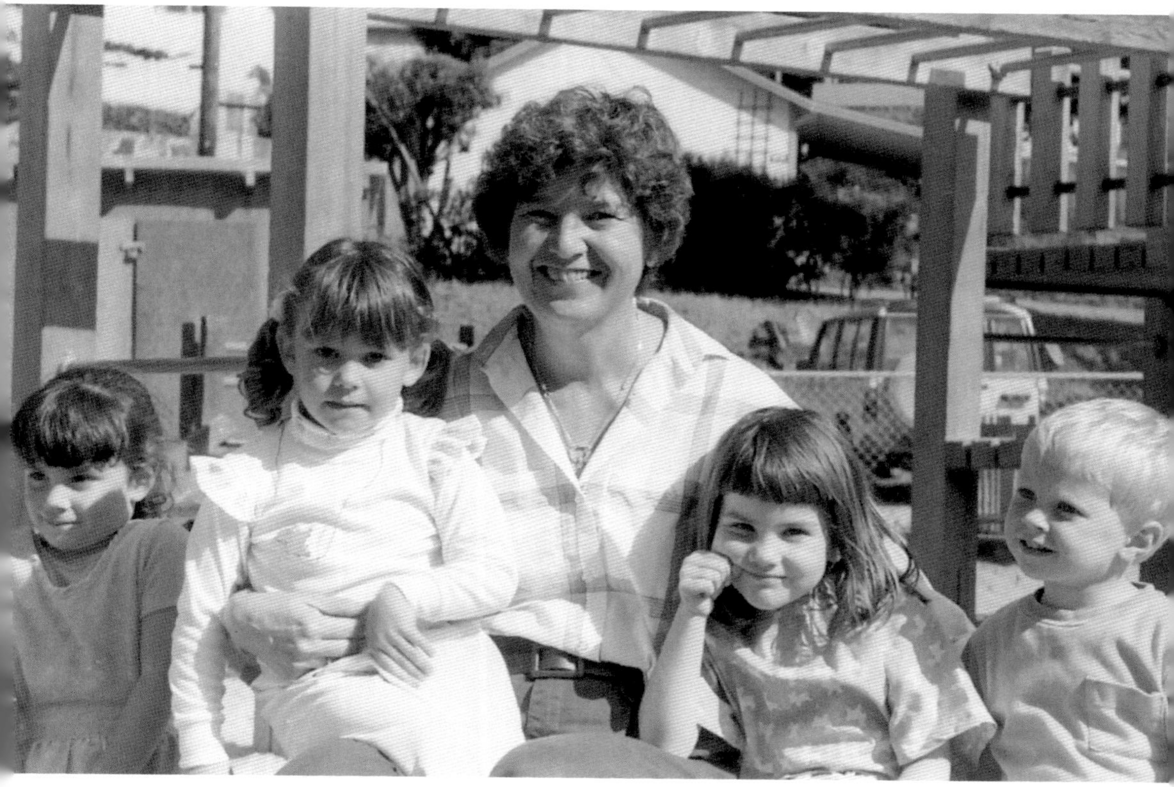

Sandra Wallace

It would not be an exaggeration to say that many parents in Pacifica owe their child-rearing skills to Sandra "Teacher Sandy" Wallace. A longtime teacher at the Co-op Nursery School, located in a World War II–era Quonset hut outfitted to be a classroom facility, she brought a professional quality to the parent education program of the Jefferson Union High School District, a component of the Co-op Nursery concept. Her unwavering belief that children deserved only best in support and educational opportunities rubbed off on every parent who put in the long hours of participation required at the Co-op. Upon her retirement, a special Congressional Recognition was given to her, along with multiple other tributes. Teacher Sandy inspired those who followed in her footsteps at the Co-op, which continues to be a popular and successful nursery school.

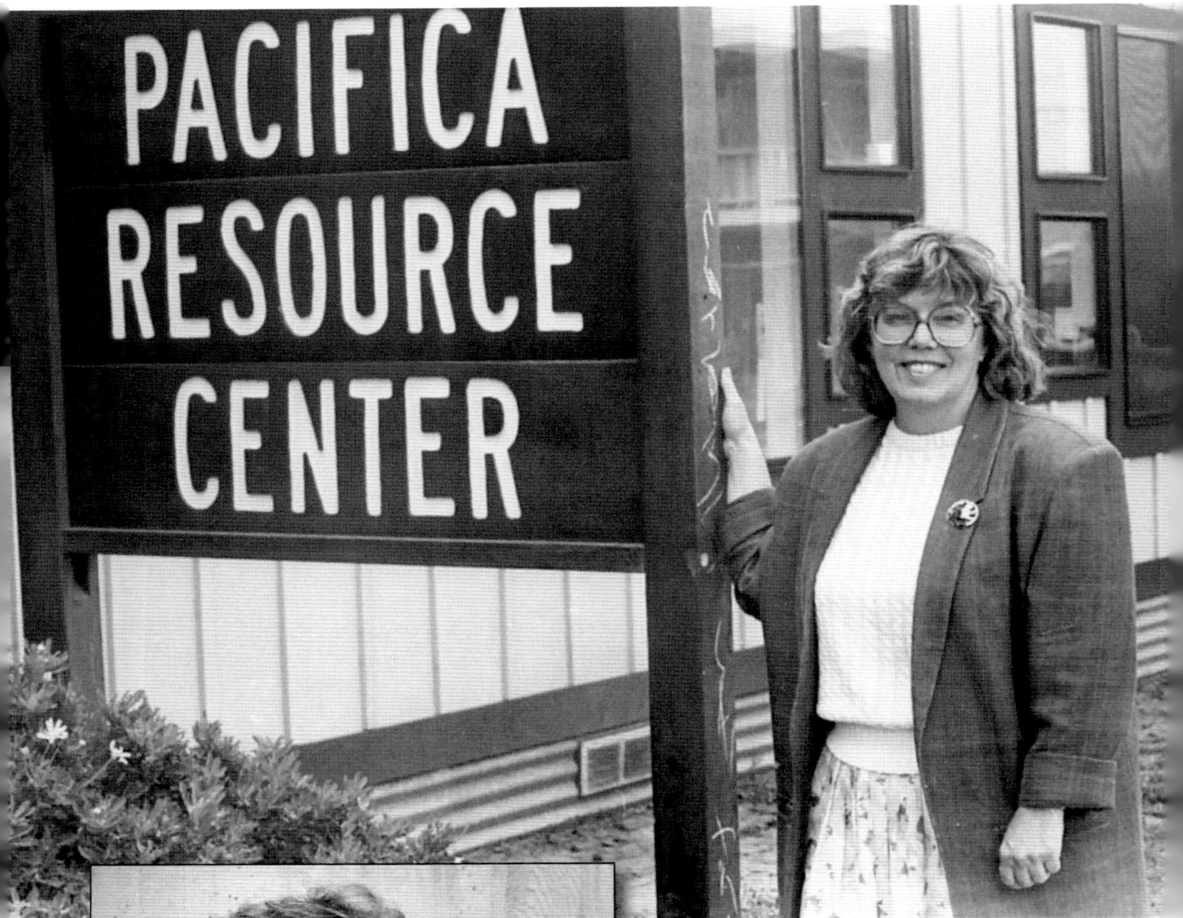

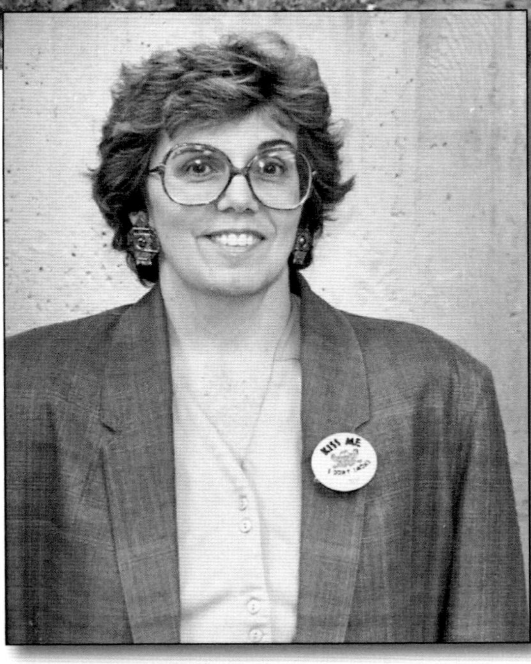

Pat Paik
Although she lives in San Bruno, Pat Paik was a powerful figure in Pacifica, sitting on the Laguna Salada Union School Board for several terms while one school was still located in San Bruno and then becoming the director of the Pacifica Resource Center, one of San Mateo County's core human service agencies helping people with food, shelter, and clothing. A constant presence at city events and a spokeswoman for the resource center, Paik helped build its reputation and popularity as a crucial safety net for Pacificans.

Gretchen Delman

A career teacher with the Laguna Salada Union School District, Gretchen Delman was also a valiant champion of equal school funding in California. A longtime official of the consortium of Low-Wealth School Districts, Delman spent countless hours lobbying legislatures and educating parents about the Byzantine formulas that fund public education in an unfair way. But she was also an exciting teacher whose personal seashell collection, gathered on trips to Sanibel Island in Florida, made students gasp in awe. Her classroom was like a shell museum, and, because of the nature of Sanibel Island, the shells originated from all around the world.

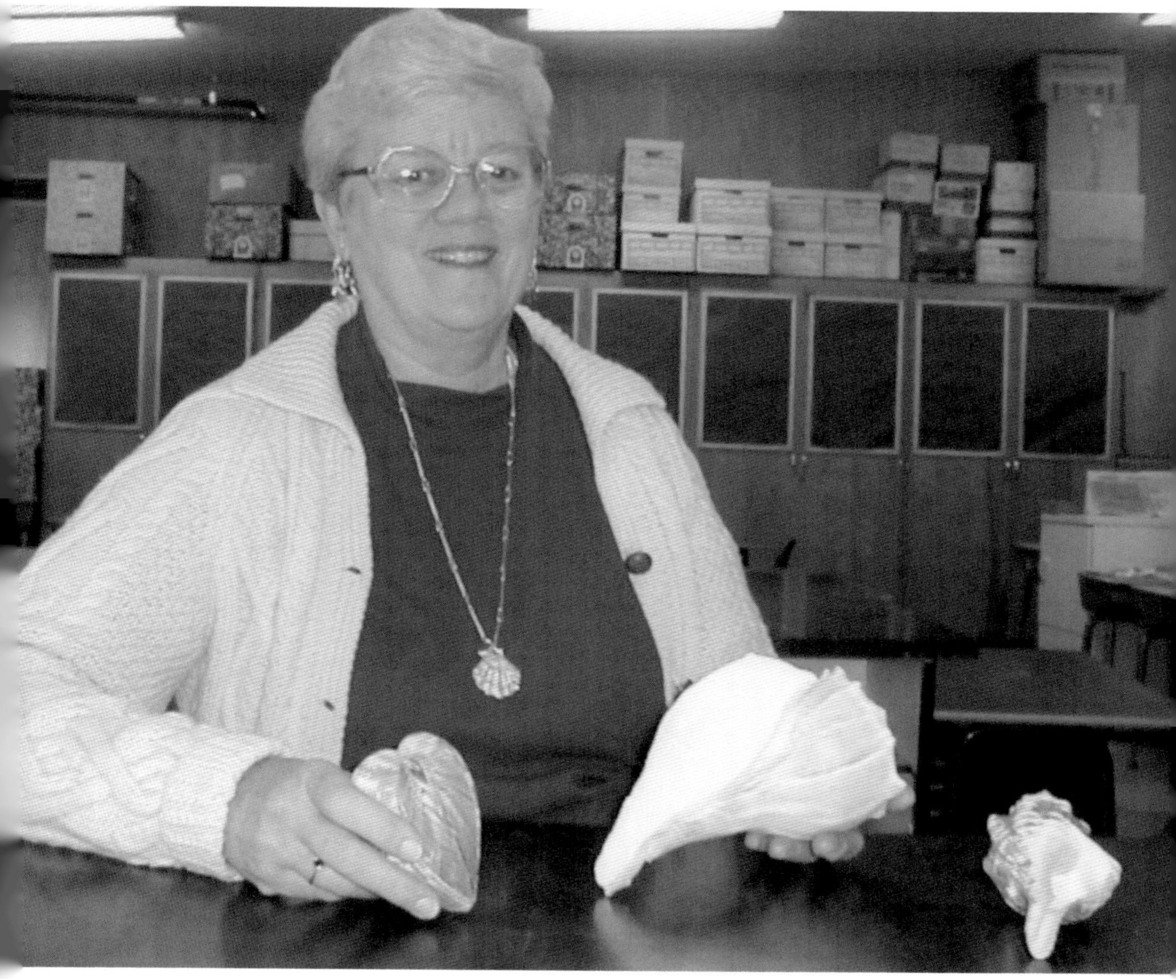

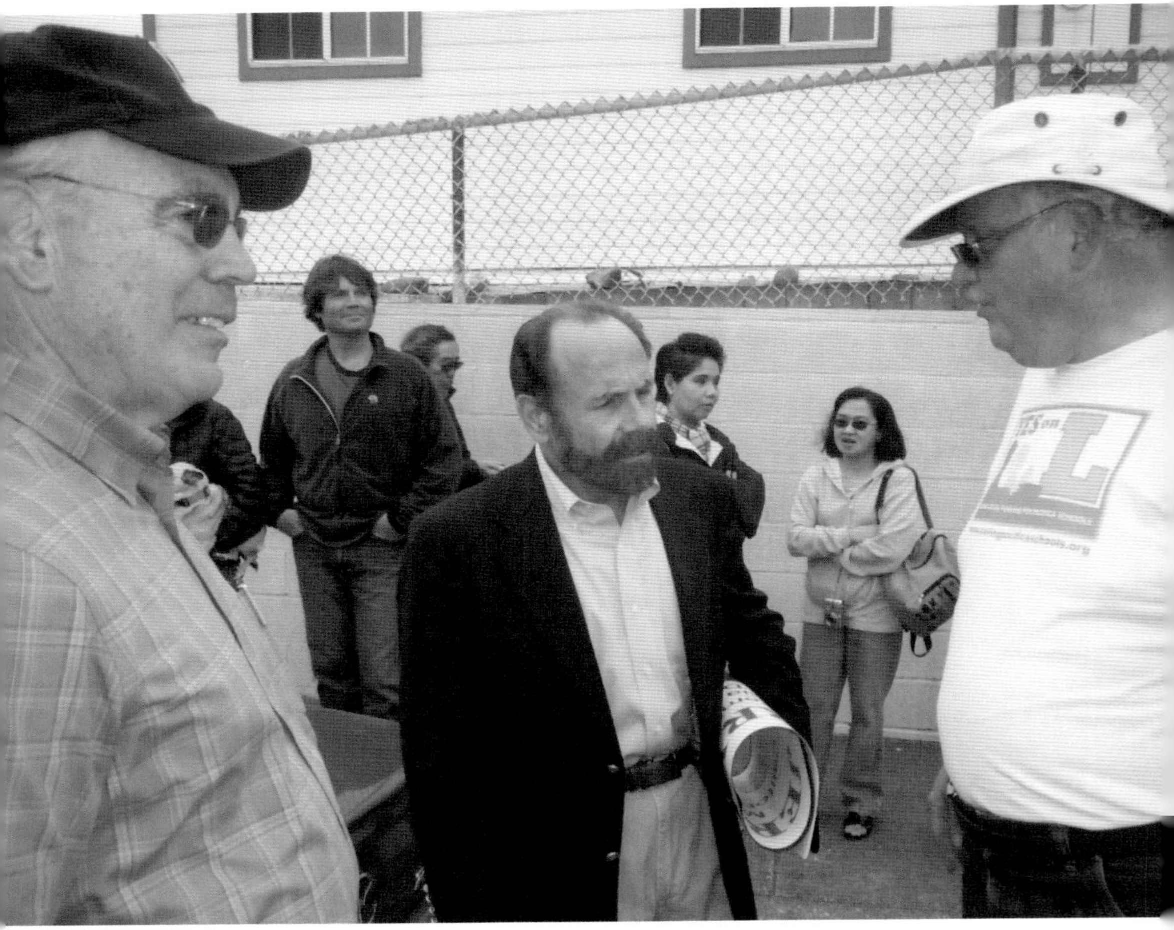

Michael O'Neill

Currently a Pacifica City Council member, Mike O'Neill sat on the Pacifica School District for more than 12 years before winning a seat on the city council. A physically imposing man, standing almost six-and-a-half feet tall, O'Neill was also on the city's planning commission for many years. Viewed by local voters as a moderate voice, O'Neill was very popular on the school board and was seen as a fiscally responsible politician. Voters often supported requests for tax increases and costly remodeling of the deteriorating schools in the district. In this photograph, O'Neill (right) is seen talking with Sen. Jerry Hill (center) and county supervisor Don Horsley (left).

CHAPTER FOUR

Pacifica Science

Pacifica is home to people who have had an international impact on the world of science and computers. The original creator of the Apple Macintosh computer, Jef Raskin, was a longtime resident and early employee at Apple. Kevin Kelly, the author and one of the founders of *Wired Magazine*, is a local. Folks who commute daily from Pacifica to Silicon Valley and San Francisco, making their mark on the high-tech world, are also avid lovers of the unique nature of the San Mateo County Coastside.

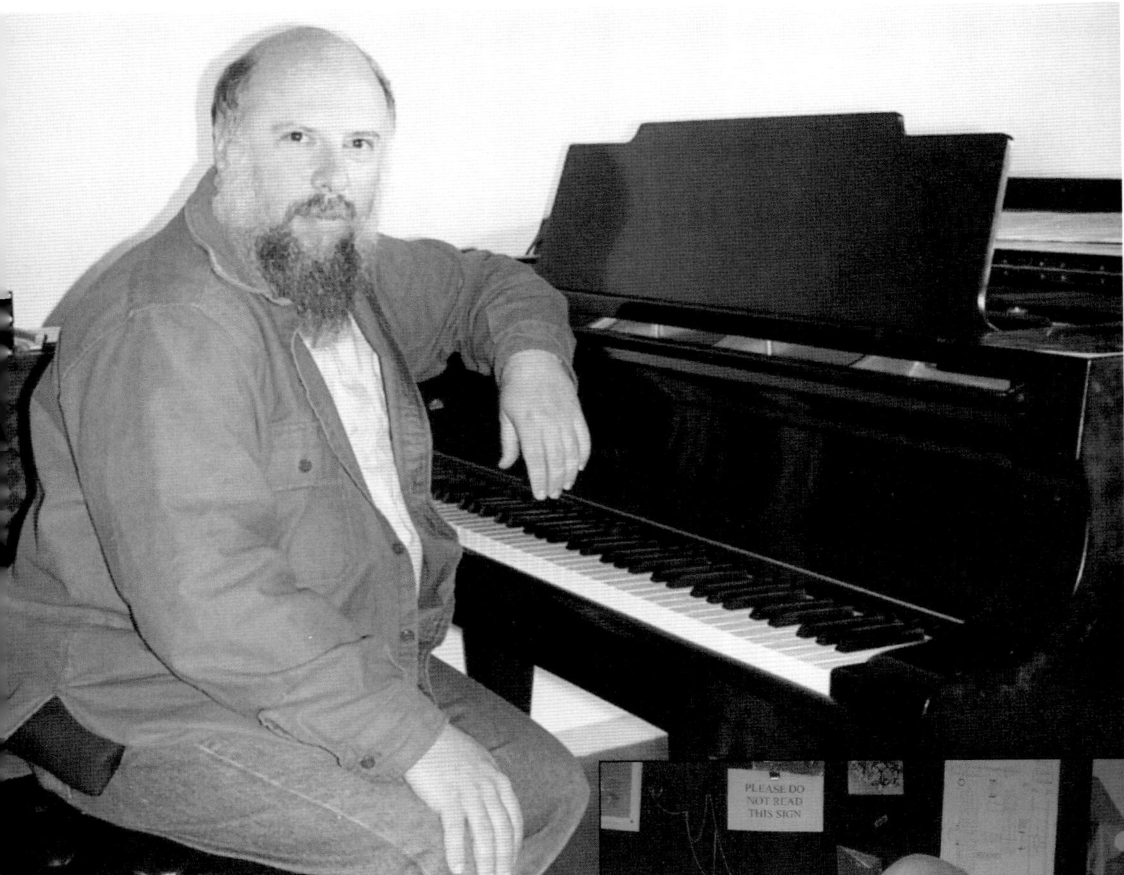

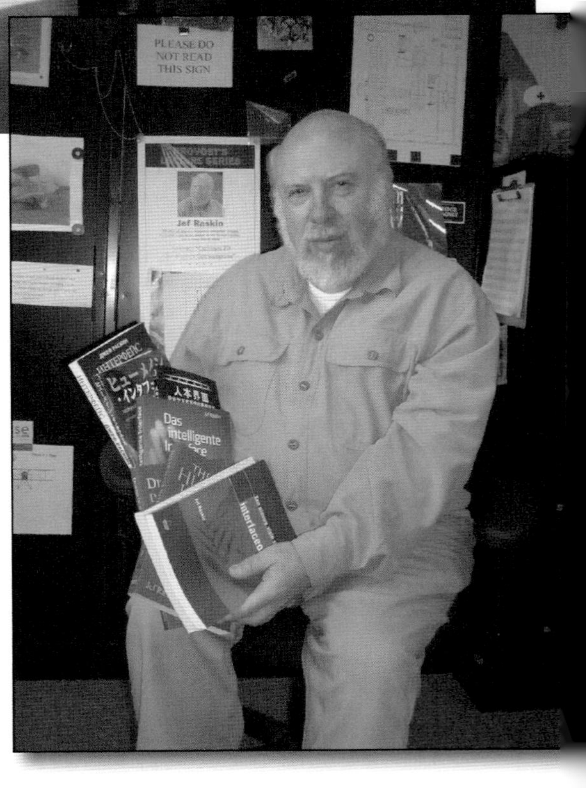

Jef Raskin
One of the earliest employees of Apple, Jef Raskin helped develop the Apple Macintosh computer. He was the one who named the project after his favorite type of real apple. A true Renaissance man, Raskin composed music, built and flew model airplanes, wrote a long-running nature column in the *Pacifica Tribune* and continued to influence the computer world through his consulting and writing work. Perhaps his book, *The Humane Interface,* will have a long-range impact on the future of computers. He founded his own computer company for a time, bringing out the Canon Cat personal computer, and influenced young geniuses, not the least of whom were his own children. His untimely death from cancer was a sad end to someone who was unquestionably one of the smartest people who ever called Pacifica home.

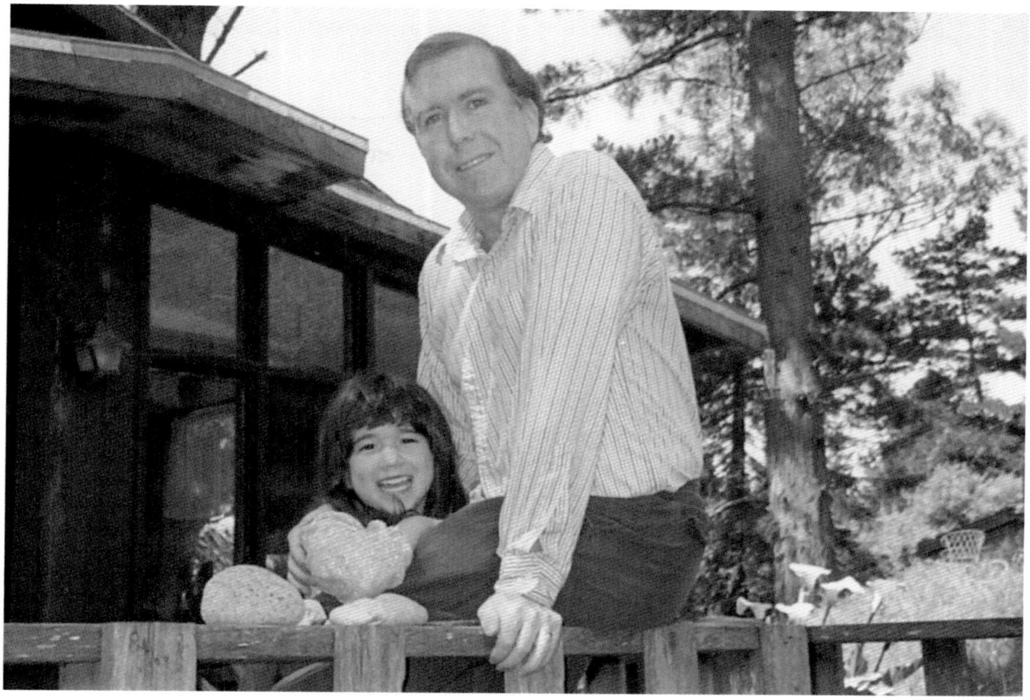

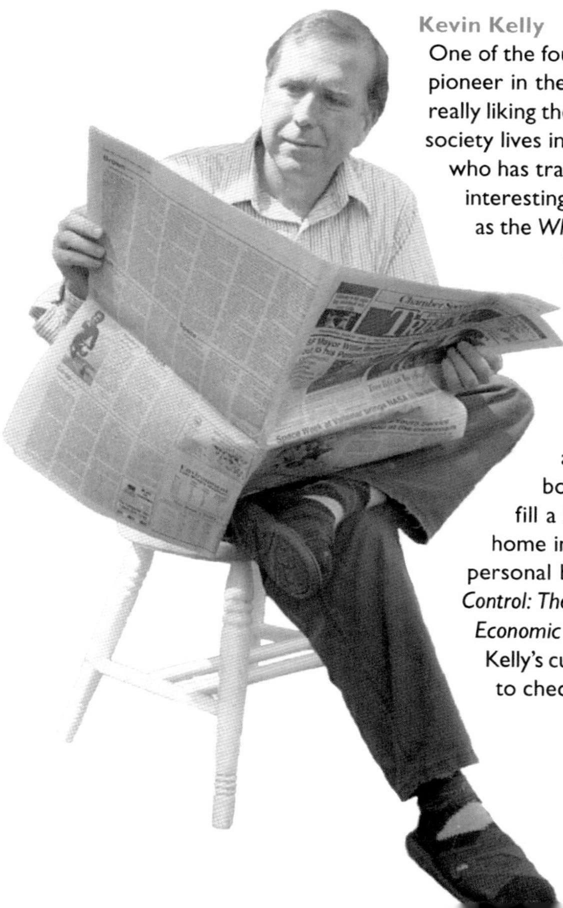

Kevin Kelly

One of the founders of *Wired Magazine*, Kevin Kelly is a true pioneer in the world of computers, but he confesses to not really liking them all that much. He is really interested in how society lives in a world full of computers. A devout Christian who has traveled extensively, Kelly has had a hand in many interesting projects that have influenced many lives, such as the *Whole Earth Catalog* and an early version of e-mail communication. He works with the Long Now Foundation, a nonprofit group dedicated to fostering long-term responsibility. He particularly likes the 10,000-year clock, designed by Danny Hillis, that symbolizes long-term thinking. He also cofounded the All Species Foundation, which is seeking to catalog and identify every living species on earth. The books, essays, and articles he has written would fill a library. In the above photograph taken at his home in Pacifica, he is with his daughter, Ping. On his personal blog, Kelly writes about his first book, *Out of Control: The New Biology of Machines, Social Systems, and the Economic World,* stating that it is growing in popularity. Kelly's curiosity and intellect warrants interested readers to check out his writing. Do an internet search.

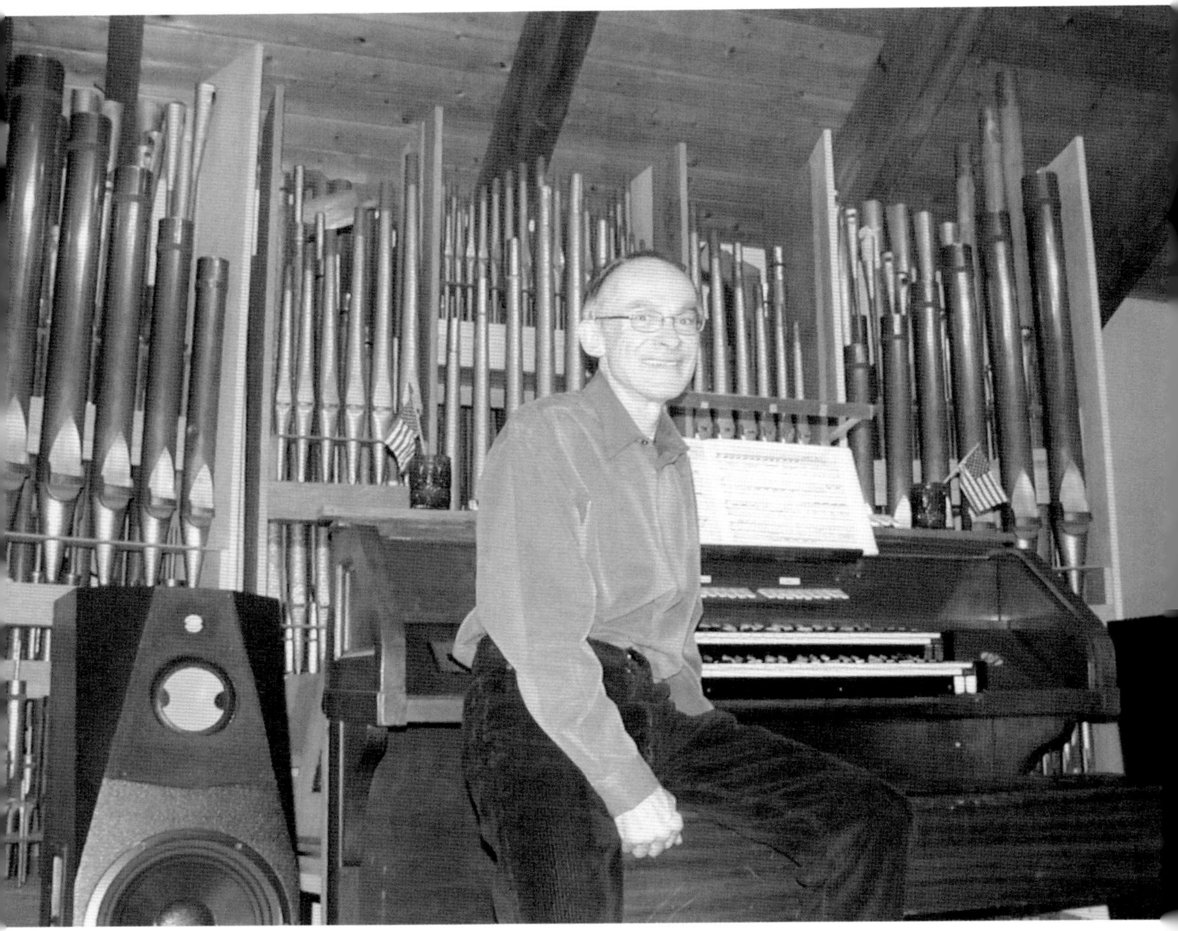

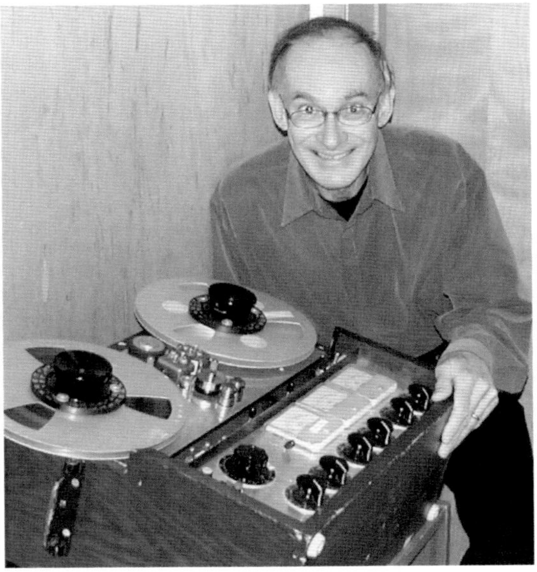

Prof. Keith Johnson

Prof. Keith Johnson records classical music of the highest level. The audio expert and technical inventor has been a part of Reference Recordings for more than 20 years. He is considered one of the top audio engineers in the world and his eight Grammy nominations and three wins prove that his amazingly accurate recording techniques bring music to life. He hand builds microphones and is known to capture performances in churches or natural environments that make the recorded sound as close to real as possible. The High Definition Compatible Digital encoding process is considered to be the most accurate recording process devised. A devoted runner as well, Prof. Keith Johnson can still be seen competing in the annual Fog Jog in Pacifica.

CHAPTER FIVE

Pacifica Business

Pacifica's nearly 40,000 residents depend primarily on the stores and shopping opportunities "over the hill." A massive retail sales tax leakage of more than 70 percent highlights what has been perhaps the most easily identifiable argument through the years: is it possible for Pacifica to have a vibrant business community while maintaining a residential town with strong environmental protection. Nonetheless, through the years, local businesses have made their mark on the personality of the city. Perhaps the most well-known establishment, Nick's, named for a man who was mayor four times and whose family continues a tradition that began in 1927, is symbolic of the city itself, clinging to a beachfront location protected by rocks from the ocean. Yet it still draws the most consistent crowd for lunch and dinner. A Pacifica business must be resourceful to be successful, attracting customers in an ever more-competitive market and an ever-growing variety of options just a few miles away.

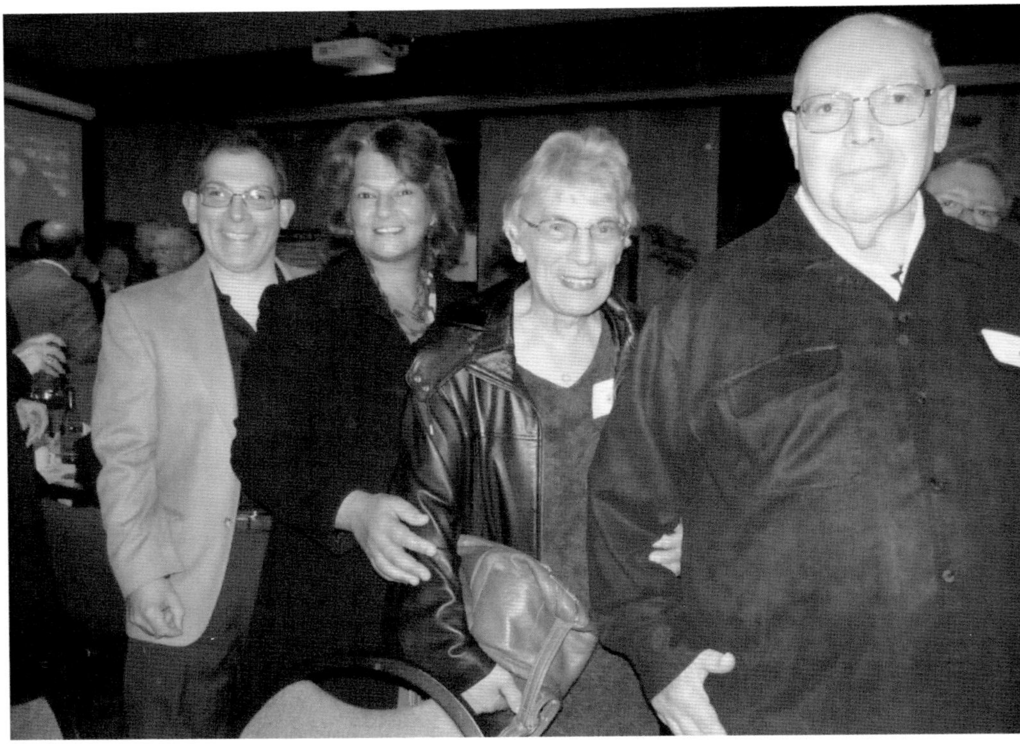

Emil Colombo

It would be hard to pick the single most popular business in Pacifica, but perhaps Colombo's Delicatessen in the Pacific Manor Shopping Center could easily be called the one with the most culinary excellence. A truly old-fashioned family deli, Colombo's is often a crowded jumble of tasty fresh meats and imported foods. Sandwiches are legendary, and the shop goes through countless loaves of fresh-baked bread to make the enormously satisfying meals. People come from throughout the Bay Area to pick up deli sandwiches and special items difficult to find in all but the most comprehensive food stores. The Colombo family still owns and operates the popular deli, which has been in operation for nearly 30 years and continues to attract local and regional customers. Emil Colombo chose the location in the Pacific Manor Shopping Center and his son, also named Emil, along with other family members, continue to offer what is a wonderful choice for shoppers. "My dad was right," said the younger Emil Colombo, succinctly summing up his father's business sense upon receiving a chamber of commerce award in 2013.

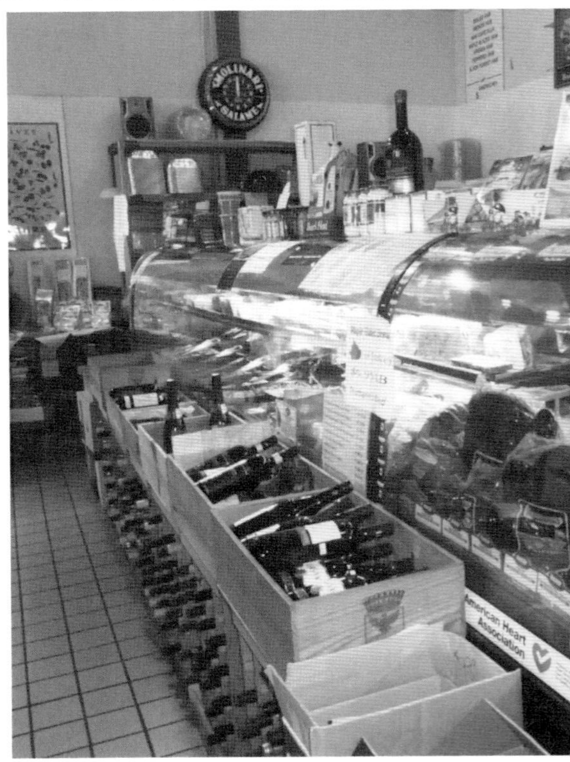

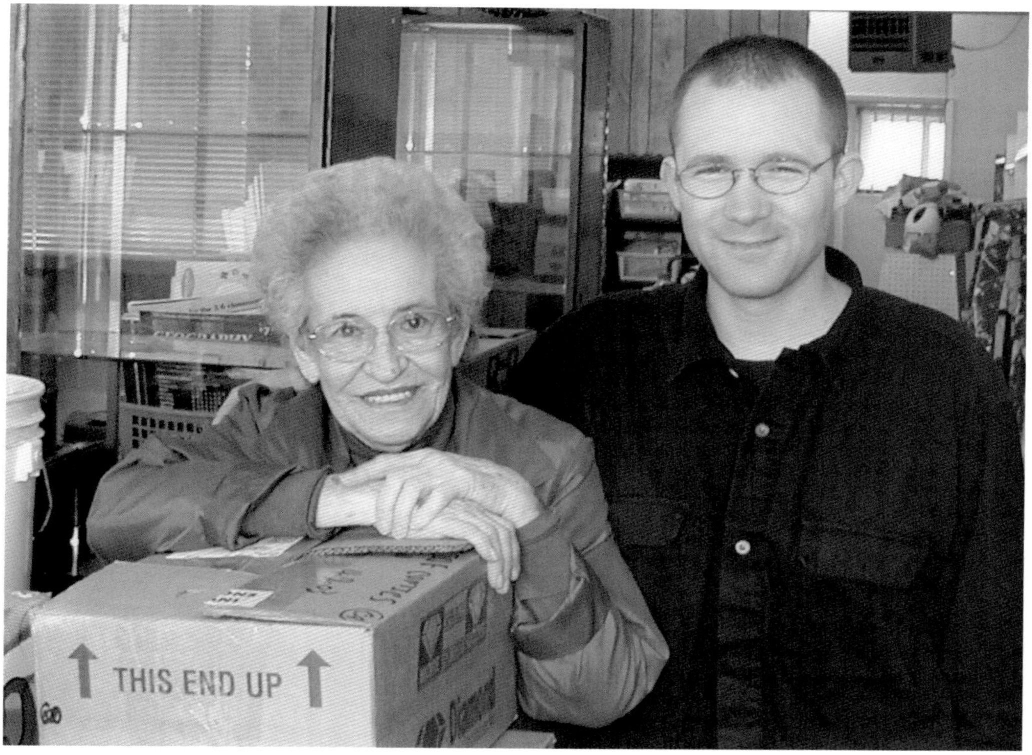

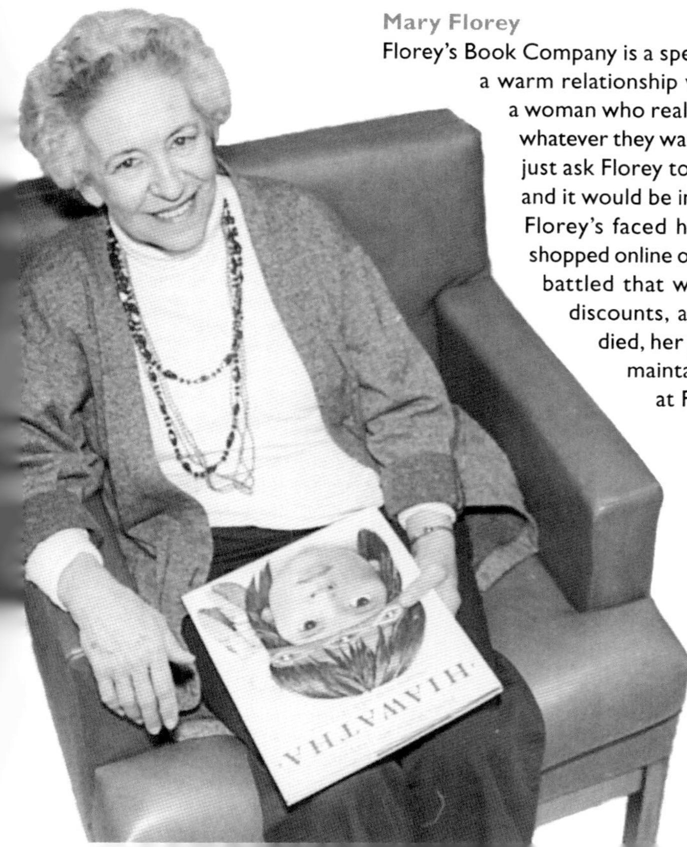

Mary Florey

Florey's Book Company is a special bookstore that has always enjoyed a warm relationship with Pacifica readers. Mary Florey was a woman who really loved reading and helping people find whatever they wanted. Before online shopping, folks could just ask Florey to research a book and order it for them and it would be in the store shortly. Like all bookstores, Florey's faced hard times as more and more people shopped online or at big-box discount stores. Mary Florey battled that with local author appearances, school discounts, and various reading groups. When she died, her grandson Aaron Schlieve took over and maintained the same comforting atmosphere at Florey's Book Company.

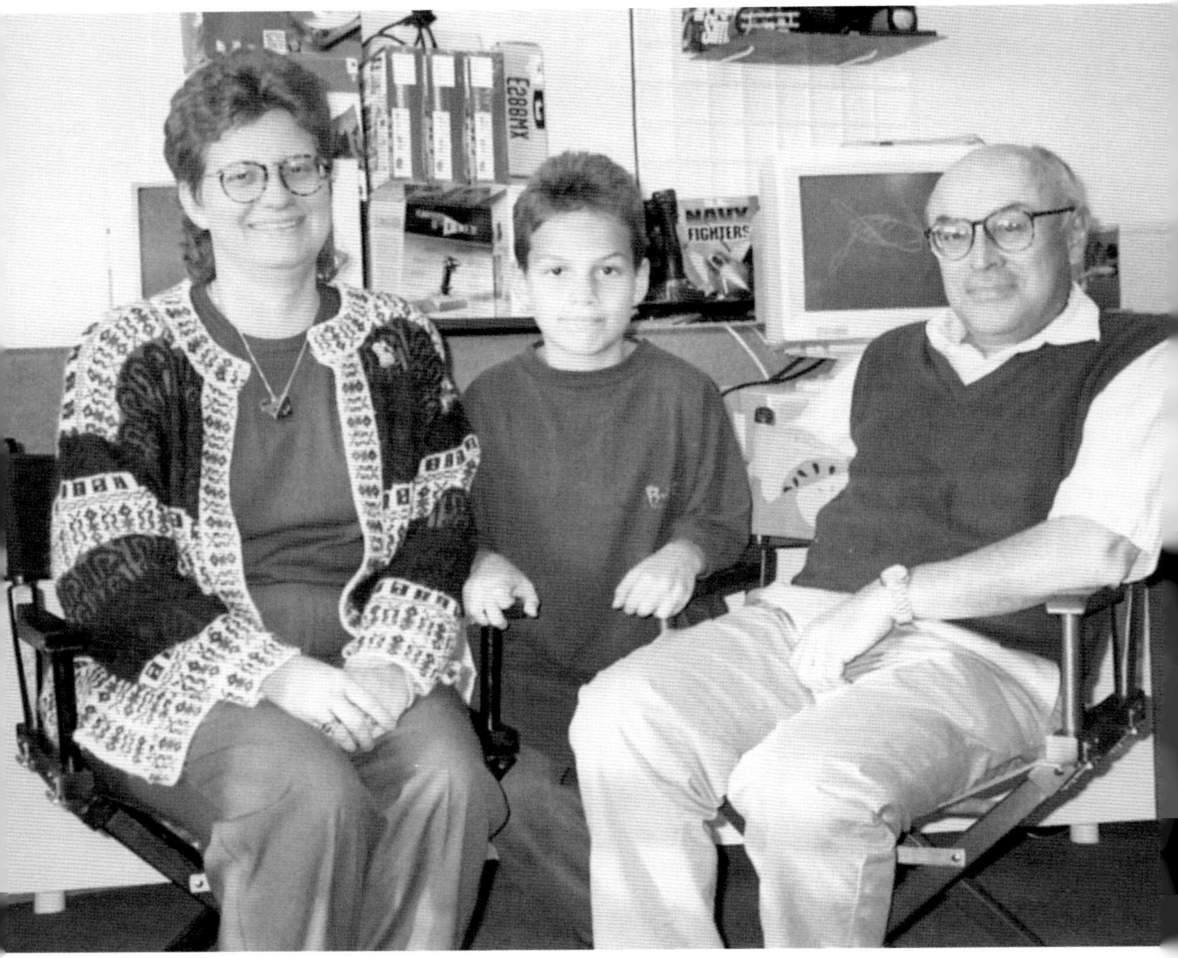

Ed and Stephanie Vinces
A senior technical specialist at Xerox for 30 years, Ed Vinces was one of the early computer professionals who helped develop what became the personal computer industry. It is no wonder that he and his wife, Stephanie, named the Pacifica company they founded in 1980 "Computer Pros." In addition to their successful business, they were deeply involved in Pacifica social and educational issues. Their popular GATE classes in animation, robotics, kinetic art, and a wide variety of other topics were beneficial in inspiring hundreds of students to pursue science and computer training. Stephanie has been active in the Pacifica Chamber of Commerce, as well as with groups as varied as the Golden Gate National Recreation Area advisory committee, the Pacifica Library Foundation, and the Embroiderers' Guild of America, San Francisco Chapter. Ed's focus continues to be providing consulting services for small business and personal computer systems.

Frank Nash and Glenn Stenstrom

The Coastside Barber Shop in Pacific Manor is an old-fashioned barbershop that has been in business for decades. Frank Nash (seated) once replaced the linoleum flooring and was amazed to see his own footprints could be seen as indentations, like those dance instructions printed on ballroom floors sometimes. He and Glenn Stenstrom (standing) work together and have a great camaraderie as they cut the hair of longtime customers as well as little boys getting their first haircut with their fathers. Stenstrom also has a reputation from his long and successful experience as a wrestler and a coach. As a student at Westmoor High School, Stenstrom became the first four-year letterman in wrestling there. With an Olympic dream, he was the silver medalist in Greco-Roman wrestling at the California state finals as well as the silver medalist in the regional Olympic trials. He attended the United States Olympic training camp in New York. As a coach, Stenstrom created wrestling programs at various schools and developed the Peninsula Grapplers wrestling club. To this day, Stenstrom's amazing physical fitness inspires and sometimes awes his friends and customers. A former marathon runner, Stenstrom is an enthusiastic advocate for fitness and is a personal testimony for keeping yourself active and in shape. (Courtesy Jane Northrop.)

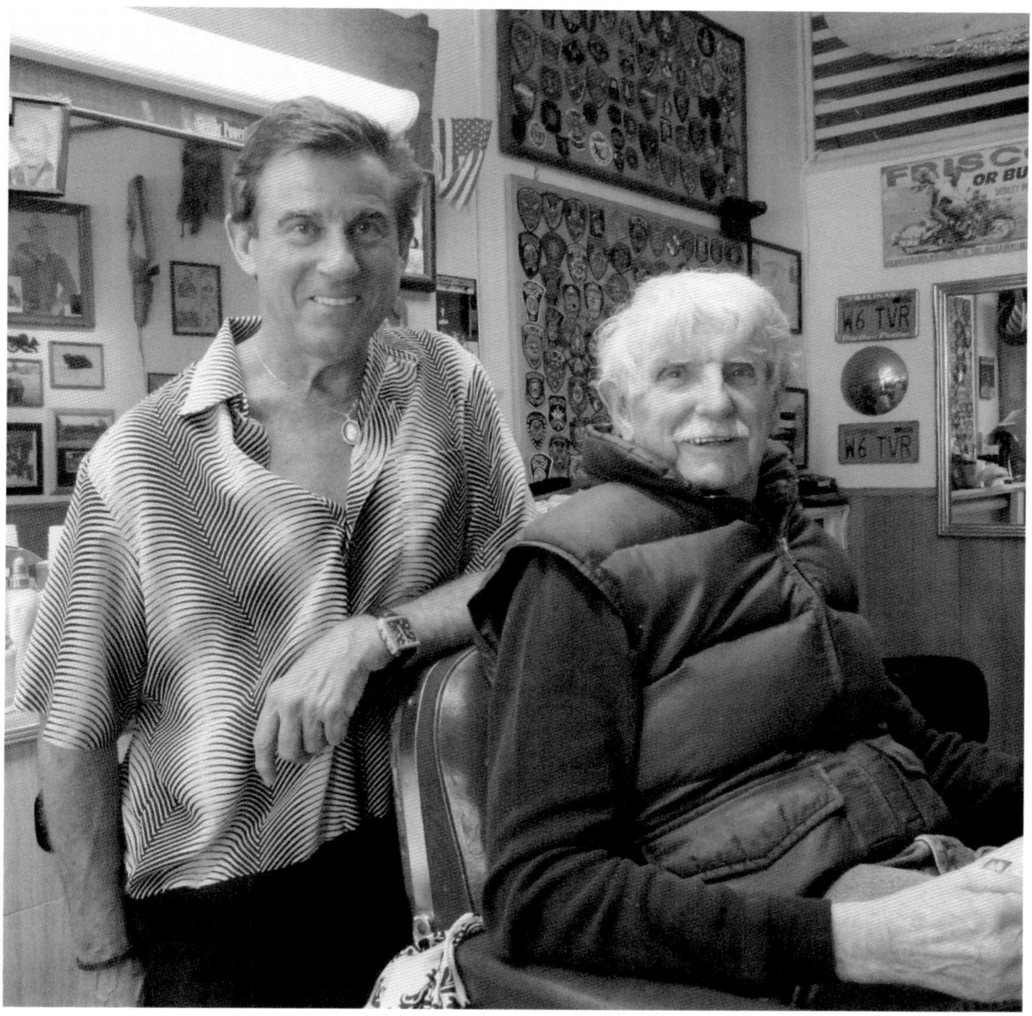

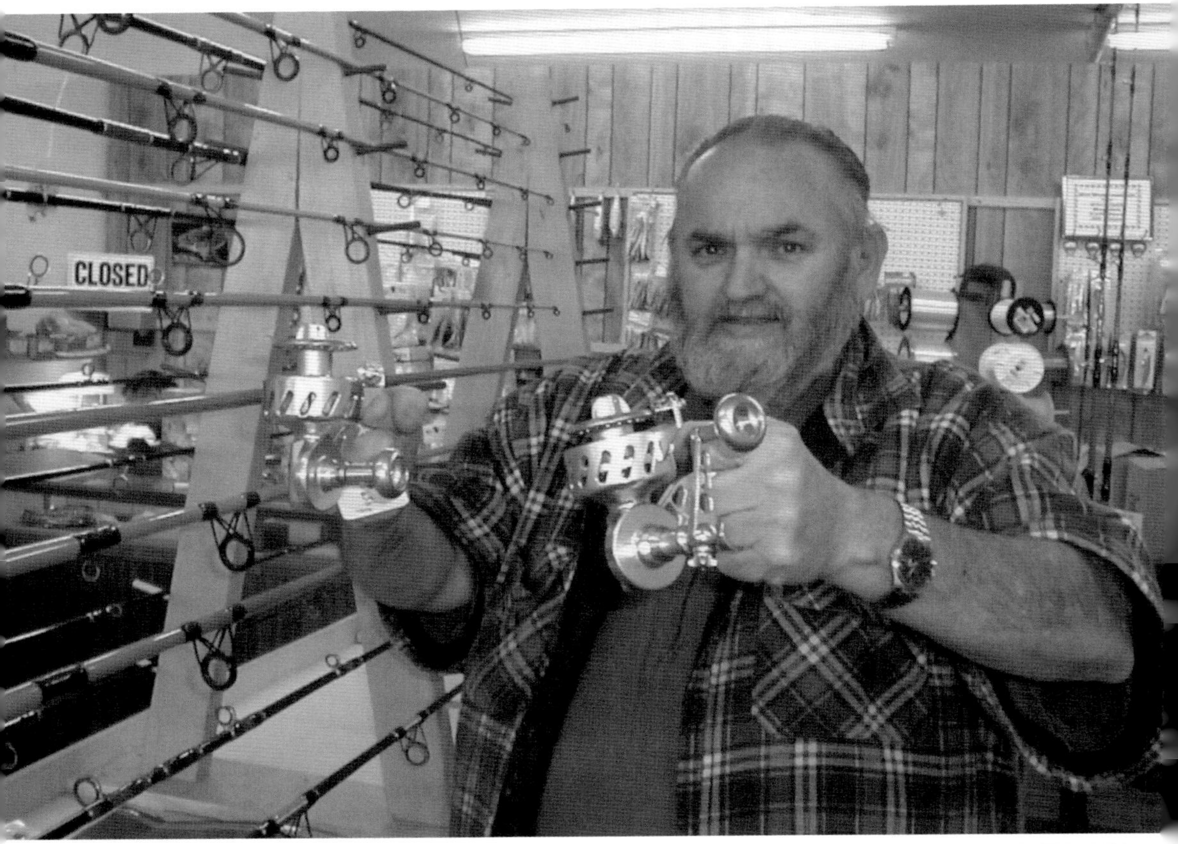

Joe and Cheryl Jimno
Fishing on the Pacifica Pier is one of the main attractions for outsiders coming to spend the day. For decades, Joe Jimno and his wife, Cheryl, helped set up folks with top-notch fishing poles, equipment, and bait. A unique shop with a mountain of memories, the Rusty Hook was a mainstay for generations of fishermen and fisherwomen in Pacifica. Once, during the 1990s, Jimno was in the news when his Sharp Park home exploded due to a gas leak. It was a truly frightening moment for the neighbors, and the Jimnos, but fortunately, they were able to continue with the Rusty Hook.

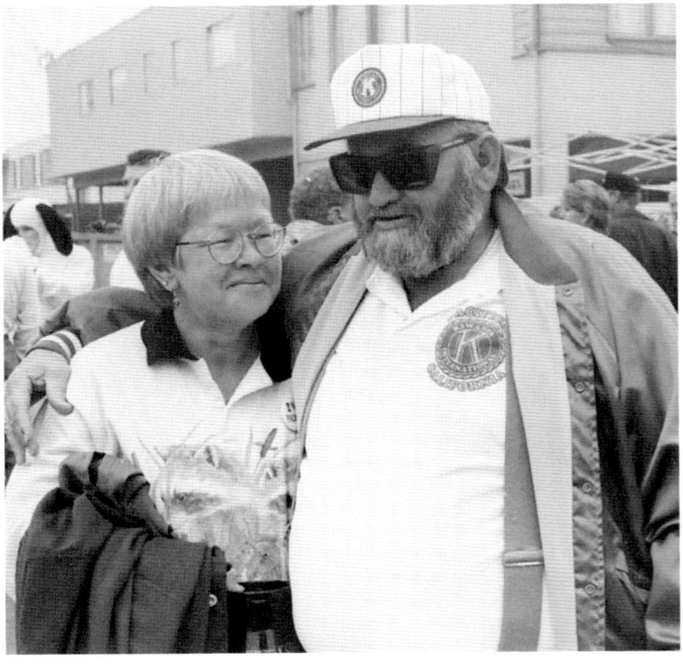

Dennis Willis

Dennis Willis likes music, movies, and television. He became a volunteer for the local cable access channel in 1981 when he was just 14 years old. His father, Jim Willis, opened a then-innovative movie rental store called Video Plus in 1986, and son Dennis ran it as a business until 2007, when it closed because of the industry-wide shift away from home video rental. "When we opened, we still had VHS and Beta tapes on the shelf," he says. "When we closed, the Blu-ray format had just been introduced. It was a good little store. Mainly, it was a good little meeting place and didn't cost a lot to operate, which is probably why it stayed around as long as it did." Willis took to the airwaves of Pacifica Community Television and created the *Soundwaves* entertainment program, keeping it going for 25 years and 500 shows. He eventually morphed this into an annual *Soundwaves Christmas Show* to raise money and food for the local Pacifica Resource Center, which continues today. "Over the years, we collected almost 40,000 items that we distributed back to the Resource Center, Toys for Tots, and a dozen other charities," says Willis. "As the economy changed, and the needs of the nonprofit centers evolved, so did the show. We set up a website with links to Bay Area charities and now pretape the show and bring in all of our own HD gear." The 2012 *Soundwaves Christmas* aired in more than half a million homes on seven different Bay Area channels. Willis is popular in the region as a knowledgeable movie critic, sharing his views on KGO radio and establishing himself as a member of the San Francisco Film Critics Circle and the Broadcast Film Critics Association. His show, *Flick Nation Radio*, keeps him in the forefront of the local entertainment industry, as do his several movie review guides. People who know him always enjoy personal conversations about the newest movies.

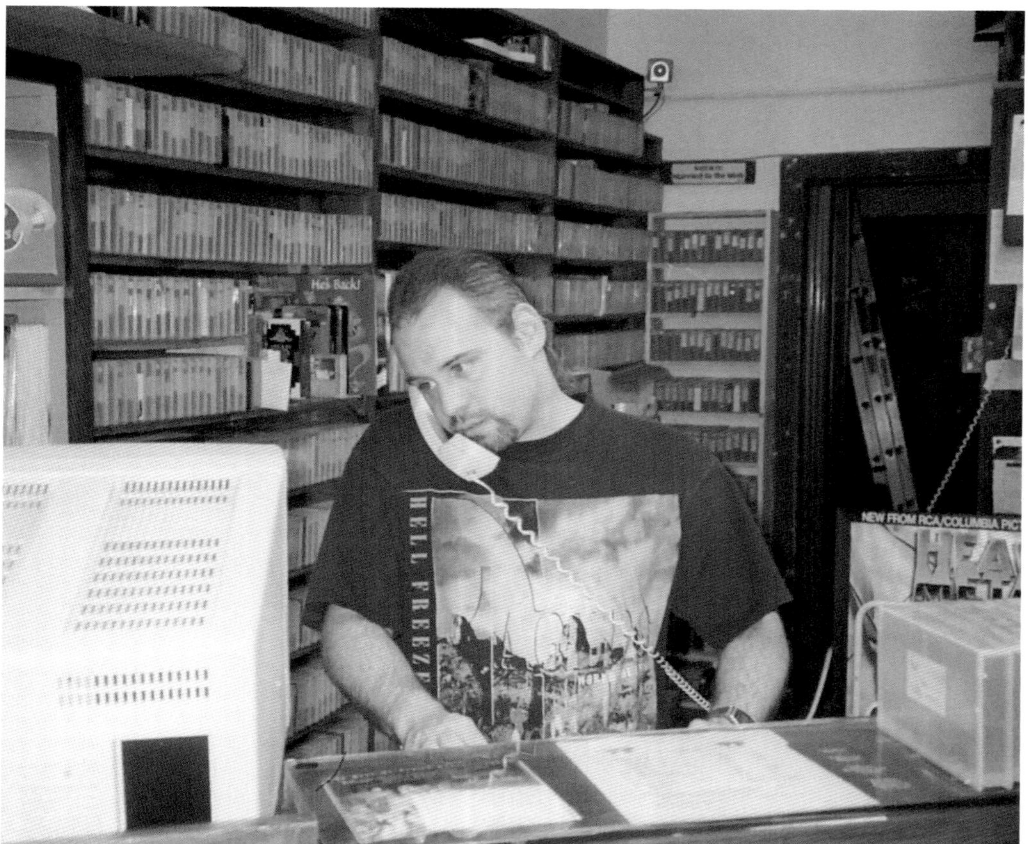

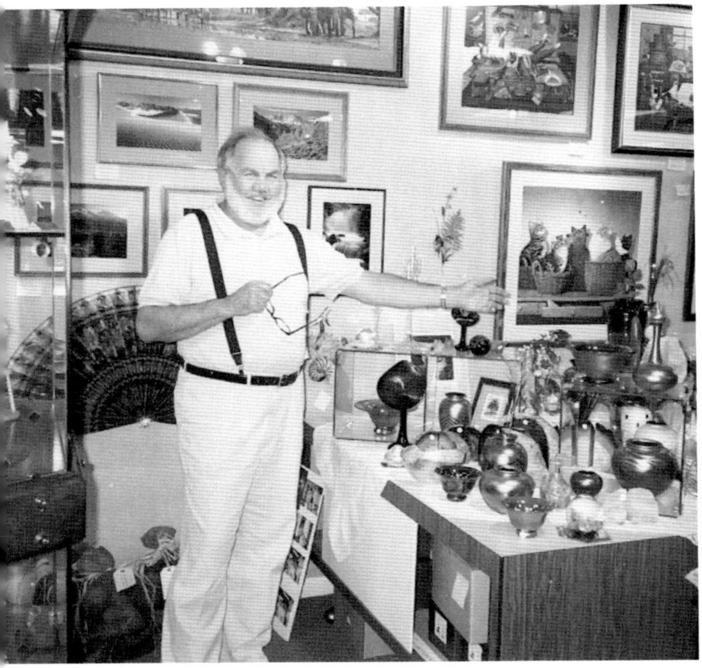

Dale and Enid Emde

The arts store known as Periwinkle was a Pacifica icon, no matter where its owners, Dale and Enid Emde, moved it. The popular store relocated to several different shopping centers during its existence, but it always maintained a vibrant outlet for arts, crafts, and framing. Son Lionel Emde, a professional musician, maintains the framing arm of the business under the same name to this day. Dale and Enid Emde, both active arts supporters in the Pacifica Arts and Heritage Council, helped shape the reputation of Pacifica as a haven for artists of all kinds. They showcased artwork, sponsored events, and brought much-needed attention to the cultural life of the city. A seasoned singer, Dale Emde was also a political activist who always wrote letters to the editor and made his opinions known to all. His son also continues that tradition.

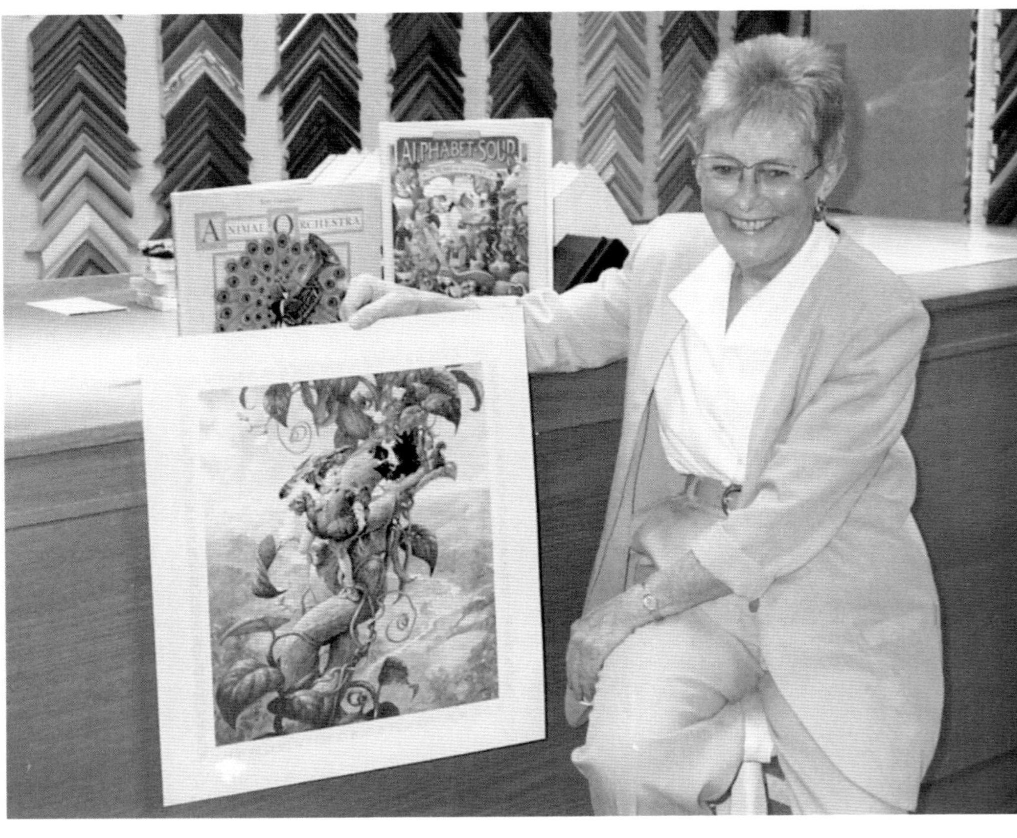

70

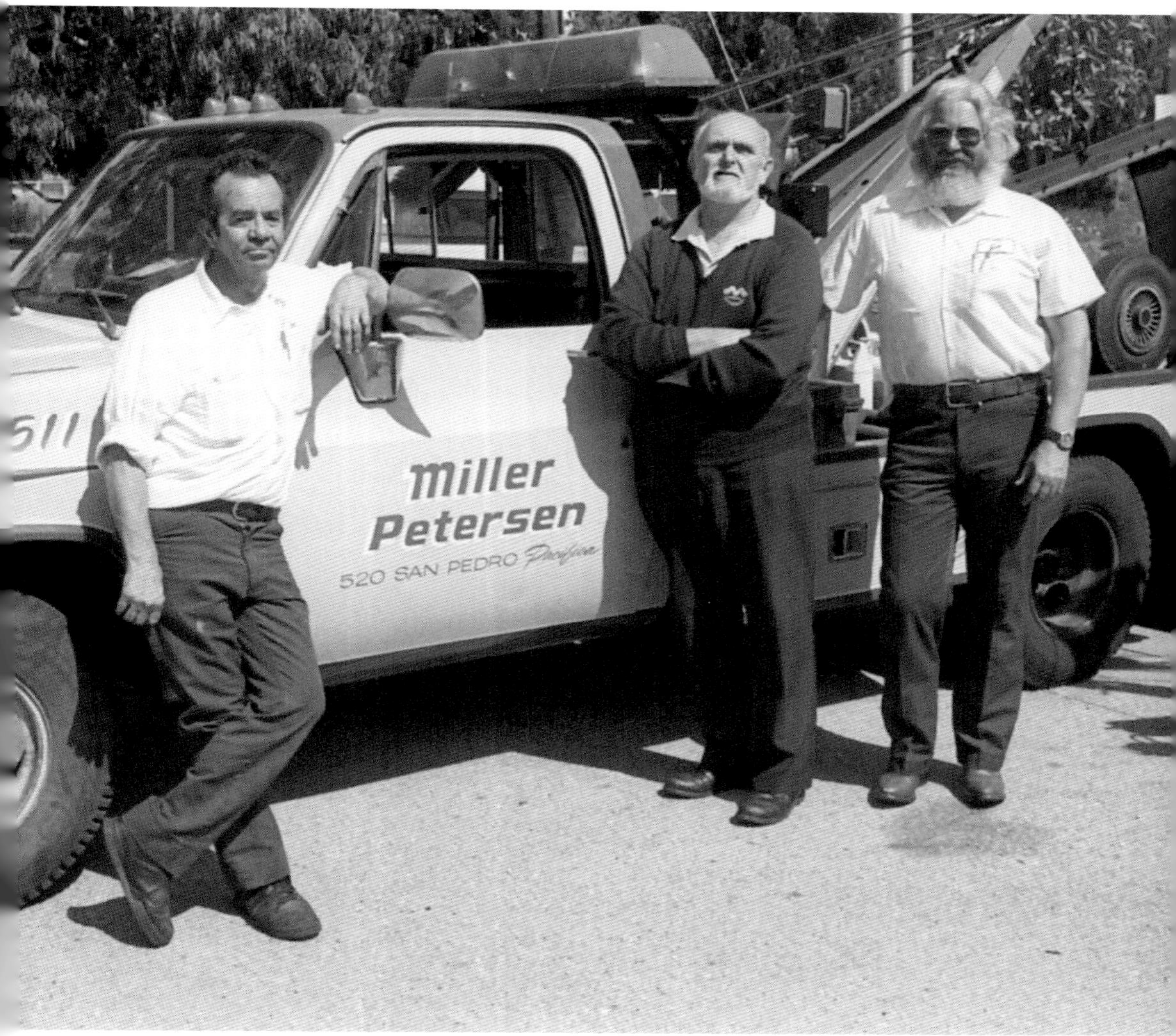

Miller and Petersen

Probably nobody knows more about cars and towing cars in Pacifica than the folks who have a decades-long history as Miller and Petersen. In 1990, the name Miller and Petersen evolved into a new incarnation at a new location on Francisco Boulevard. However, the legacy stretches back longer than Pacifica itself. Fred Petersen retired that year, but his name remained as Warren Miller moved the towing and auto-repair business in partnership with Ron O'Brien. One of the early car dealerships in Pacifica, Miller and Petersen sold Chrysler-Plymouth vehicles and GMC trucks. Today, there are no automobile dealerships left in Pacifica. When Miller first looked at the original Pedro Point location of the business in the 1950s, he remembers thinking, "All I saw was horses, a grocery store and a wooden sidewalk. I asked Freddie, 'are you out of your mind?'" They outlasted seven other dealerships and got out of the car sales business themselves in 1983. Miller and Petersen is a repair shop and towing company today. In the photograph, from left, are Fred Petersen, Warren Miller, and Ron O'Brien.

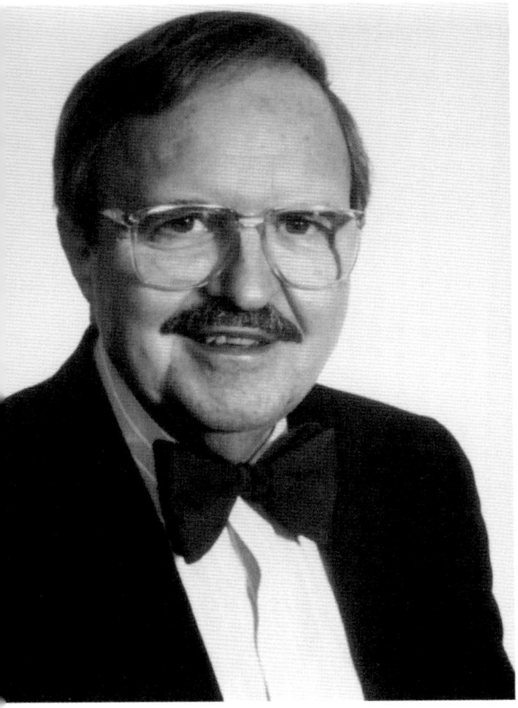

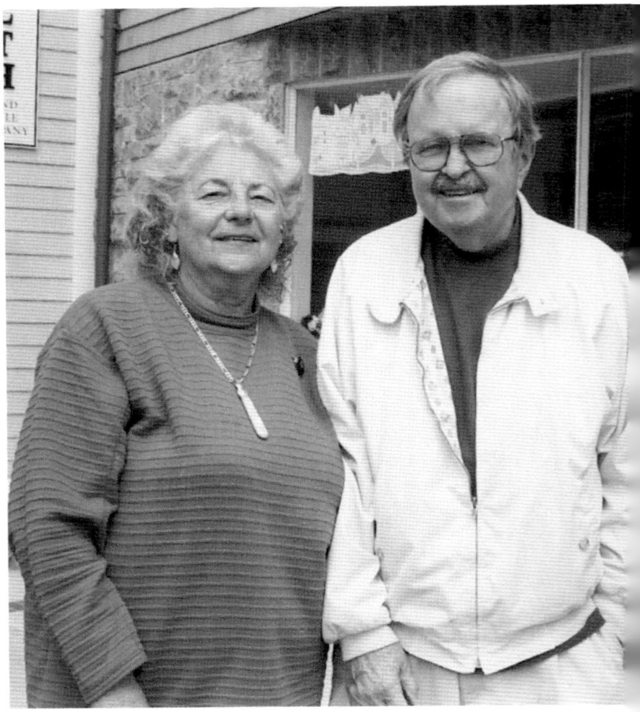

Bill Drake

Few people have the kind of impact on their community that Bill Drake, the owner, editor, and publisher of the *Pacifica Tribune* from 1959 until 1988, had. While the paper was a standard weekly community newspaper, Drake made sure it had all the information on Wednesday morning that Pacificans needed. It was jam-packed with just about everything that filled the lives of people in the community and could easily have been a daily considering the amount of information included. It was joked that if a cat was hit by a car in Pacifica, there would be a story including the cat's name and something about its personality. Drake and his wife, Peggy, bought the paper just two years after the City of Pacifica was incorporated, and they embarked on a mission to help grow the town while building the subscriber base as well. Drake included comprehensive sports coverage, which pleased the thousands of youngsters and their families in the many neighborhood schools. He also was deeply involved in coverage of the political scene and candidates always courted the newspaper's endorsements or griped when they did not receive it. Pacificans said that the *Tribune* was the glue that kept the community united, since the various communities making up the town were separated and distinct. Folks in Linda Mar often only knew about Fairmont through what they read in the *Tribune*. Sadly, Drake faced the tragedy of both his wife and daughter dying near the time he was retiring and hoping to enjoy the fruits of his labor. He eventually married his longtime friend and associate Jackie Ellis, (right). Like many people whose life revolves around a devoted dedication to an all-encompassing career, Bill Drake had a difficult time giving up the constant involvement with every detail of Pacifica, but his legacy of keeping several generations of Pacificans riveted to their Wednesday morning community newspaper is one of the true legends of the coast-side city.

Elaine Larsen

An ongoing presence at the *Pacifica Tribune* for 26 years, Elaine Larsen brought her journalism skills and an empathetic ear to community news that is hard to rival. As a young reporter hired by then-publisher and owner Bill Drake, Larsen learned the ins and outs of Pacifica, covering everything from politics to police. Born in Palo Alto, she worked at her high school newspaper and went on to UC-Berkeley and later earned a master's degree in journalism from Northwestern University in Chicago. "Bill Drake taught me more than any college course," she said. "As a police reporter, I kept my ear to the police scanner and spent time with police on ride-alongs out in the field." Adapting to the changing nature of newspapers, she was promoted to editor and publisher, all the while keeping up with advancing technologies and challenges. In 2013, she received a Community Hero award from Pacifica Community Television. "What I am most proud of are all the stories we've published about people in town overcoming adversity or helping promote a worthy cause. That's what makes the *Tribune* a true community newspaper."

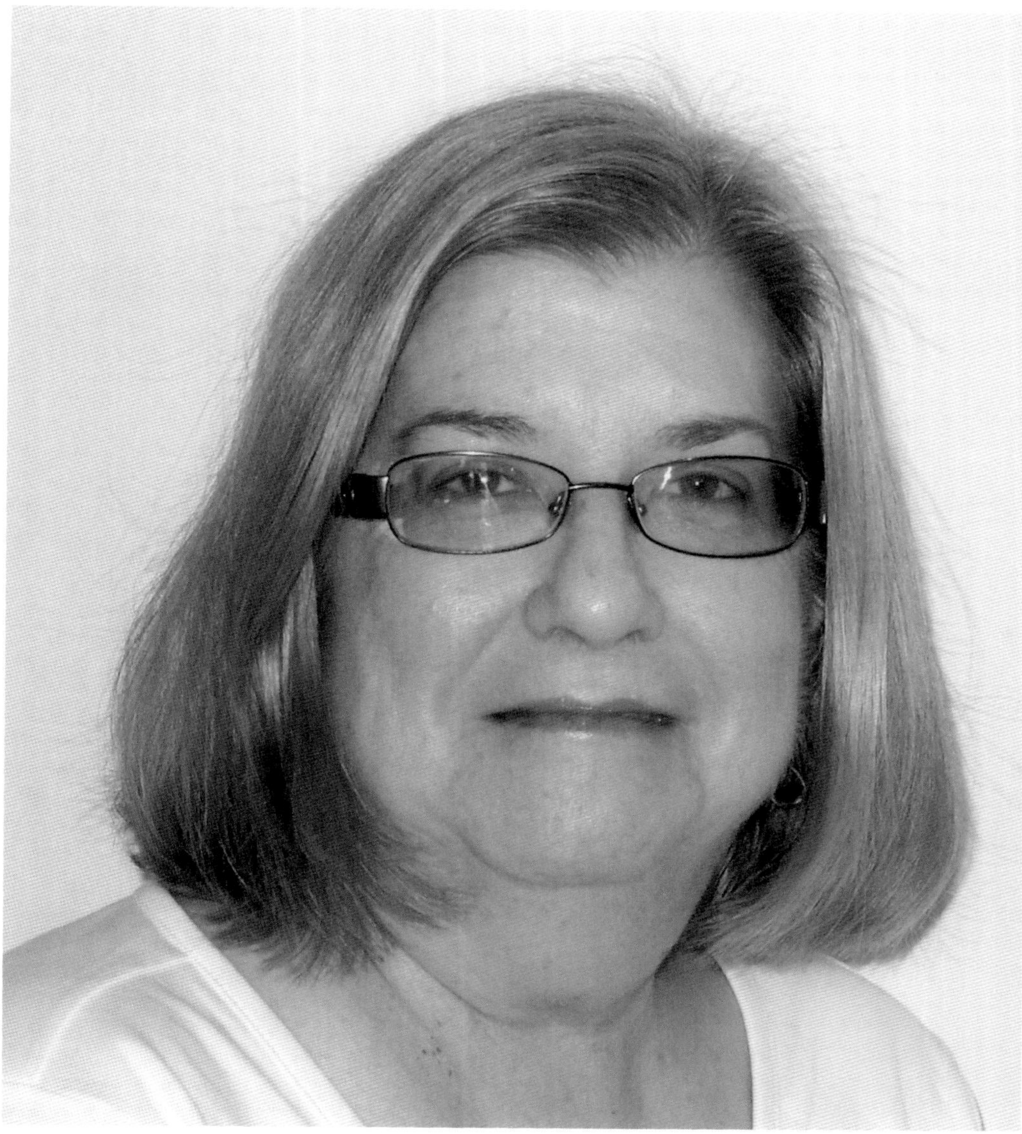

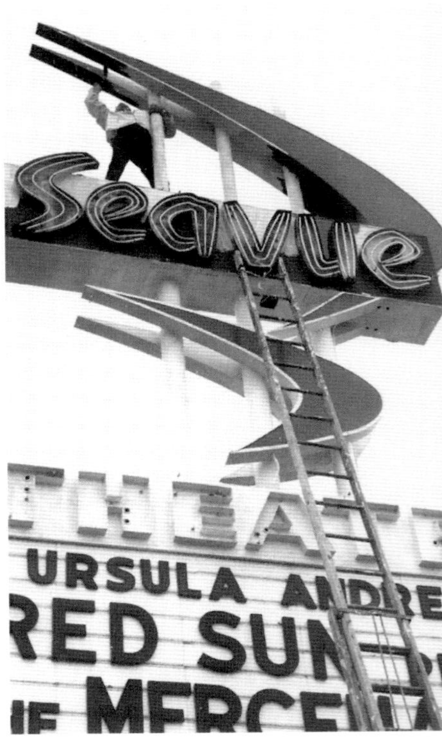

Seavue Theater

The first movie theater on the coast, the Seavue Theatre was a single-screen motion picture house, decorated with marine life murals on the inside walls and capable of showing first run movies. Pacificans grew up watching films there, even after it was split into a two-screen theater, known as the Seavue Twin. Competition from larger movie chains "over the hill" and an unsuccessful string of efforts to show classic or second-run films marked the end of the once-popular facility and it was eventually torn down and replaced by a Walgreens. The popularity of the movie theater to generations of Pacificans can still be seen through a Facebook page devoted to people reminiscing about their experiences there. It is one of the few businesses that seemed to have its own personality that was not related to a specific individual, and while it disappeared to history, it is not forgotten.

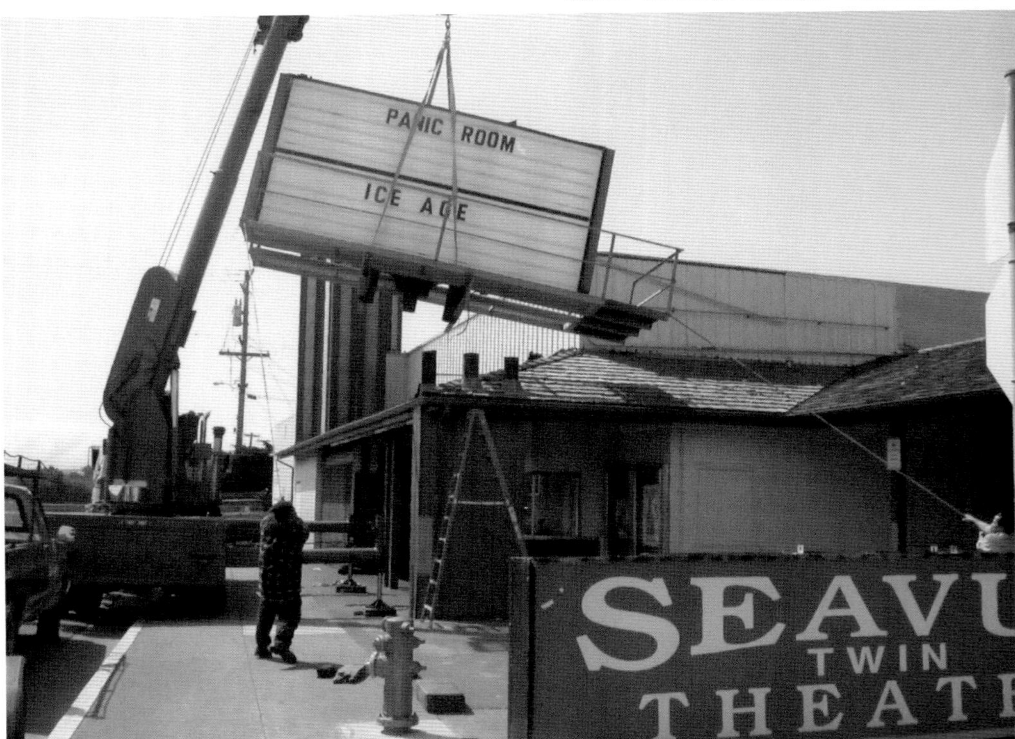

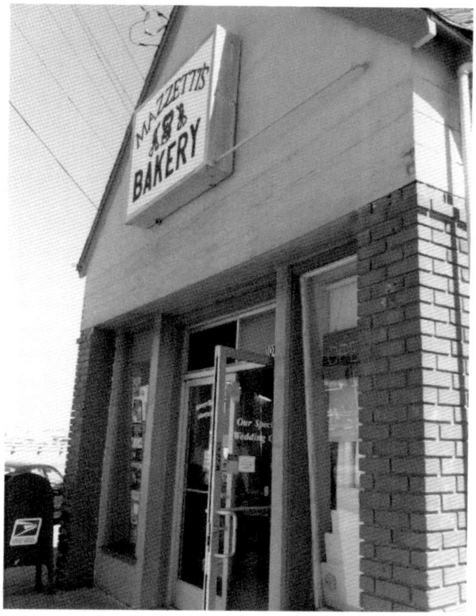

Julie Mazzetti

Julie Mazzetti runs the family-named Mazzetti's Bakery continuing a long tradition of local ownership for one of Pacifica's most beloved businesses. In addition to countless wedding cakes, cupcakes, and tasty treats, Mazzetti's serves as a sort of community meeting spot, with politicians and the public regularly having morning coffee and hashing out the news of the day.

In one of the original buildings left standing after the Highway 1 ditch cut through Pacific Manor in the 1960s, Mazzetti's still has an incredibly high, multigenerational support from Pacificans with a sweet tooth. During the holidays, the pumpkin pies literally fly out of Mazzetti's, much to the delight of customers and the business.

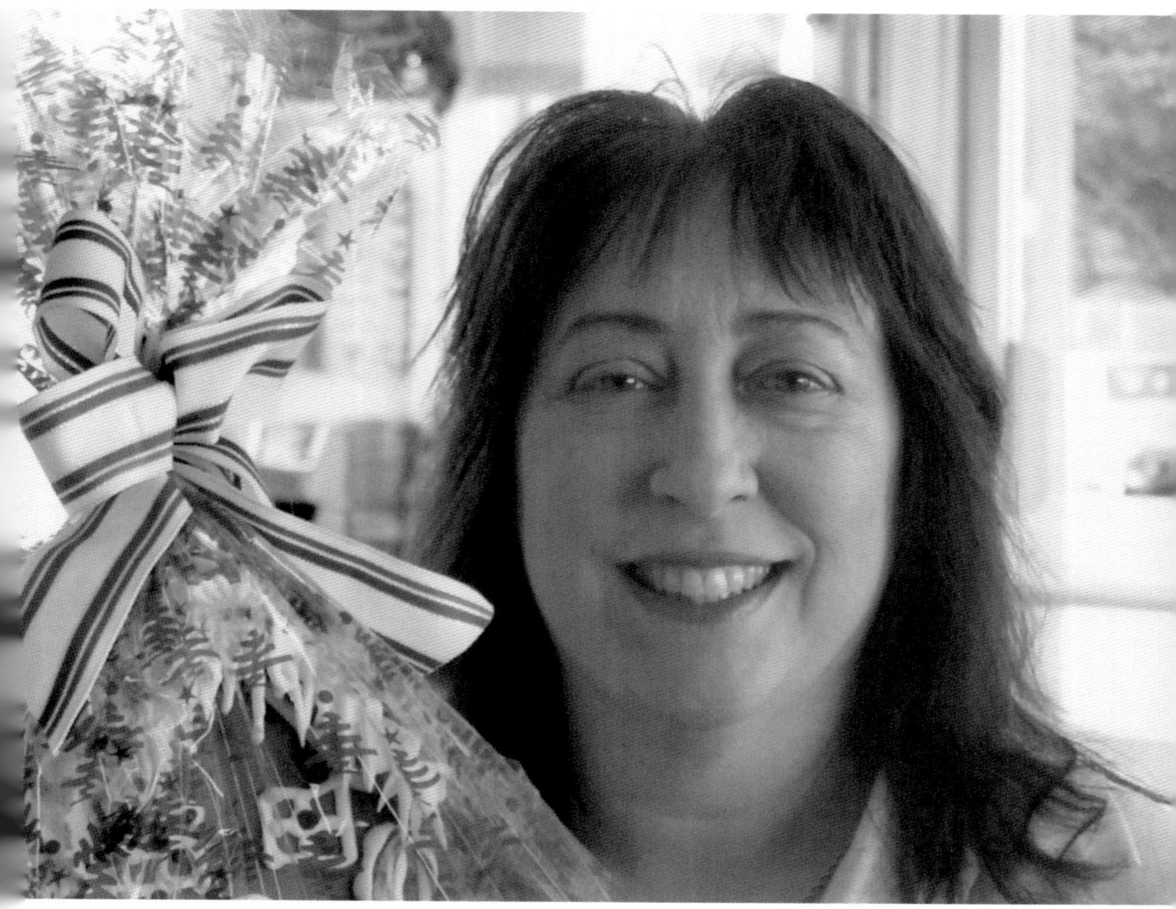

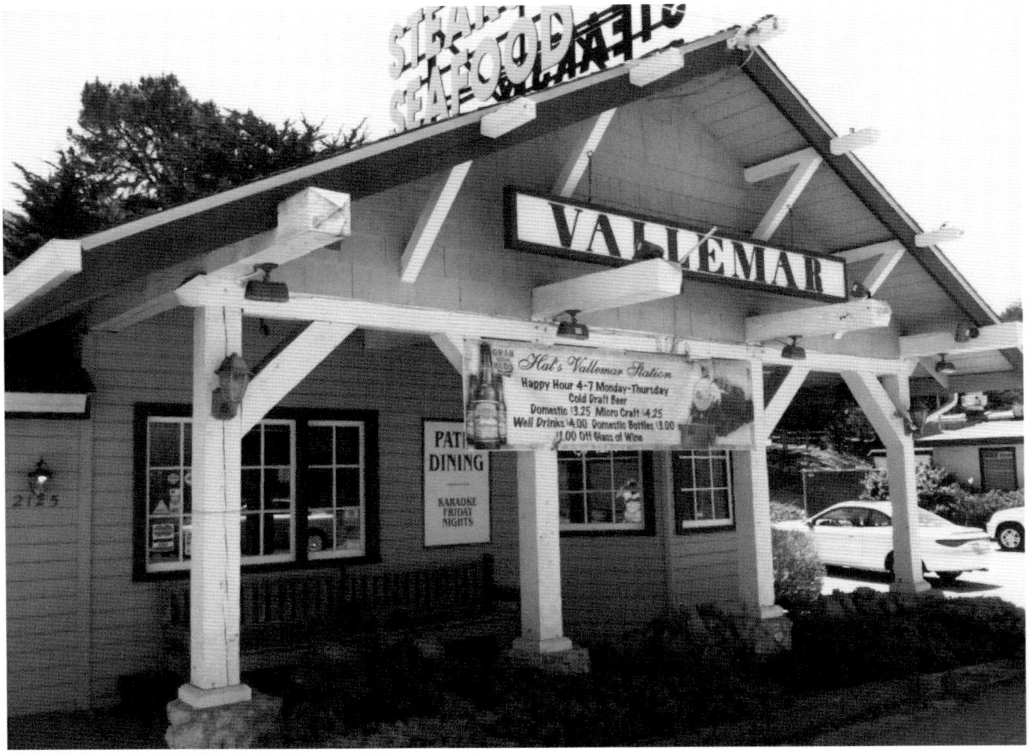

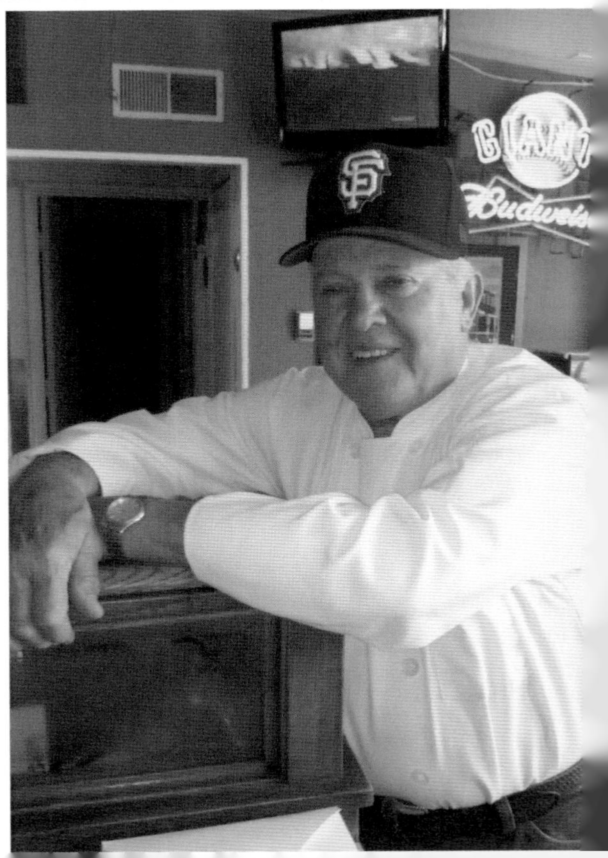

Hal Ash

Hal Ash is a restaurateur and proprietor of the Vallemar Station, a popular local restaurant in the former Ocean Shore Railroad station on Highway 1 at Vallemar. He also happens to be the primary cook there. He and his wife, Barbara, also ran the Rose Room in Pedro Point for many years. Once, the visiting president of Ireland stopped in for a visit. In addition to having a popular bar and restaurant, Ash kept the historic railroad station in great shape and a vivid reminder of the Ocean Shore Railroad.

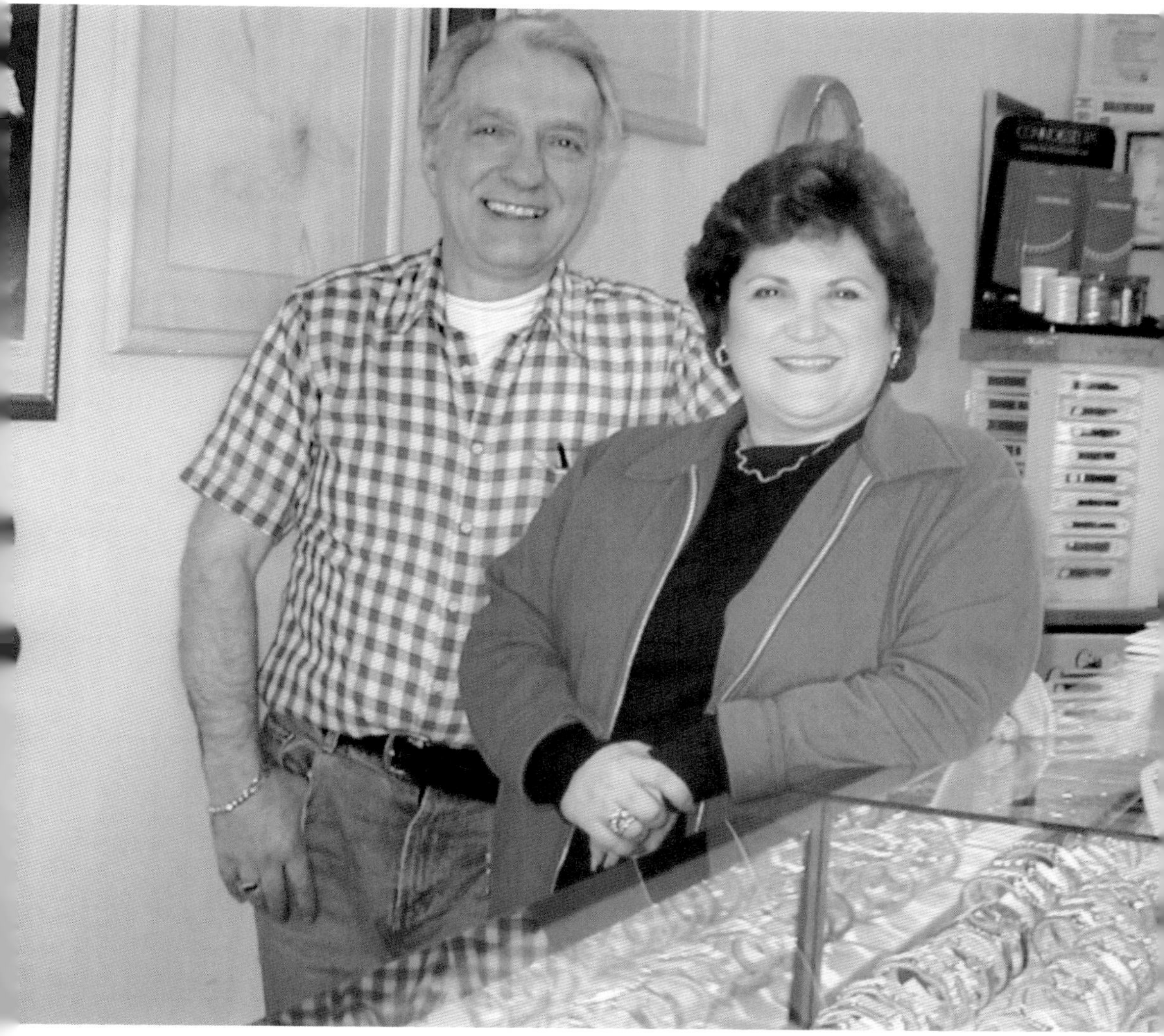

Maria and Phillip Ampola

Maria and Phillip Ampola created their Jewels Forever store in the Linda Mar Shopping Center in the face of ever-increasing competition from over the hill jewelry stores. By focusing on the local economy and creating a truly down home appeal, they have managed to stay in business for 23 years. In addition to the unique, Pacifica-themed jewelry they offer, such as pendants with waves and collectibles of Pacifica, Phillip is a skilled artisan capable of repairing or refurbishing just about any piece of jewelry or watch. He works on site and can often complete many repairs while the customer waits.

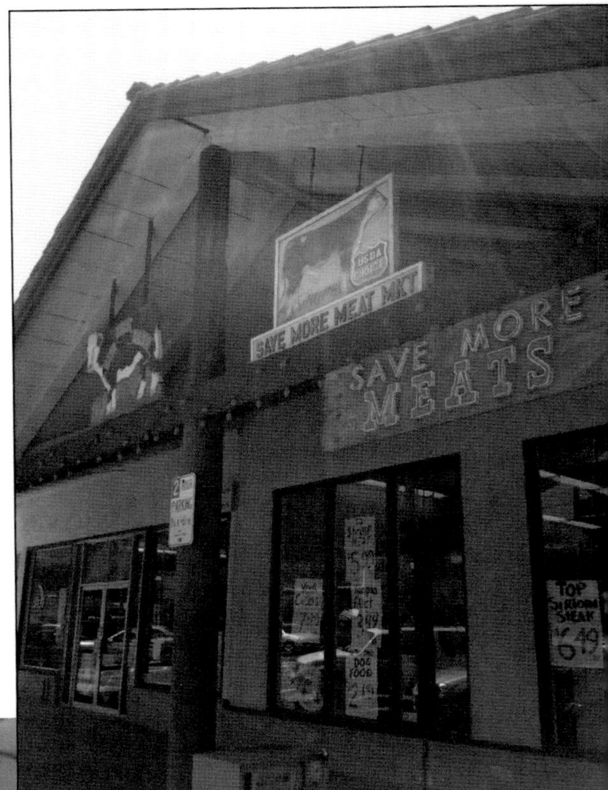

Matthew Lee

One of the truly long lasting businesses in Pacifica, the Lee family's Save More Meats is an old-fashioned, quality butcher shop specializing in a wide variety of quality meat and poultry products. Family-owned and operated, Save More Meats continues to provide discerning shoppers with specialized cuts of meat with Matthew Lee following in his father, George Lee's, footsteps.

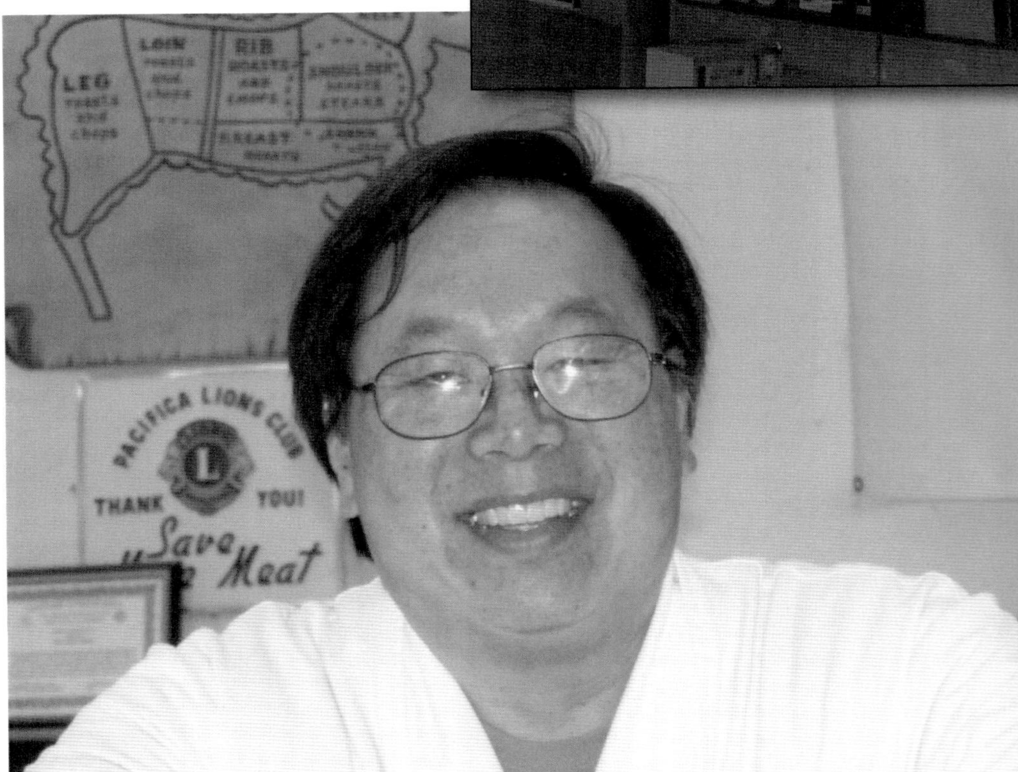

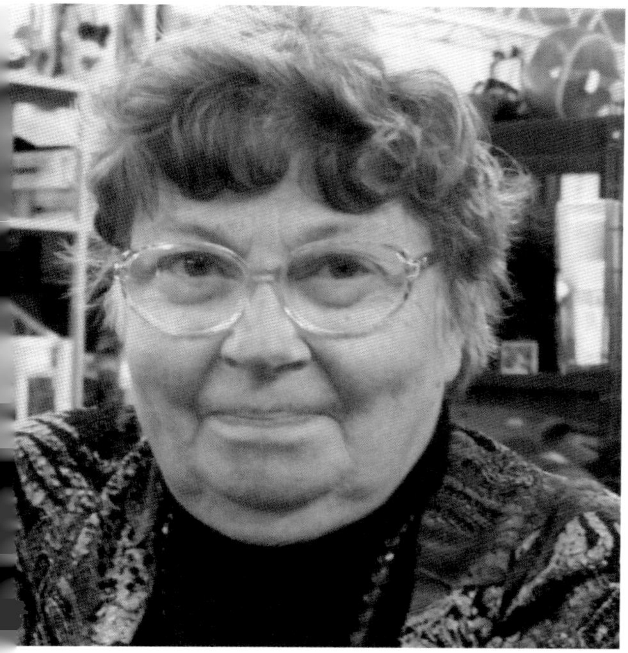

Sarah Glew

Manor Music, in the Pacific Manor Shopping Center, has been in business for decades in two different locations at the center. Owned and operated by Sarah Glew, the comprehensive music store features just about every brand of guitar and electronic organ imaginable. Musicians from throughout the Bay Area use Manor Music as a go-to rental facility for amplifiers and concert equipment, while music students rent band instruments, get sheet music, and find every accessory they need. It is a legendary music store, which brings attention to Pacifica in a very specific business niche. In addition to running her store, Glew has always been active in the unusual organization of property owners and business owners that manage the hybrid shopping center. While each storefront is actually a separate building, the parking lot is owned by the shopping center association.

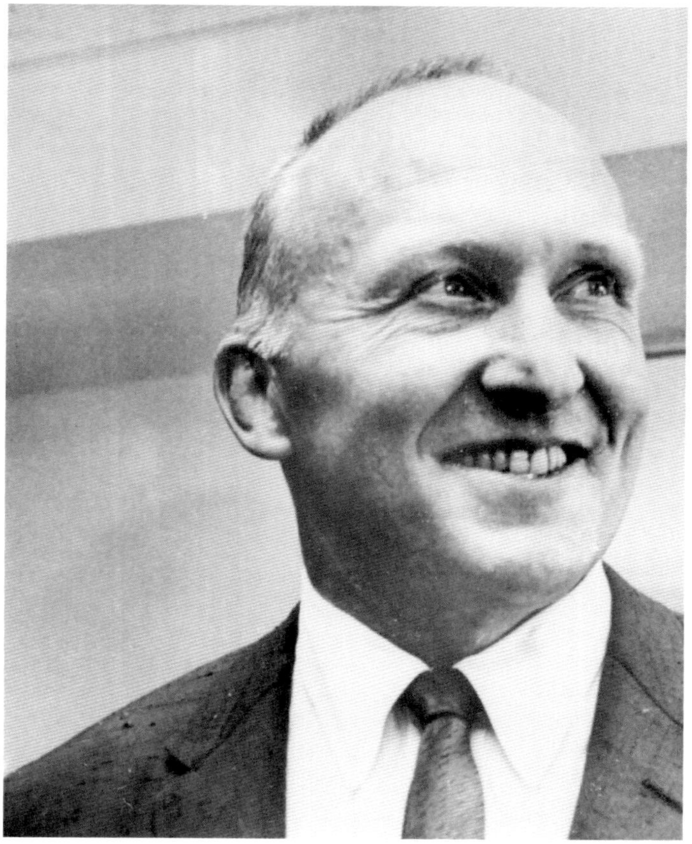

Andres Oddstad

The original developer of the Linda Mar residential suburb, Andres Oddstad was tragically killed in a car accident in the East Bay at the age of 44, putting an end to what many viewed was becoming a major development career that would have competed with Henry Doelger, who built so much of Daly City. Oddstad purchased seven Pedro Valley ranches, creating the Linda Mar subdivision. His company also built the Eureka Square Shopping Center and the relatively more upscale Park Pacifica residential community. His name is on a major boulevard through the back of the valley, a former elementary school, and a public park.

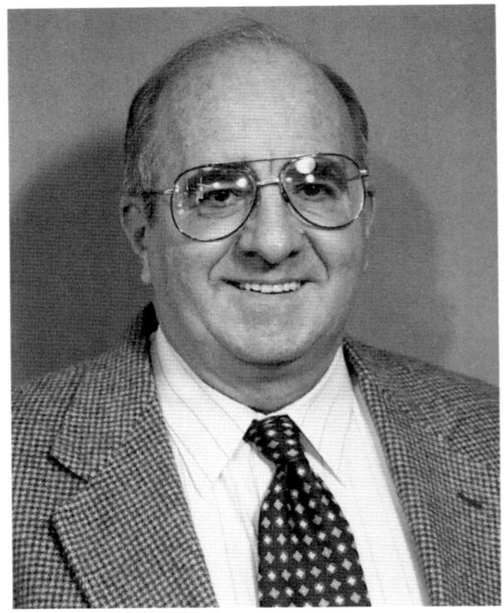

Loyle Mueller

The longtime director of the Pacifica Chamber of Commerce, Loyle Mueller helped promote the city and the local businesses from a tiny office above the Anderson Store building for years. Eventually, the chamber moved into posher digs in the Redevelopment District in Rockaway Beach, with several directors following in Mueller's footsteps. An unassuming gentleman with a soft-spoken demeanor, Mueller was a strong advocate for everything Pacifica and helped guide the chamber into a more diverse future.

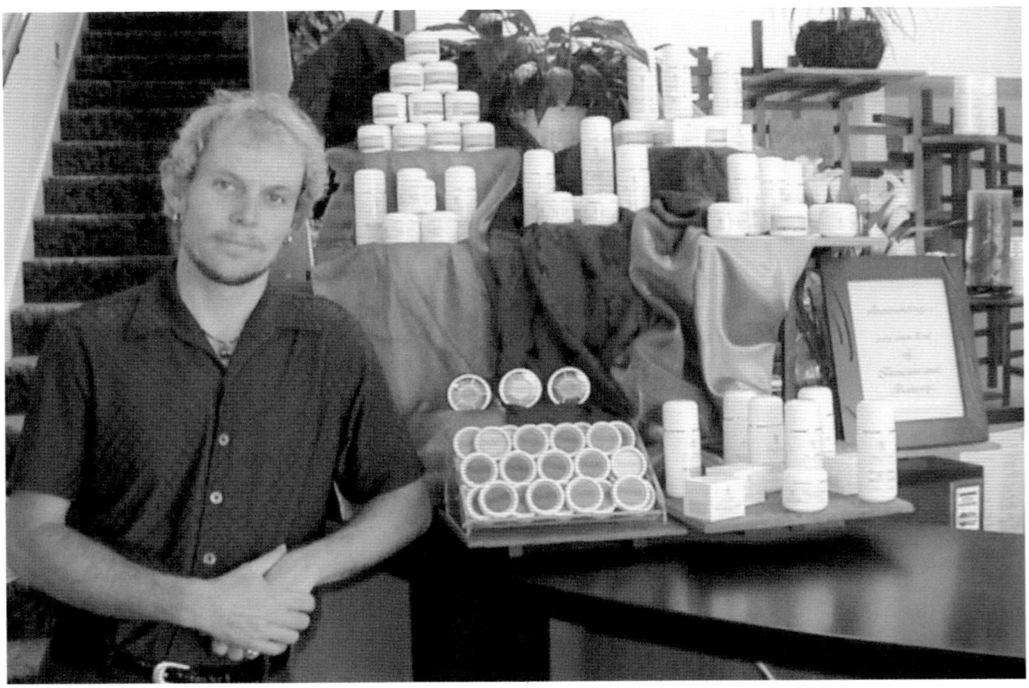

Paul Strom

Paul Strom's hair salon is an example of a specialized business that is only in Pacifica because the owner happened to live in the town. Coming from San Francisco, Strom established an upscale salon, which some thought would never find customers in the small town of Pacifica. Two decades and countless stylings later, the Paul Strom Salon continues to be one of the icon businesses of the Rockaway Plaza, even though it is tucked away in the back of the building. A longtime member of the chamber of commerce, Strom has also been an active voice in the business community and is a talented musician as well. *Elle* magazine once listed this salon as "one of the best places across the country."

CHAPTER SIX

Pacifica Sports

While there are legendary local sports figures who have made reputations on a larger scale, the countless high school and college athletes who contribute to the story of Pacifica is astonishing. Horace Hinshaw, a local legend, chronicled the achievements of athletes for decades, single-handedly creating the Pacifica Sports Hall of Fame and inducting more than 100 individuals into it through the years. High school coaches, especially football coach Bill Gray, have had an immense impact on the community and generations of young people gained experience in sports through them.

With thousands of school children being inspired by soccer, baseball, surfing, and every other sport imaginable, it is no wonder that so many people have made careers out of coaching or playing.

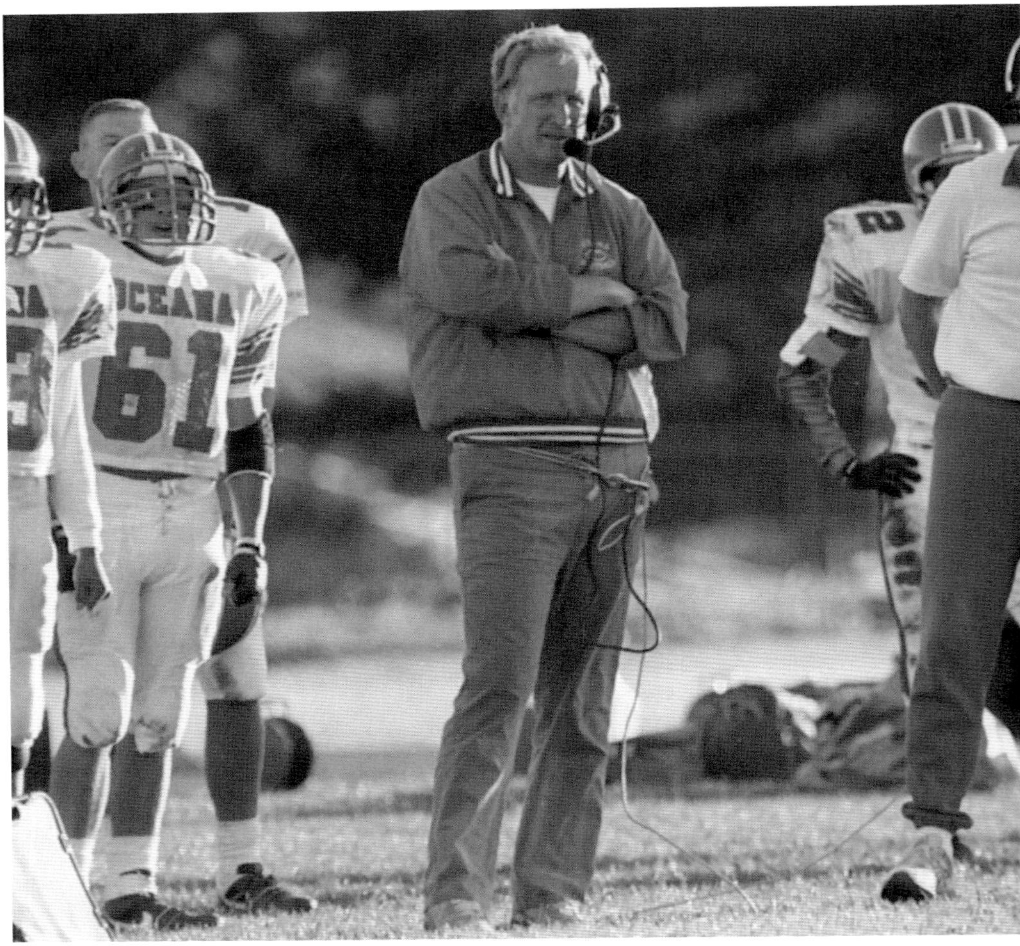

Coach Bill Gray (ABOVE AND OPPOSITE PAGE)
Bill Gray is the quintessential high school coach. He is the "gold standard" that others aspire to be like when they choose to teach students the joy and rewards of participating in sports. His career at both Oceana and Terra Nova High Schools is the story of building dominant football programs while inspiring youngsters to do their best on and off the field. He became the head football coach at Oceana in 1974, but he also forged a top-notch wrestling program there that brought national attention to the Pacifica school. Two students earned state championship titles under his guidance—a record that stands to this day. Gray was so dedicated to his coaching career that he often was viewed as the dominant force at his school. He was able to forge strong links with the business community, which in turn raised funds to support the athletic programs. His defense of the safe-and-sane fireworks sales in Pacifica helped defeat several attempts to eliminate the community's involvement in the highly successful fundraising program. Seldom seen wearing anything other than a sweat suit, Gray became one of the most prominent personalities in Pacifica, being honored by community groups and sports organizations. A 2013 award from the Pacifica Chamber of Commerce was so heartfelt, it brought tears to his eyes, as he admitted that he loved the community and he loved what he did. Generations of young men and women were inspired through their involvement with sports and their interaction with Bill Gray as their coach.

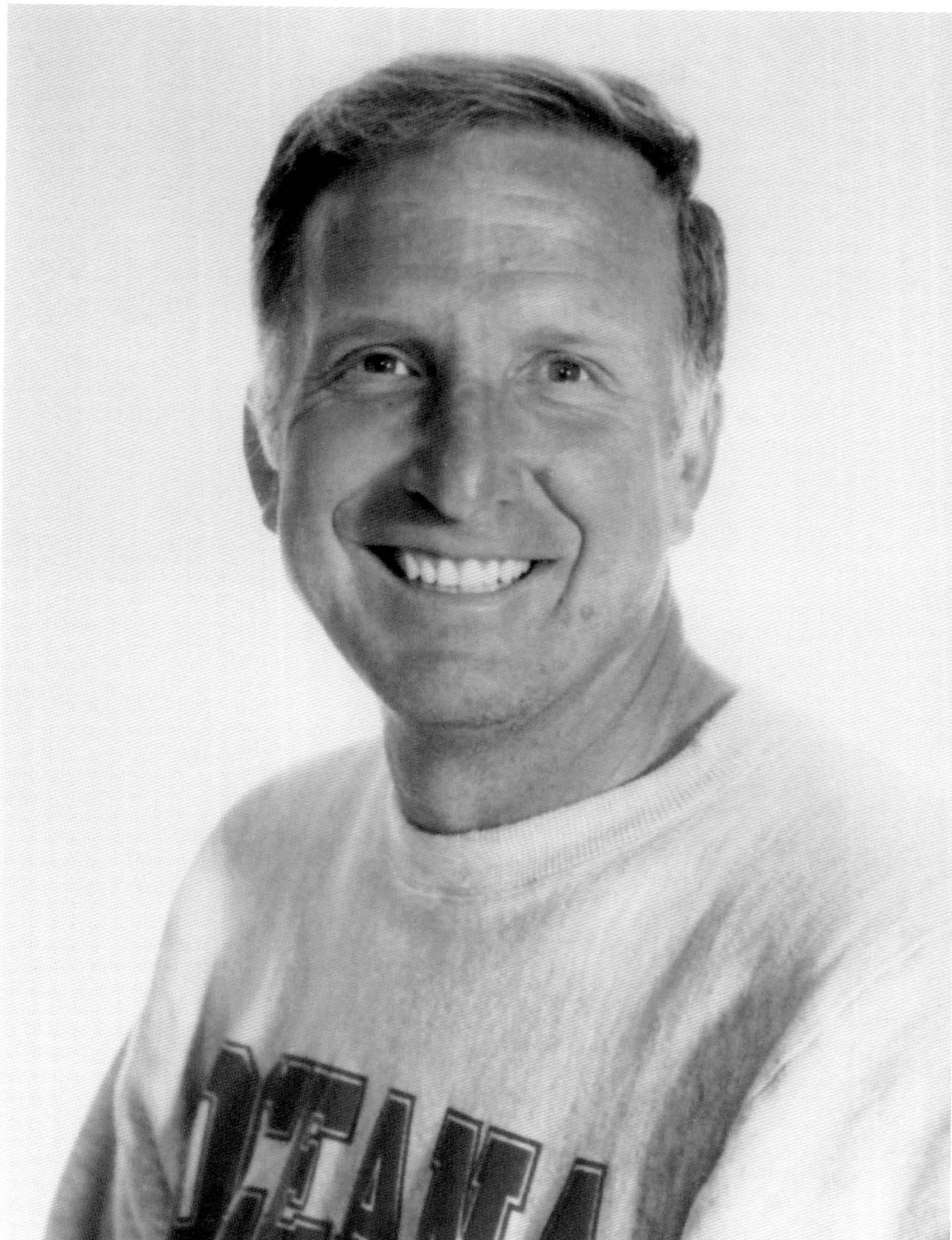

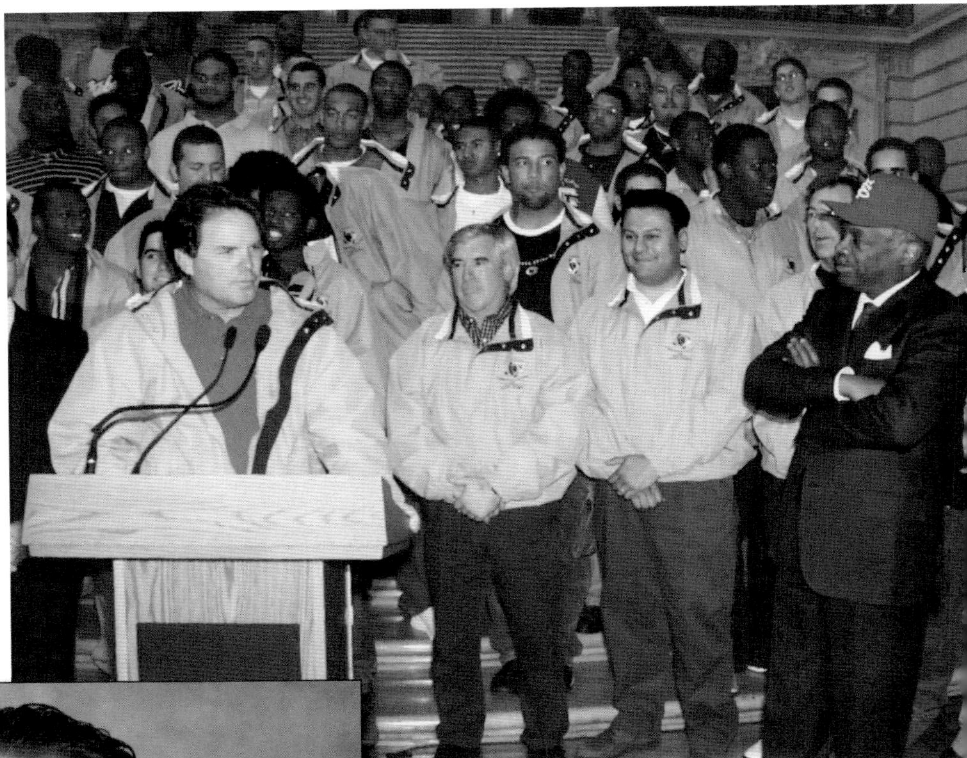

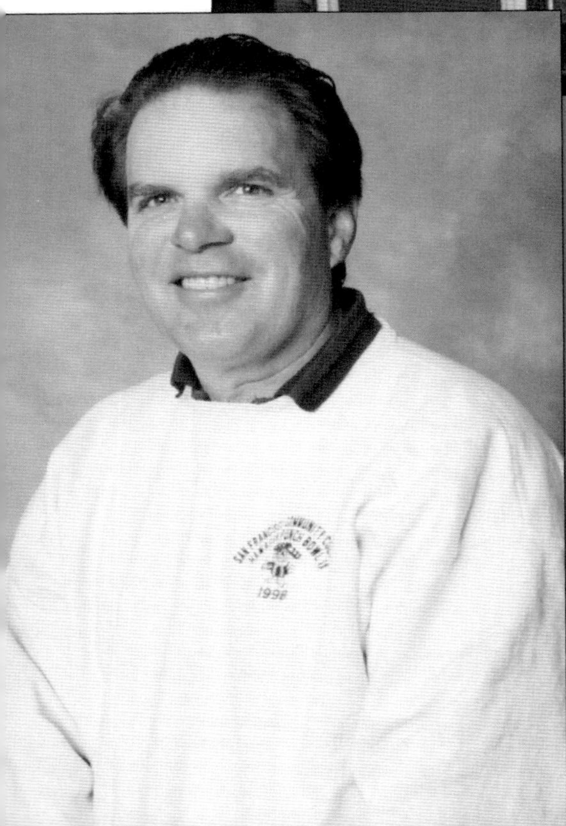

Coach George Rush
City College of San Francisco is where George Rush made his mark as a college coach. Taking over the football program there in 1977, George Rush took his teams to eight Golden Gate Conference championships. In 1998, City College was ranked No. 1 in the State and No. 1 in Northern California by the Junior College Athletic Bureau Coaches poll. His stellar performance as a coach brought attention to the City College that was rare for a two-year community college. "Coach of the Year" honors became a recurring title for Rush: in 1998, he earned his seventh conference title. He also worked to develop his athletes as scholars, and he helped his students go on to four-year schools with many earning scholarships. As the City College of San Francisco athletic director, which he became in 1989, George Rush was able to shape the entire college's athletic program and manage the development of the multi-million dollar stadium renovation project.

Horace Hinshaw

Horace Hinshaw's favorite word is "super." It is the word he uses to describe just about anything, including how he feels and what he thinks about sports. A career with the United States Post Office as an official spokesperson did not get in the way of Hinshaw creating perhaps the most comprehensive community coverage of local sports for any weekly newspaper in the country. In his spare time, he was the sports editor of the *Pacifica Tribune* from 1970 to 1988, and again in the 2000s following his retirement from the post office, Hinshaw was the No. 1 fan for every kid or adult who was involved in sports in any way at all in Pacifica. He created the Pacifica Sports Hall of Fame in 1990 and continued to shepherd that project, culling an ongoing awareness of what coaches, student athletes, and professionals did with their careers. The popularity of the annual banquet forced it to locate outside of Pacifica, which has no banquet halls large enough to handle the crowd. Hinshaw campaigned for increased sports fields in the city, dreamed about a comprehensive athletic facility, and was a cofounder of the American Youth Soccer Organization in Pacifica.

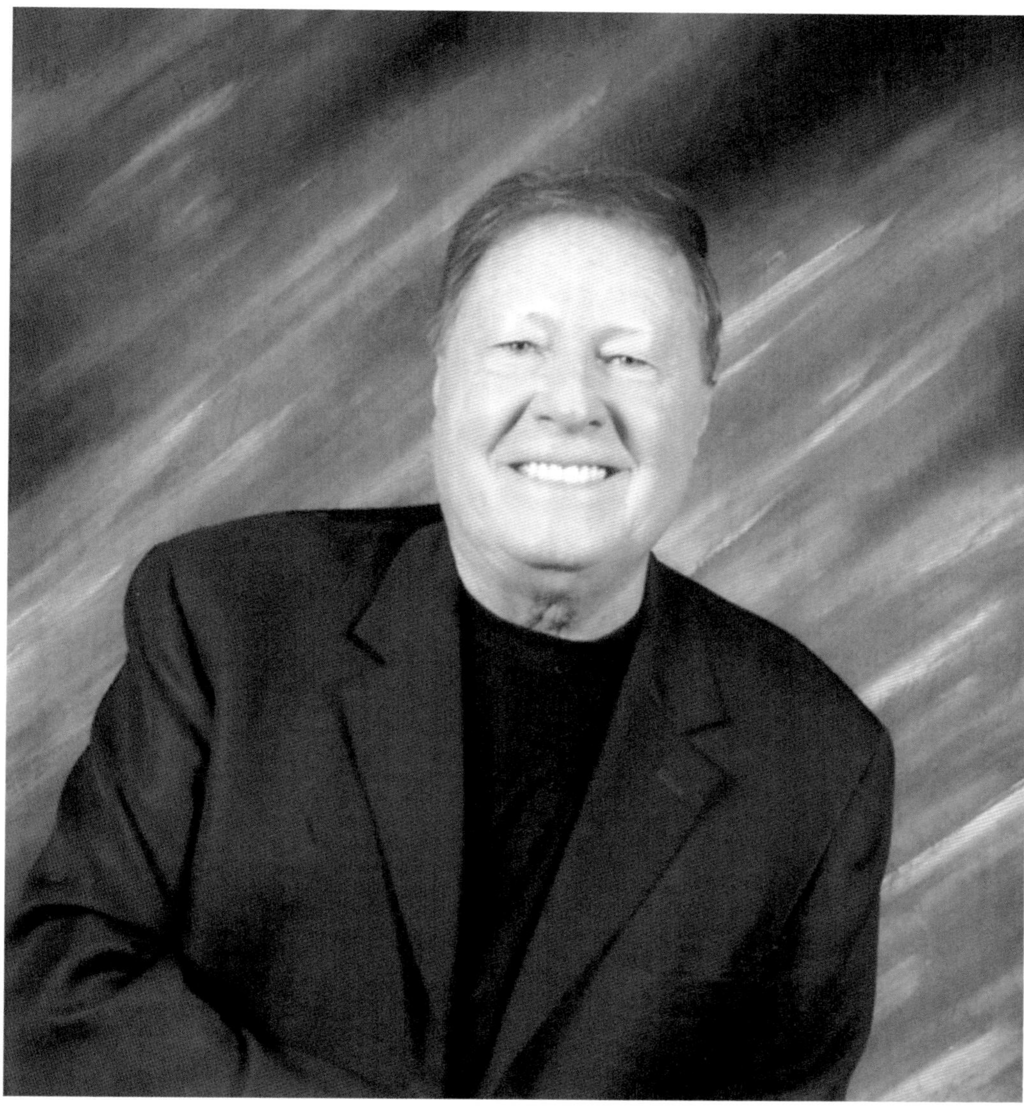

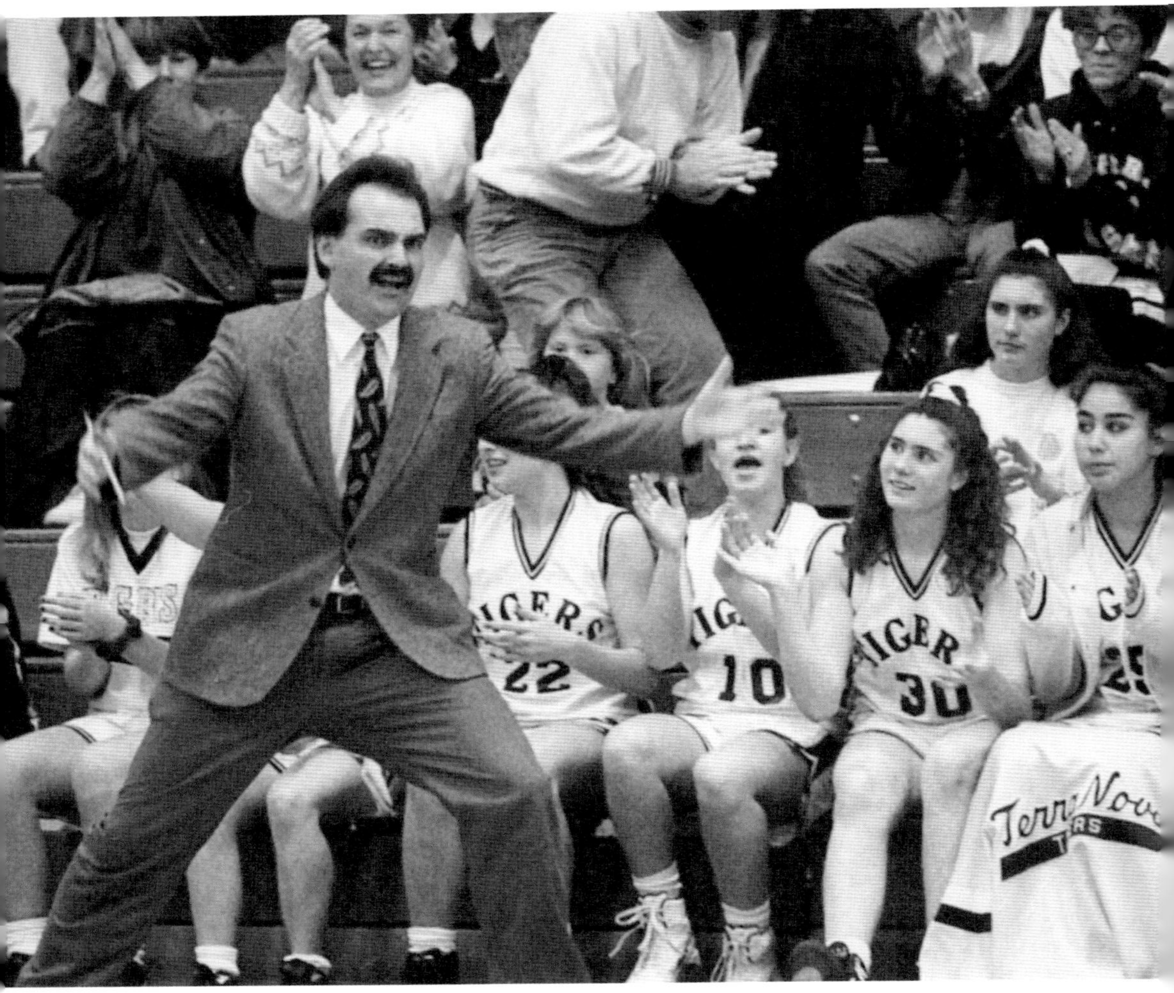

Coach Bill Lepeltak (ABOVE AND OPPOSITE PAGE)
Bill Lepeltak brings the same personal intensity to coaching middle school, high school, or college athletes. That excitement inspires his athletes and leads to winning teams and successful student athletes. A recent San Mateo County Coach of the Year award highlighted the impact Bill Lepeltak has had on the youth sports community. Hired to help Horace Hinshaw report on school sports when he was still in high school, Lepeltak went on to have a career in coaching while still maintaining his connection to the weekly *Pacifica Tribune* as a correspondent and sports reporter. "The award means a lot because there are a lot of coaches who could have received the award," Lepeltak said when he learned of his county-wide recognition. A high school and college coach, as well as an in-demand referee, Lepeltak also worked with middle school students and helped establish a successful program at Ingrid B. Lacy Middle School. From Oceana High School to Terra Nova and even Notre Dame de Namur University, Lepeltak brought his supportive coaching style to a broad range of students. He makes sports fun and creates top athletes as well as provides opportunities for students who are often overlooked. "I'm very happy. I wake up every morning and look forward to coming to work," he said in a newspaper article about his coach of the year award. "I'm having fun. How many people can say they get to play for a living?"

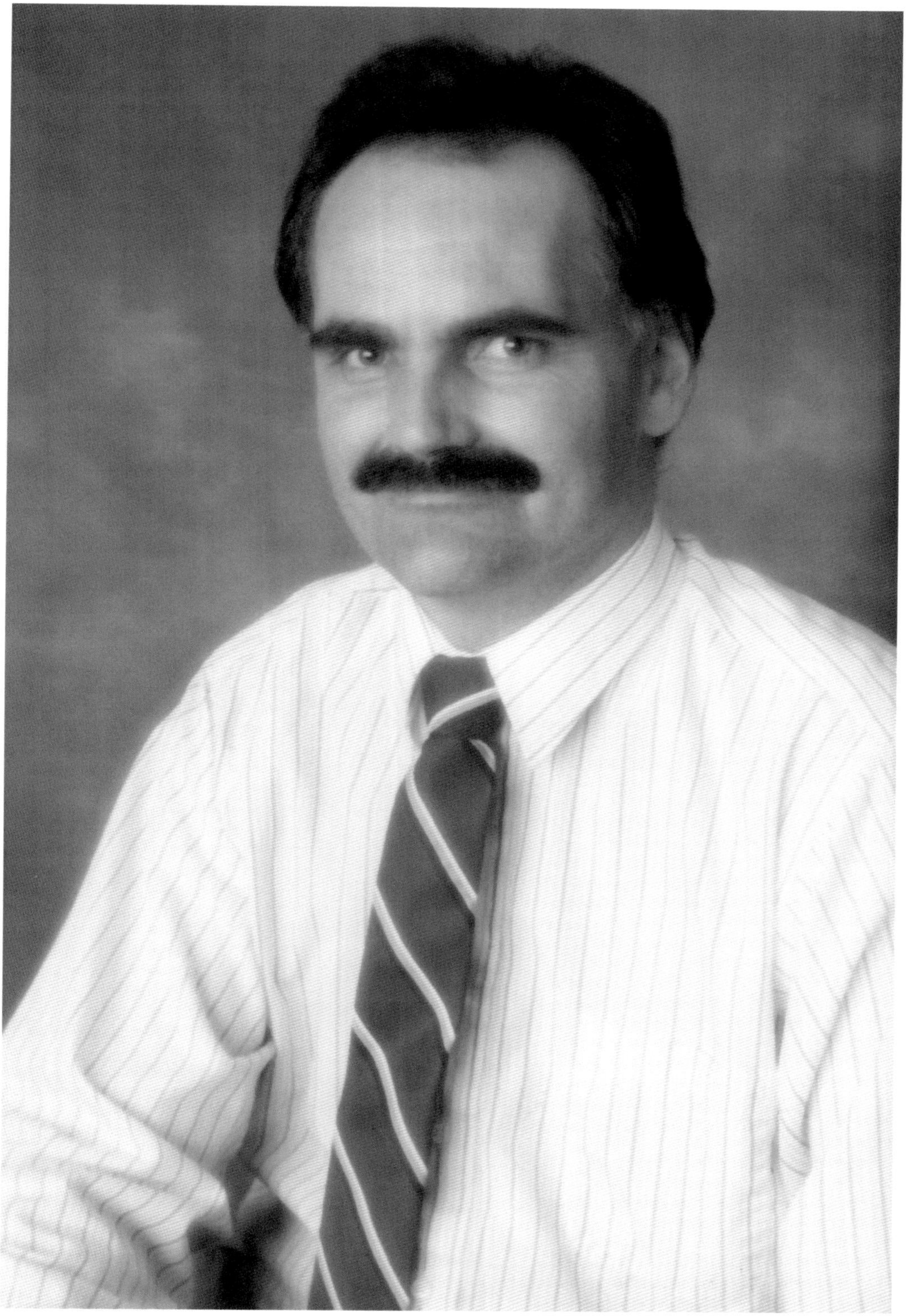

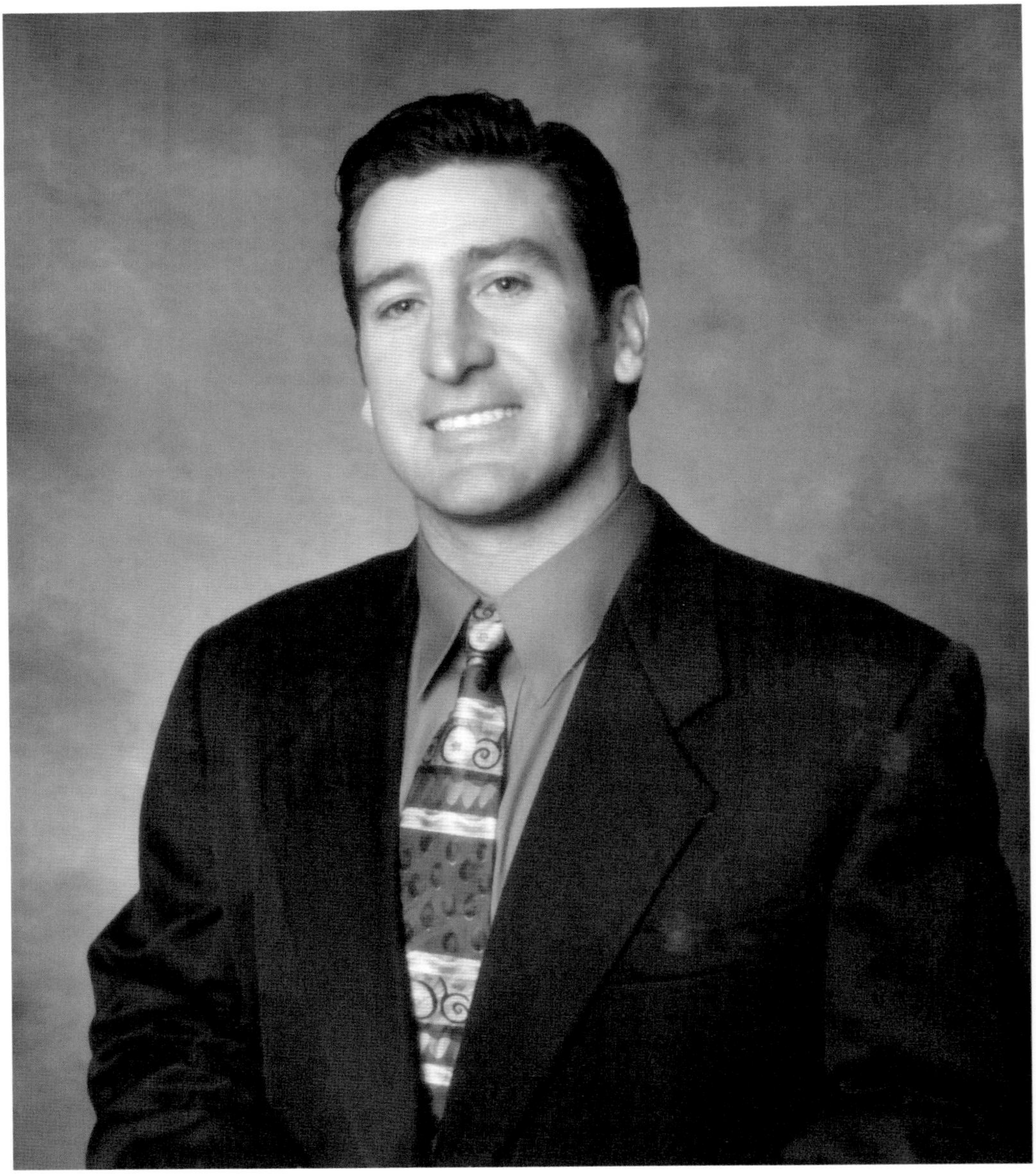

Tom Piccolotti

A mainstay on the elected board of the North Coast County Water District for many years, Tom Piccolotti is still known for his exceptional athletic success as a high school student and semipro football player. As an Oceana High School wrestler, Piccolotti was the California State Wrestling Champion in 1985, following in the footsteps of Johnny Piccolotti's win two years earlier. He was named one of the top all-around athletes in San Mateo County during his senior year. Also an excellent football and baseball player in high school, Piccolotti played both sports at Skyline College and College of San Mateo. He joined the San Mateo Outlaws, a semipro football team, and earned most valuable player honors while a player. Eventually, he shifted to coaching the team. A career in public works for the City of Daly City blends nicely with his civic activity as a board member on the North Coast County Water District. His daughter Marina followed in his footsteps as a champion wrestler.

Lou Piccolotti

The patriarch of the Piccolotti family, Lou Piccolotti coached youth sports in Pacifica for more than four decades. Known as "Mr. Pic," he would always make sure every team had a sponsor and every athlete had a chance to play. A semipro baseball player prior to incorporation of the City of Pacifica, Piccolotti began coaching young players in the 1950s. Every youth league benefited from his experience and dedication. A Little League baseball field was named after him in Fairway Park and he received endless commendations and honors, including recognition from the San Mateo County Board of Supervisors. He inspired countless young athletes, especially the many younger members of his extended family. Of the players he coached through the years, he said, "They are all champions for their efforts; they are a very special part of my life."

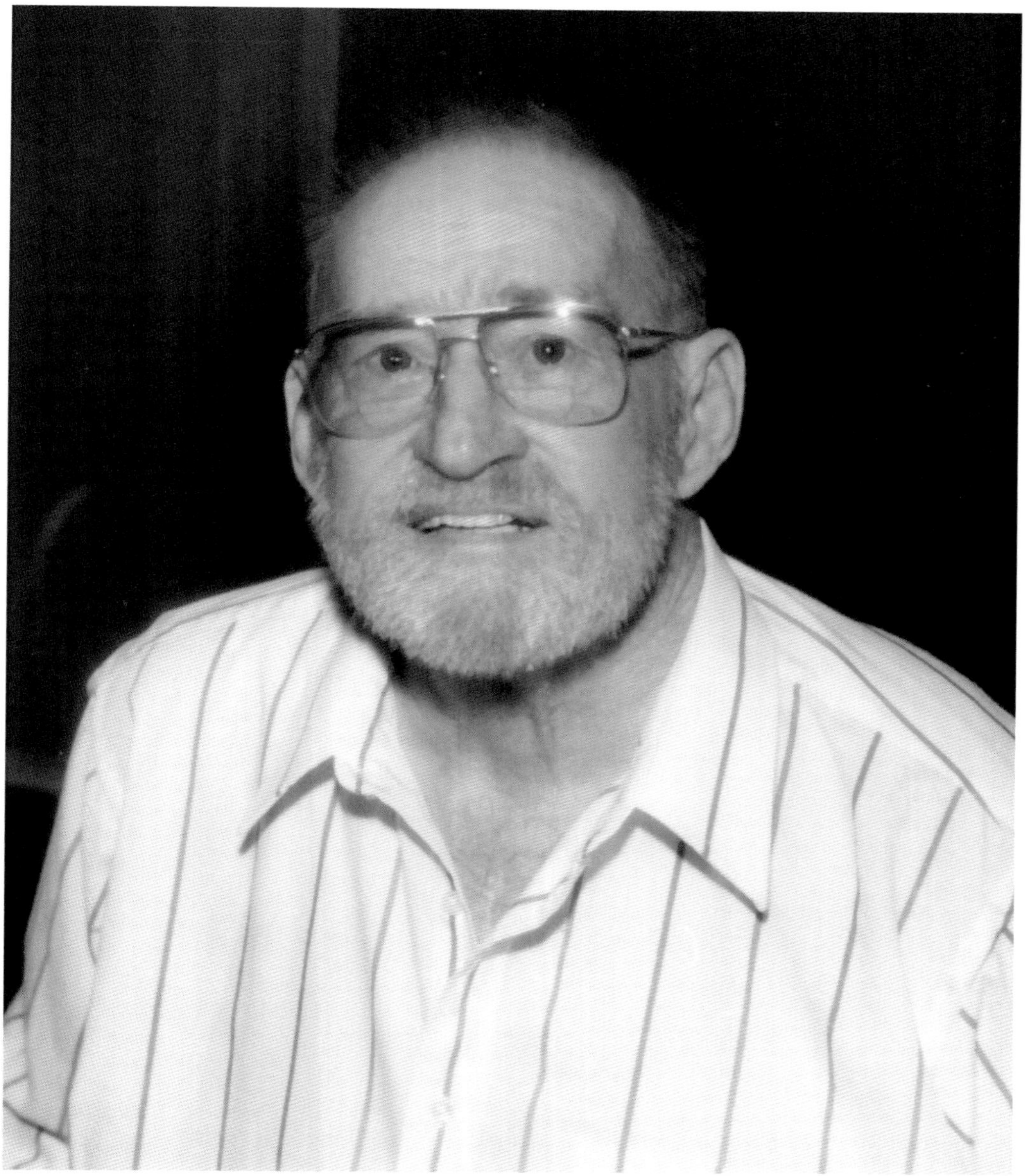

Johnny Piccolotti

Another great wrestler in the Piccolotti family, Johnny Piccolotti earned the title of California State Wrestling Champion in 1983, becoming the first Oceana athlete to win a state championship. He completed an unbeaten season, although he said it took Coach Bill Gray's encouragement for him to commit to the sport. During his four-year high school career, Piccolotti established a 121–11 win/loss record. An all-around athlete, he also played baseball and basketball. Unsurprisingly, he excelled at both of them, being named to the All-Northern Peninsula League first team in baseball and Most Valuable Player title in basketball.

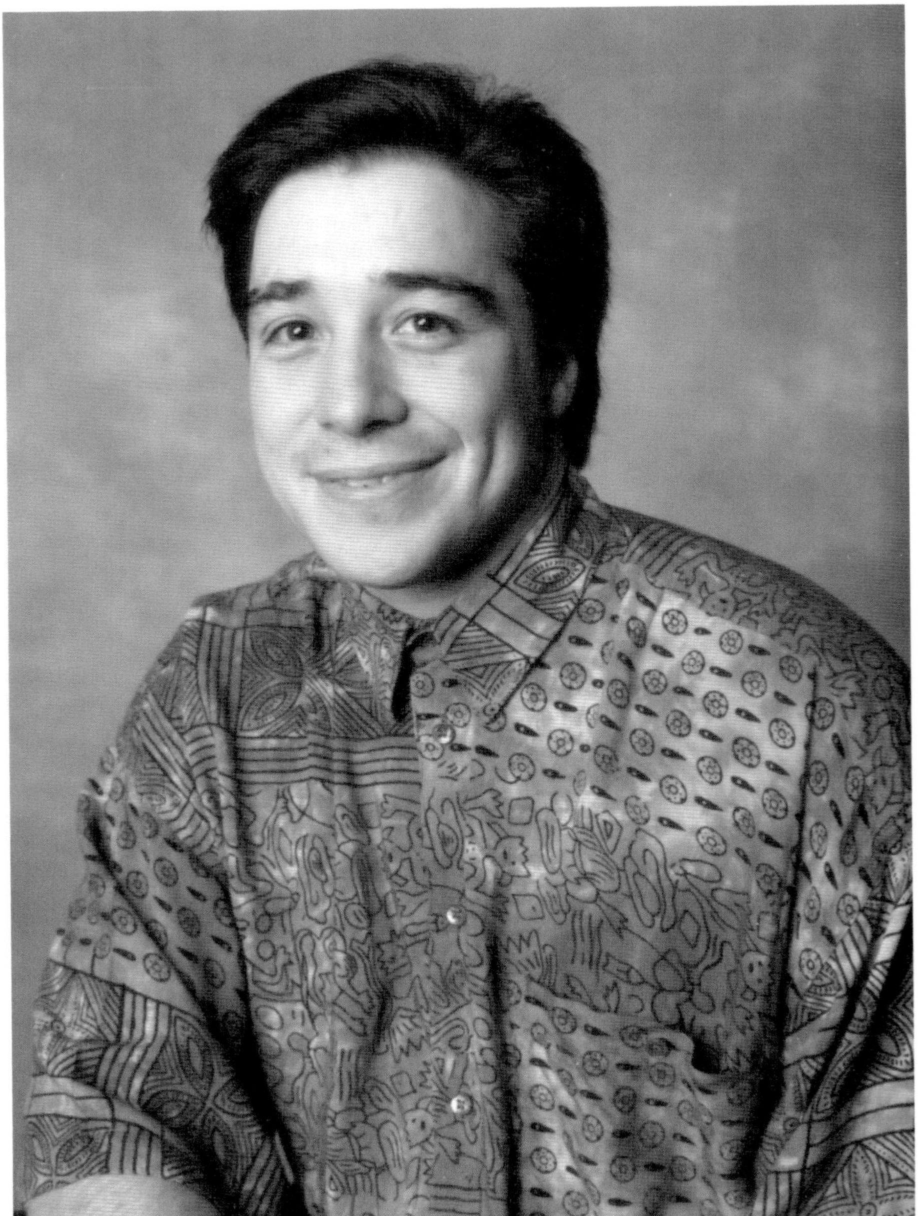

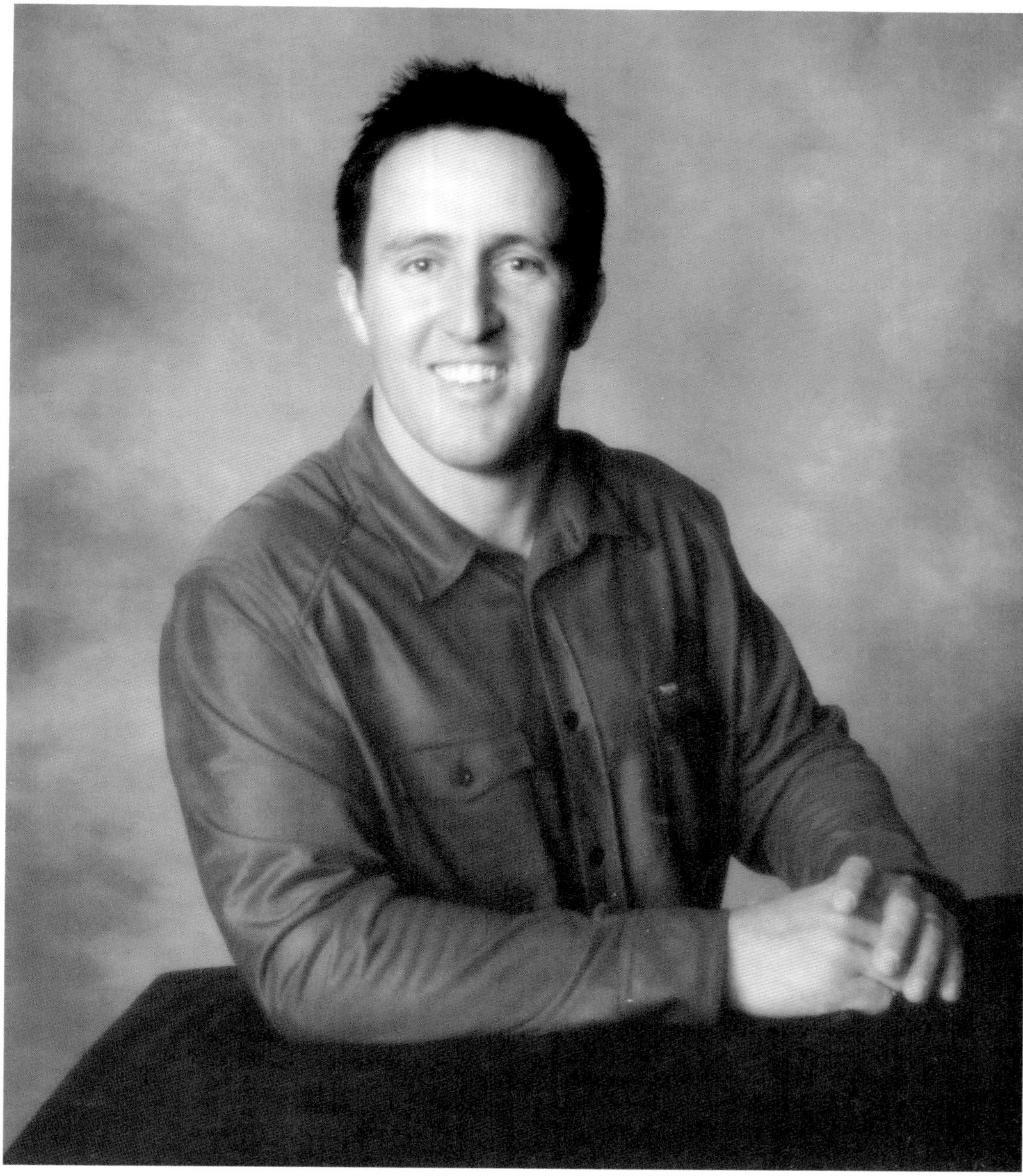

Jason Piccolotti

The athletic dynamics of the Piccolotti family include Jason Piccolotti, whose football prowess was a determining factor in the City College of San Francisco's 1994 perfect season. He did the same thing for his Oceana High School football team four years earlier. Under the guidance of the City College of San Francisco coach George Rush, Piccolotti's memorable season in 1994 included being named most valuable player of the Coast Conference, completing 59 percent of his pass attempts for 2,662 yards. He scored 31 touchdowns that year, running in four himself. In between high school and college, Piccolotti played on the semiprofessional Outlaws team, leading them to the West Coast Amateur Football League championship in 1992. Coach Rush claimed that Jason Piccolotti was "one of the top two or three. He is a leader. He is calm under pressure and the bigger the game, the greater Jason plays. Those are things you either have or you do not and Jason has them."

Manny Hazard

Emmanuel "Manny" Hazard was a top athlete at Oceana High School, leading his team to its first-ever league championship in 1987. Under high school coach Bill Gray, he excelled, but then he went to City College of San Francisco and continued his growth as an athlete under Coach George Rush. By the time he was at the University of Houston in 1989, where he received a scholarship, he was one of the best pass receivers in the country. He caught 22 touchdown passes for 1,689 yards, playing with quarterback Andre Ware, who went on to win the Heisman Trophy for Houston. Hazard went on to play for the Toronto Argonauts, and two other Canadian Football League teams before retiring in 1996. Like so many other top athletes from Pacifica, he claims that Bill Gray and George Rush coached him to his success. "Without their support and guidance, I would not have been blessed and able to achieve the goals I have accomplished," he said.

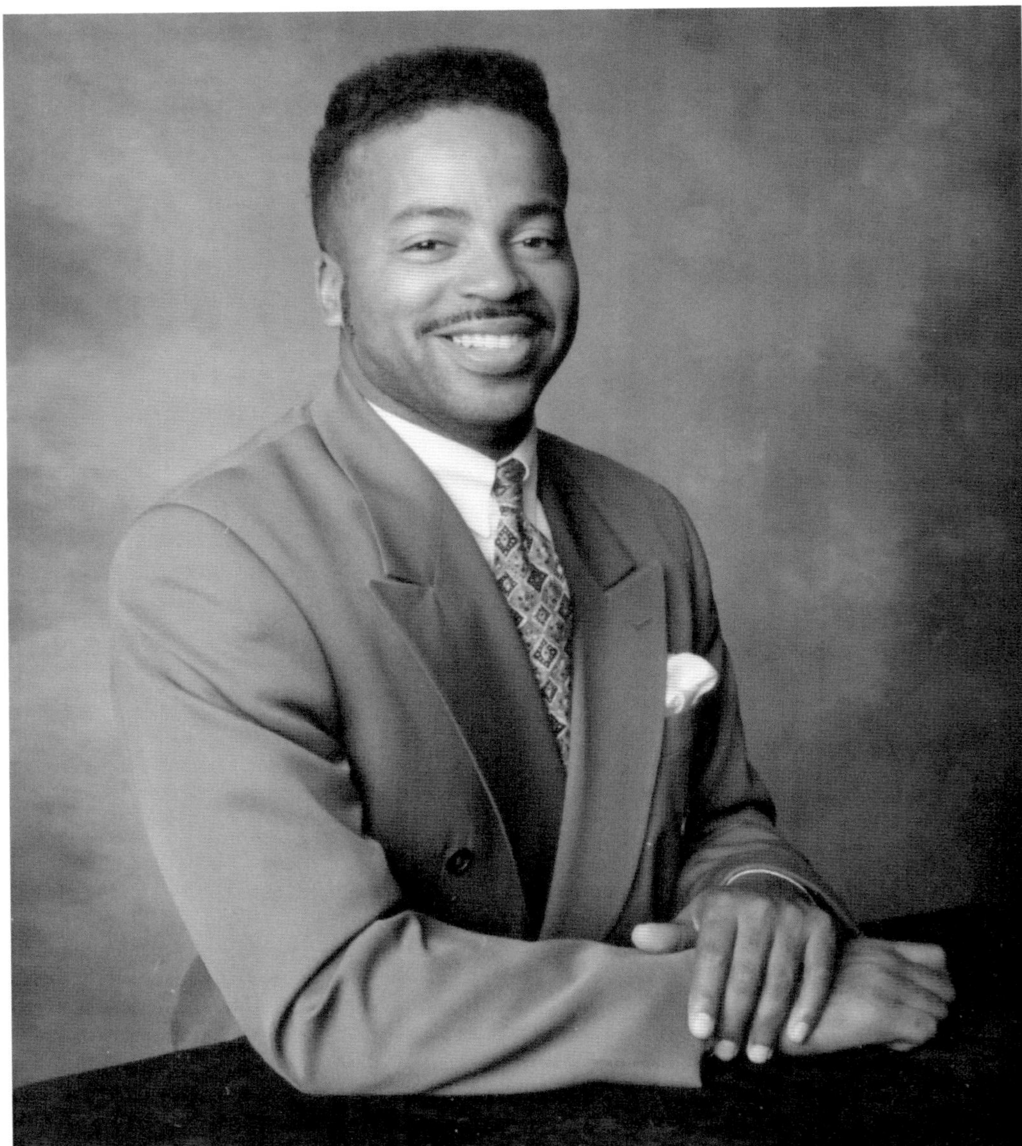

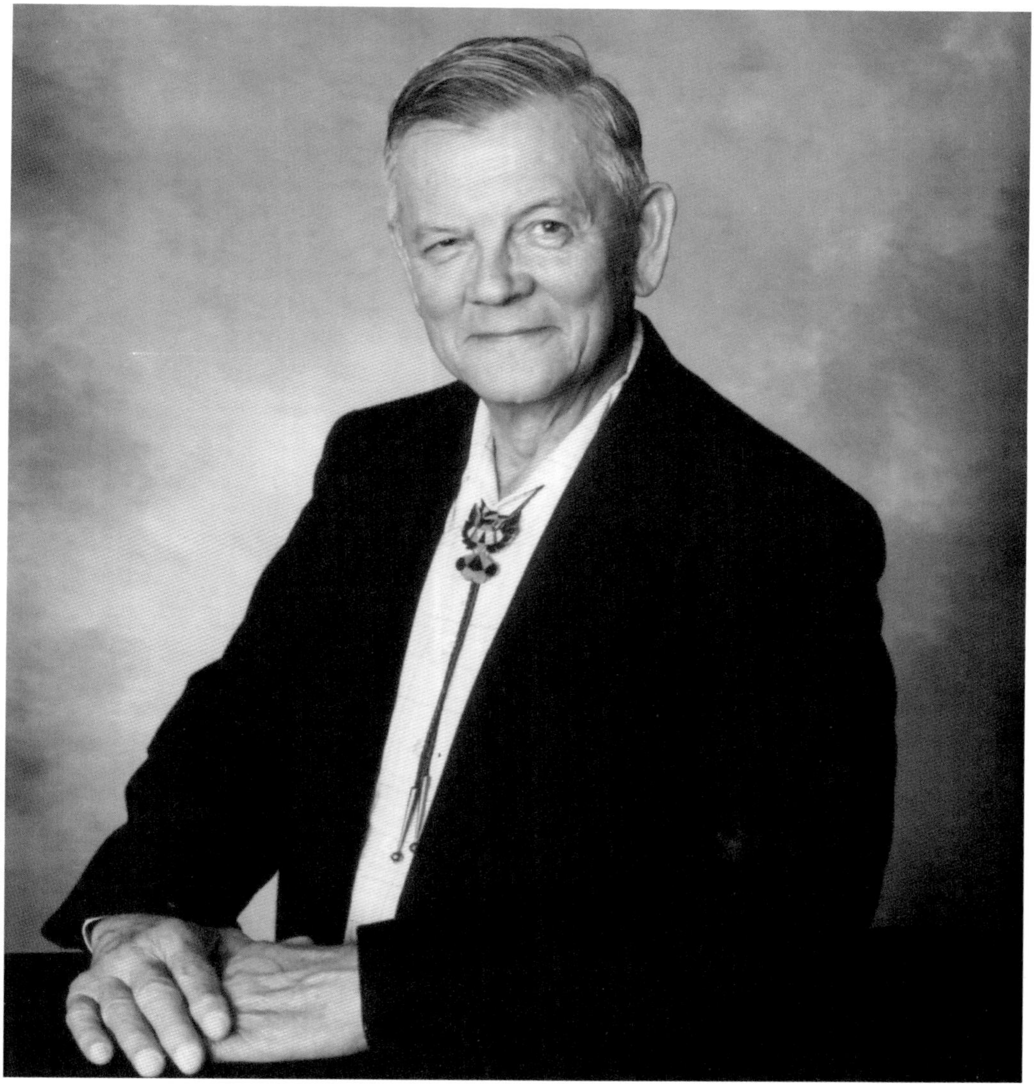

Rudy Pickell

An exceptional community volunteer, Rudy Pickell typifies what it means to be committed to his hometown. He established the American League baseball program in 1975 and then managed the American Legion Pacifica Post 238–sponsored team, bringing two of his loves together. As a coach, he excelled and some of his young players went on to great success in high school, college, and even professional sports. A veteran, Pickell also managed the annual American Legion Essay Contest for high school students and was active in all aspects of the local veterans social group. He also was a longtime member and past president of the Pacifica Lions Club. Like several other different Pacificans, Pickell took his turn organizing and managing the annual Pacific Coast Fog Fest, which had been originated by a professional events company but eventually needed a locally controlled nonprofit to take over. Pickell was the first chairman of Pacifica Festivals, Inc., which operated the Fog Fest for six years. His professional career was running a sheet metal company in Pacifica, but his true fame in Pacifica was through youth baseball and patriotic support of the American Legion, among other social groups. His other claim to fame is being the father of Debi Durst, a professional comedienne married to political satirist Will Durst.

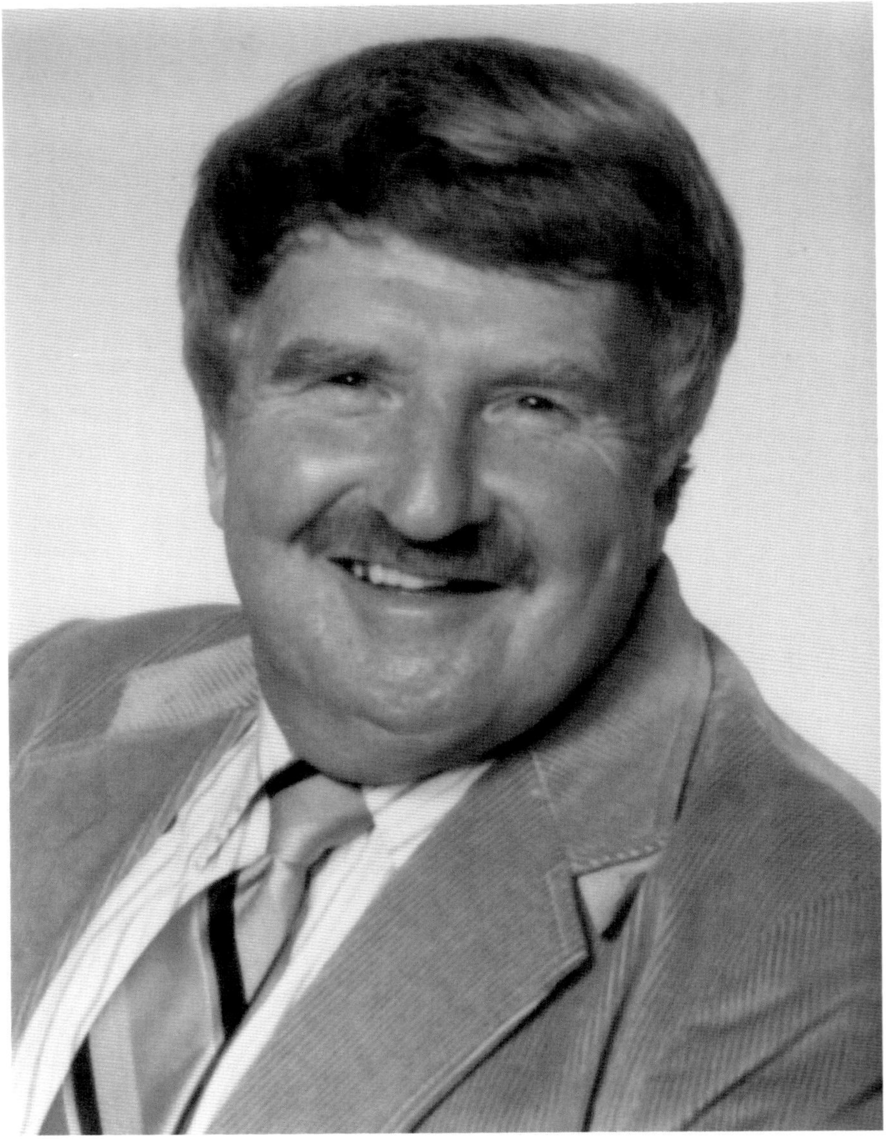

Don Beck

Don Beck always seems to have a whistle around his neck. For more than 31 years, he was an active volunteer in the development of youth sports, promoting his vision that the joy of athletics comes from participation and improvement, not just winning. Also an educator, Beck worked in the Laguna Salada Union School District for 27 years, serving as vice principal at Linda Mar School for 17 years. Seeing a need and an opportunity, Beck founded the Junior Olympics within the school district, creating an active rivalry and physical fitness outlet for thousands of children. He also cofounded the American Youth Soccer Organization (AYSO) in Pacifica, which could arguably be called the single largest youth organization in town. His smiling face at the finish line of countless races encouraged runners of all ages, and his own jogging devotion helped inspire and shape generations of runners. He founded a popular running club and taught a backpacking course for the more adventurous. Thousands of Pacificans can thank Don Beck for their lifelong interest in physical fitness.

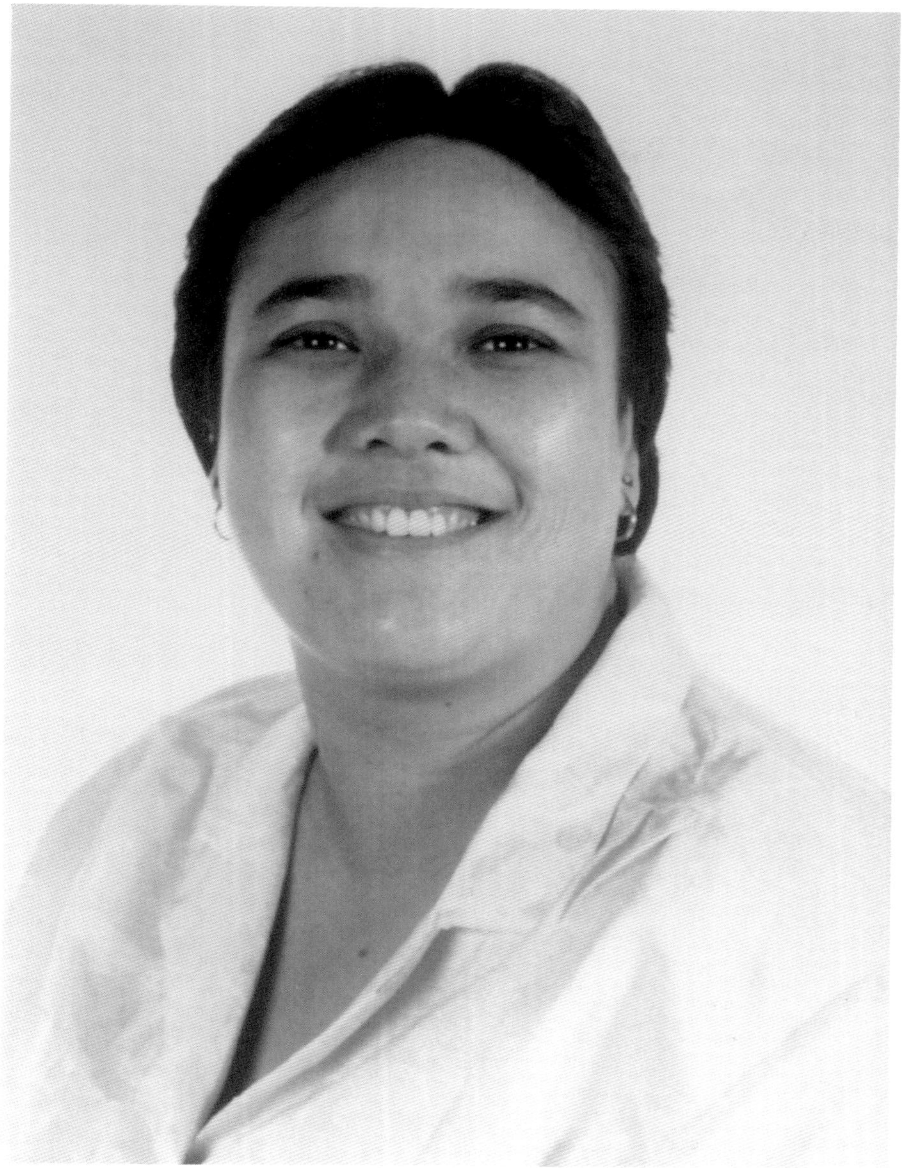

Tonia Moe

One of the rare breeds of student athletes who goes on to coach at her alma mater, Tonia Moe made her mark at Terra Nova High School in both worlds. Born in Hong Kong, Moe came to Pacifica in 1972 and immediately became a star athlete at the high school in volleyball, basketball, and badminton. After her graduation, she went on to San Francisco State University, but she soon came back to Terra Nova as a coach. A nine-year career at the school saw her team earn a North Peninsula League championship in basketball and a record scoring streak in volleyball. That team also won a league championship, eventually moving on to the state competition in Sacramento, a feat unmatched in Terra Nova history. When she retired, she said she was going to devote more time to her family and a business which specialized in athletic uniforms and equipment. She was a charter member of the Pacifica Sports Hall of Fame, inducted in 1991.

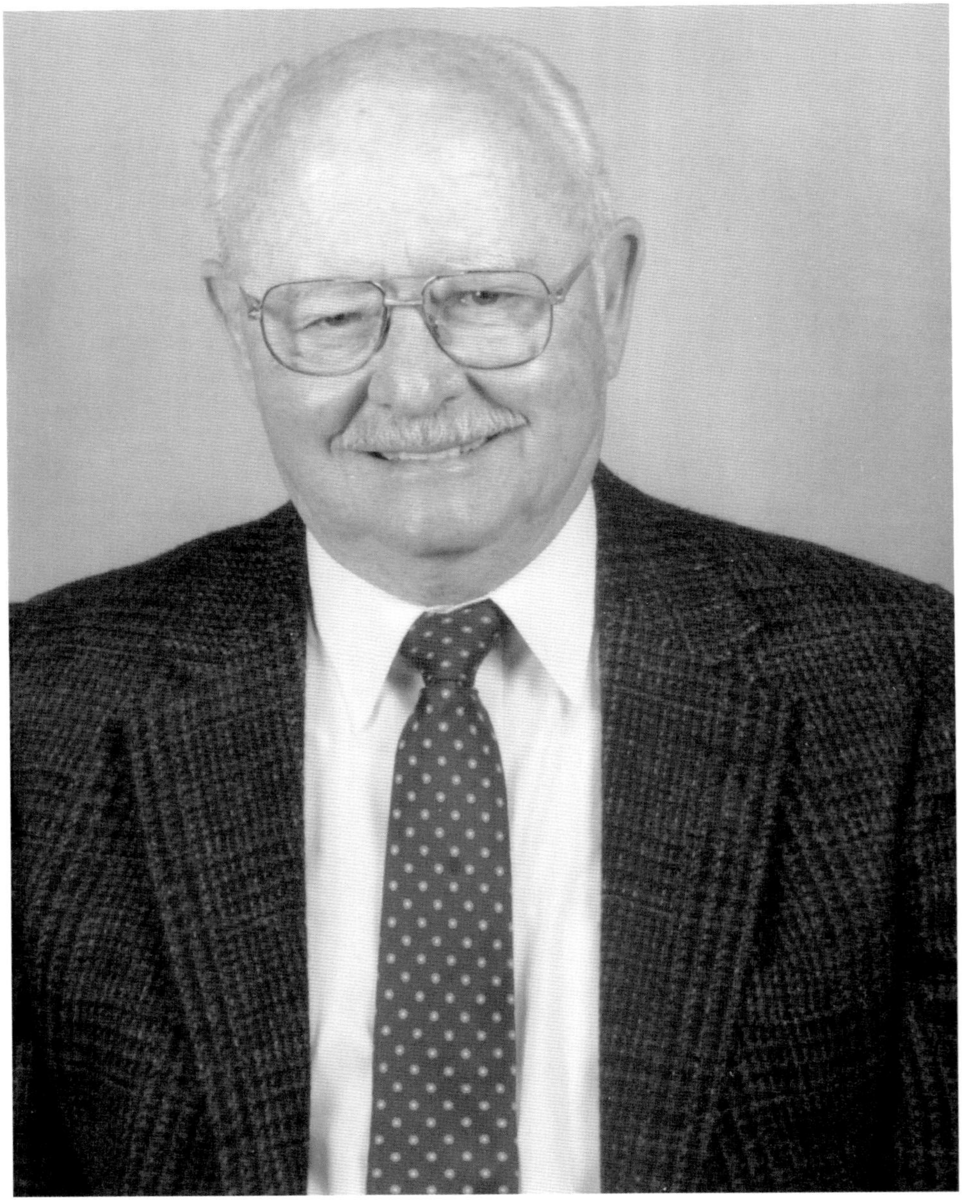

Ernest Ribera
A career educator with the Jefferson Union High School District (JUHSD), Ernest Ribera spent six years as the principal of Oceana High School. A coach as well as an administrator, Ribera guided cross-country teams to championship seasons at Westmoor High School and coached freshmen and sophomore football players at Jefferson High School. He was the very first assistant principal at the newly opened Terra Nova High School in 1960 and he ended his career as the assistant district superintendent at the JUHSD. He also served on the San Mateo County Parks and Recreation Commission. "The thrill of participation in a competitive sport is a sound motivational factor," he said to young athletes. "If you win, you are happy. If you lose, the pain goes away. So win or lose, give it your best effort. That will be your true satisfaction."

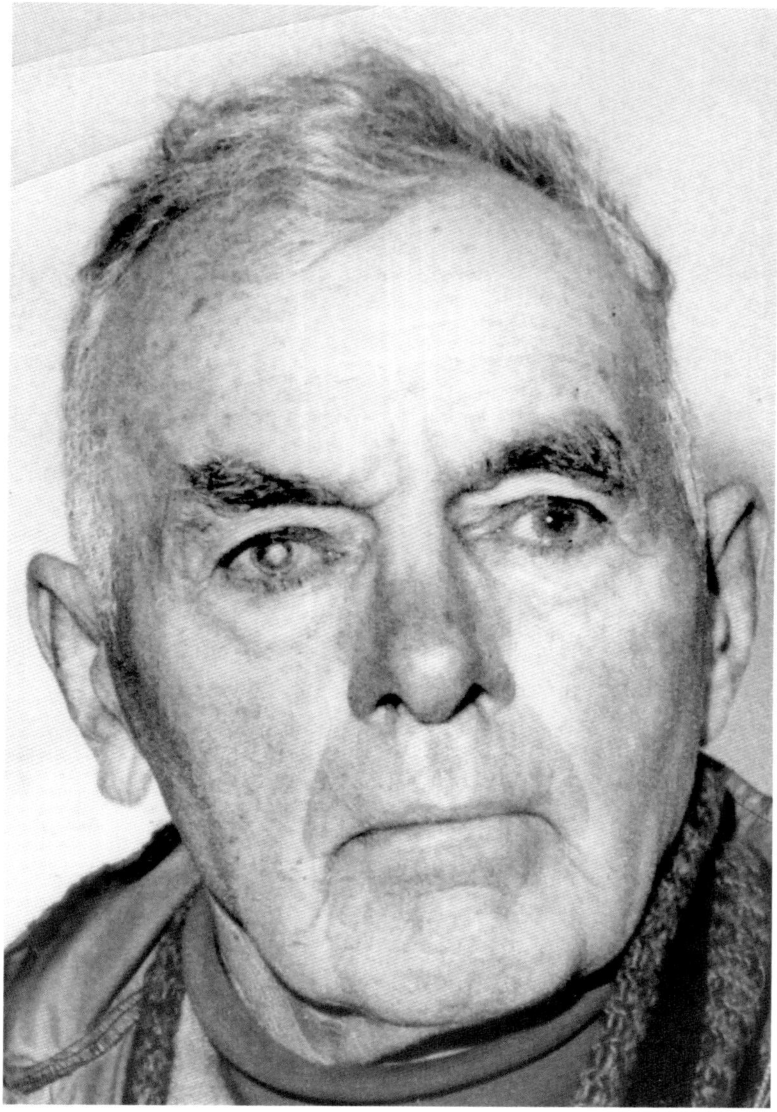

Elmer Harris

One of the grand old men of Pacifica, Elmer Harris was 96 when he died in 1989, leaving a legacy as a champion golfer and sports enthusiast. A high school coach, Harris did not take up golf until he retired in 1949, which gives some small sense of his longevity. In 1984, he was inducted into the San Francisco Prep Hall of Fame, which trumpeted his activities at several San Francisco high schools. His high school coaching legacy stretches back to 1917, when he worked in the Oakland School District and organized the Oakland Boys Club basketball league. But it was not until he was featured in *Sports Illustrated* as a top 75-and-older golfer that his fame grew even more. As a senior golfer, he won seven world titles. In Pacifica, he organized and taught golf classes at Sharp Park Golf Course and the long gone Pedro Point driving range. His lifelong devotion to youth sports and his late success in golf is nothing if not inspirational. Harris also was tireless in his activities for the Pacifica Parks, Beaches, and Recreation Department, organizing everything from ballroom dancing to chess. People remember Elmer Harris for his spirit, his teaching career, and his friendship.

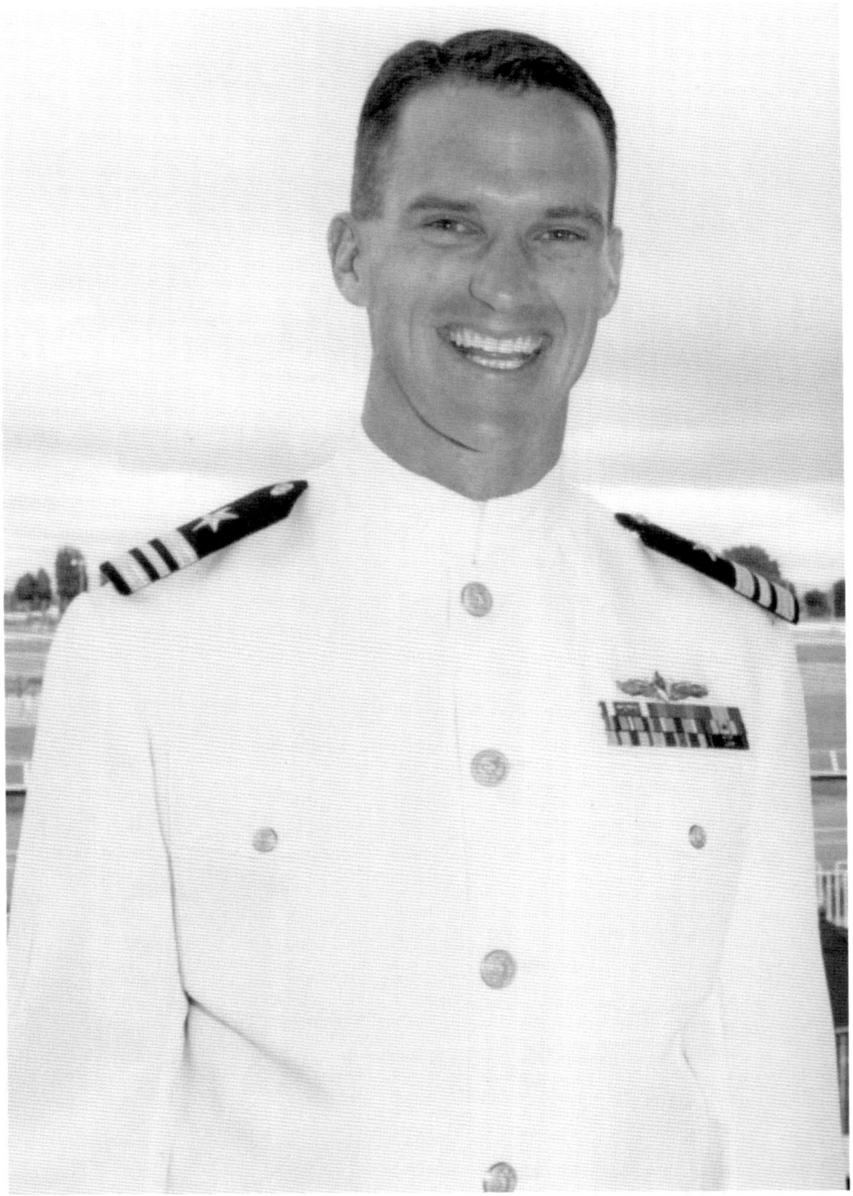

Bill Byrne

A standout quarterback on the United States Naval Academy's football team, Bill Byrne distinguished himself as the Terra Nova High School football quarterback first. He led the Tigers to a 1981 North Peninsula League championship before earning a spot at the Naval Academy. He became the starting quarterback in 1984 at Annapolis and put together perhaps the strongest season ever for a Navy starter. He set the school record for single-game completions with 37 in 52 attempts for 399 yards and two touchdowns against Syracuse. His prowess earned him the honor of being named the 1985 All-East Conference quarterback, a first for a Navy player. When he graduated, he was tapped as the fifth most successful academy quarterback. His Naval career was shaped by his exceptional leadership qualities typified on the field. He was the recipient of the City of Philadelphia Outstanding Leadership Award in 1986.

Carl Vallero

Perhaps one of the greatest coaches for Pacifica Youth Baseball, Carl Vallero guided a local team to the Joe DiMaggio League California Championship in 1970, snagging the city's first ever trophy in that prestigious league. It had been Vallero who introduced Joe DiMaggio baseball to Pacifica six years earlier. As a younger man, Vallero was a professional baseball player himself, signing with the Cleveland Indians in 1946. He continued in baseball as a scout for the Milwaukee Braves, the Seattle Pilots, and the San Francisco Giants. Being a youth coach in Pacifica for 30 years helped create countless young athletes, some of whom owe their professional careers to Carl Vallero.

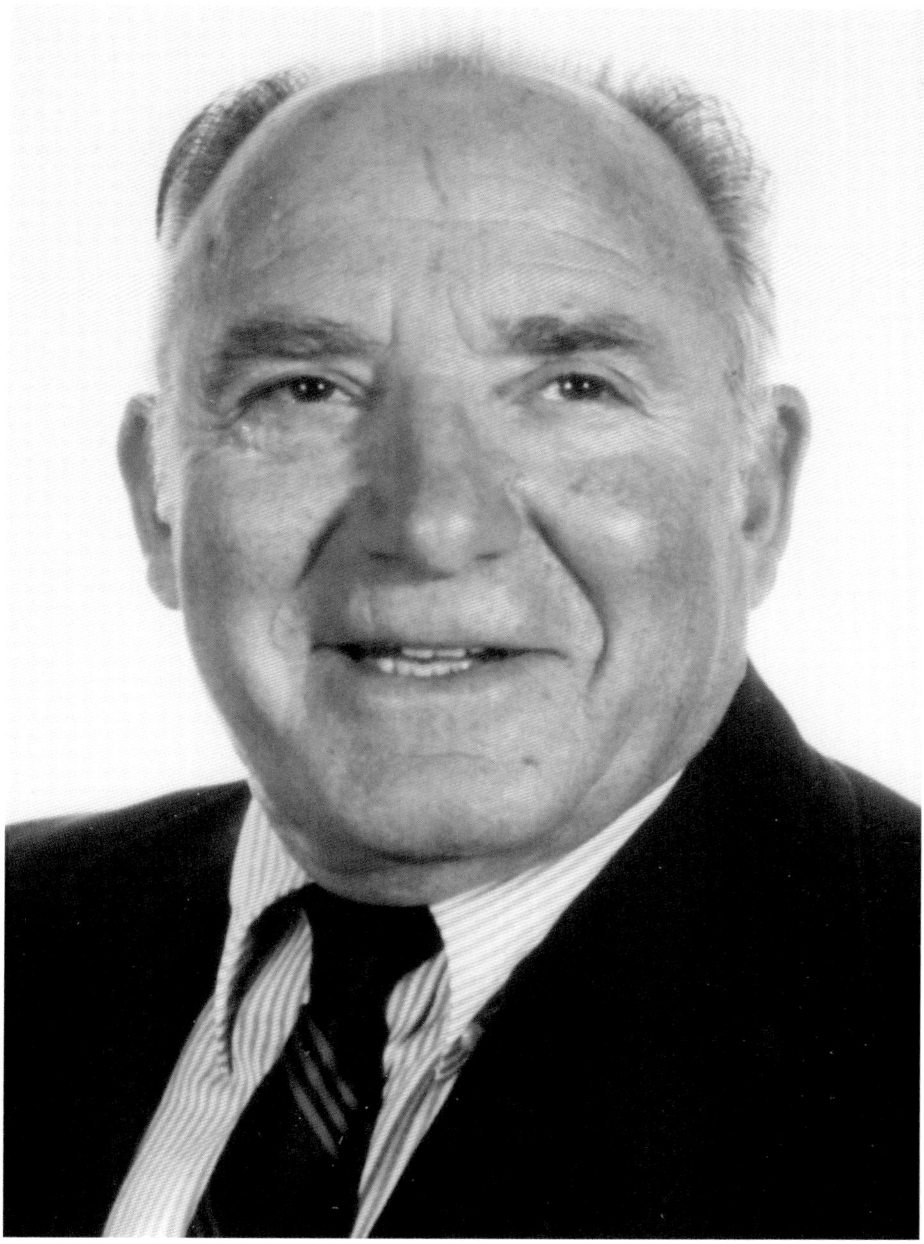

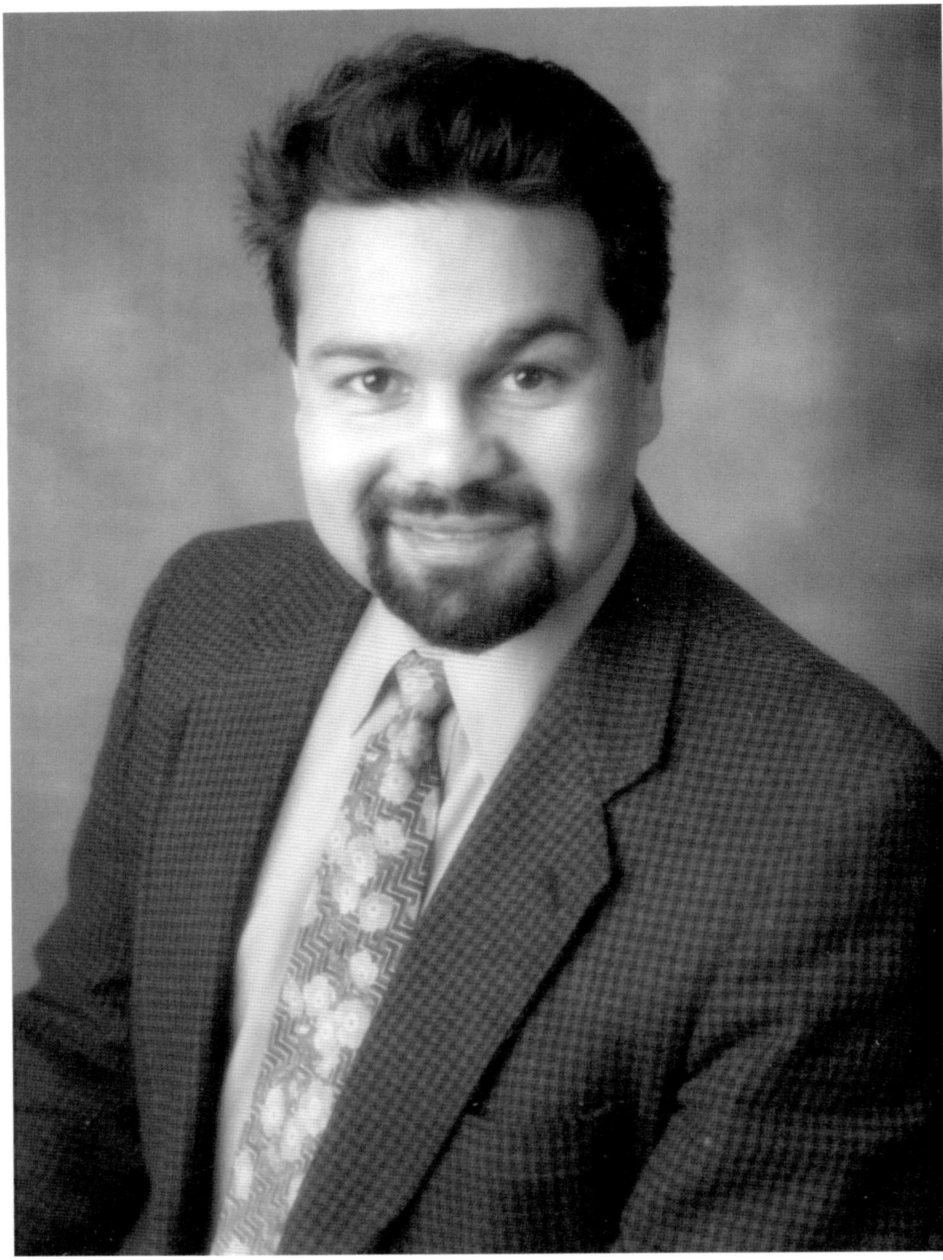

Johnny Nava

Known as the "Pride of Pacifica," Johnny Nava was a native son who succeeded in the world of boxing. In 1983, the first professional boxing match held in Pacifica took place at Oceana High. Nava won that match by a decision and went on to have a career record of 22 victories. He was 15 when he began to box and made his amateur debut in the 1979 Golden Gloves tournament. His sporting career ended in the late 1980s, but Nava continued to train another San Mateo County boxer—Eddie Croft, who eventually was considered one of the top 10 in world rankings. Nava went on to have a career in the insurance business.

CHAPTER SEVEN

Pacifica Community Leaders

The social fabric of Pacifica, range from active civic clubs to the parent organizations at the public and private schools play and crucial part in the personality of the city. From the Lions Club to the Rotary Club and even the Beta Sigma Phi women's sorority, the civic activity of Pacificans is astonishing. Many individuals have displayed leadership in these groups, crafting individual reputations that are widely known. The Pacificans Care organization, which raises money for a variety of charities, is also a well-regarded group. Noteworthy in the town is the effectiveness of the Pacifica Resource Center, a core agency that assists the less-fortunate residents with food and shelter needs. The overall community reveres the resource center, coming out in force whenever budgetary concerns threaten its existence.

Individuals who have made an impact on the community are as varied as the community itself. Religious leaders, civic activists, artists, and writers have become widely known for their purposeful lives.
This is a sampling of some of those fascinating Pacificans.

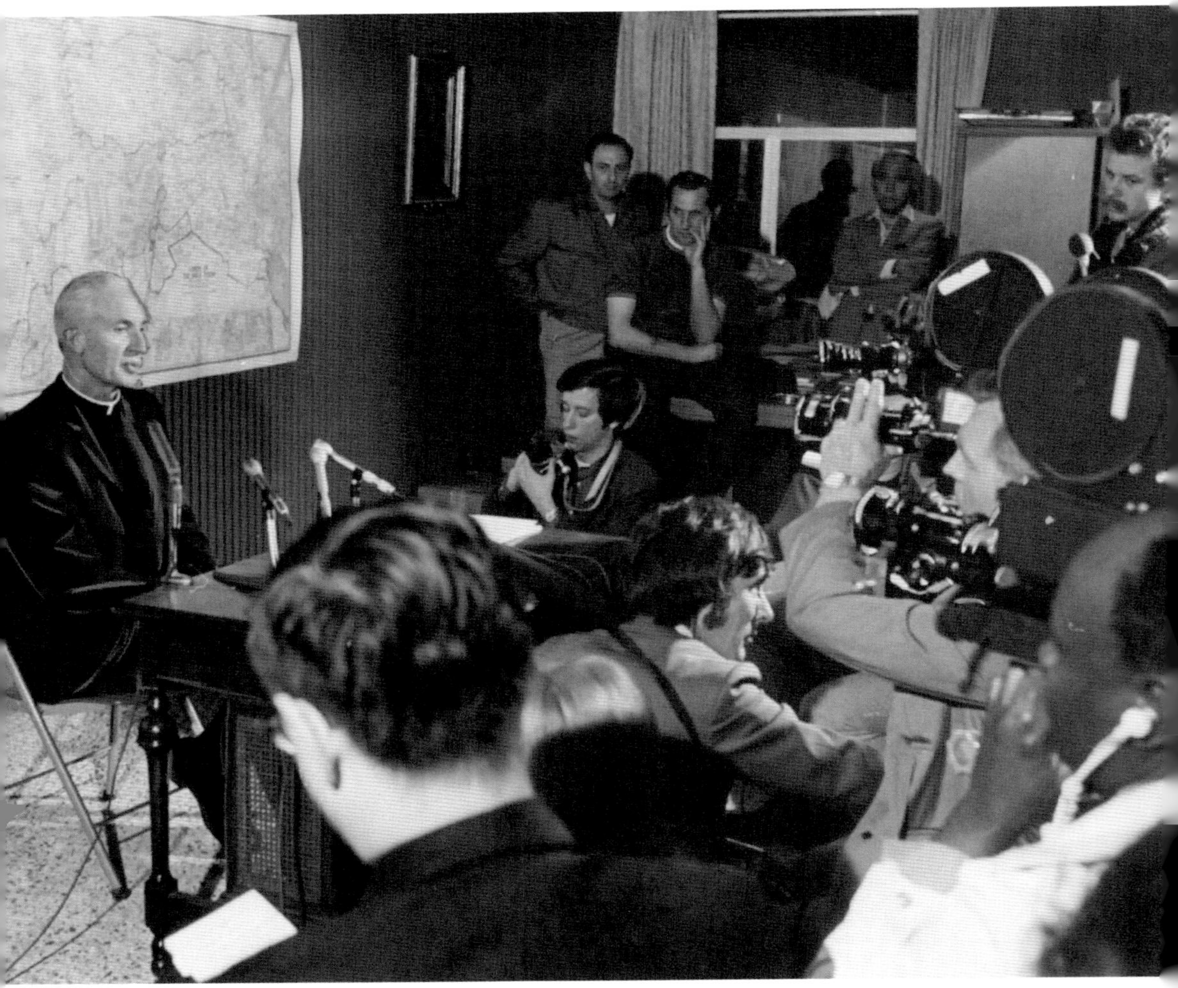

Fr. Robert Duryea (ABOVE AND OPPOSITE PAGE)
In contrast to the ongoing tragedy of Catholic priests being in the news for child sexual abuse, a Pacifica priest caught the attention of the national news media for having a sexually related secret as well. Fr. Robert Duryea created a firestorm of publicity when he revealed in 1971 that he had a secret family and was married to a woman he loved. A priest for 25 years, Father Duryea was at St. Peter's Catholic Church in Pacifica when his secret was revealed and the city became ground zero for the fascinating story. San Francisco Archbishop Joseph McGucken immediately excommunicated the Pacifica priest, who was 49 at the time with a 30-year-old wife and a five-year-old son. Father Duryea wrote about his experiences in articles for the *San Francisco Chronicle* entitled "I Was a Married Priest" and went on to work for a family counseling center in Fremont, California. He died in 2001 in Los Gatos, California. Oddly enough, Robert Duryea's brother John Duryea was also a priest, serving in Palo Alto, California. John also shared the same secret as his brother, maintaining a secret marriage of his own. Fr. John Duryea was excommunicated by Archbishop McGucken in 1976 for falling in love and marrying Eve De Bona. He died in Mexico in 2006. Fr. Robert Duryea in Pacifica and Fr. John Duryea in Palo Alto were both well-loved priests in their communities whose transgressions against the church consisted of having a wife and family.

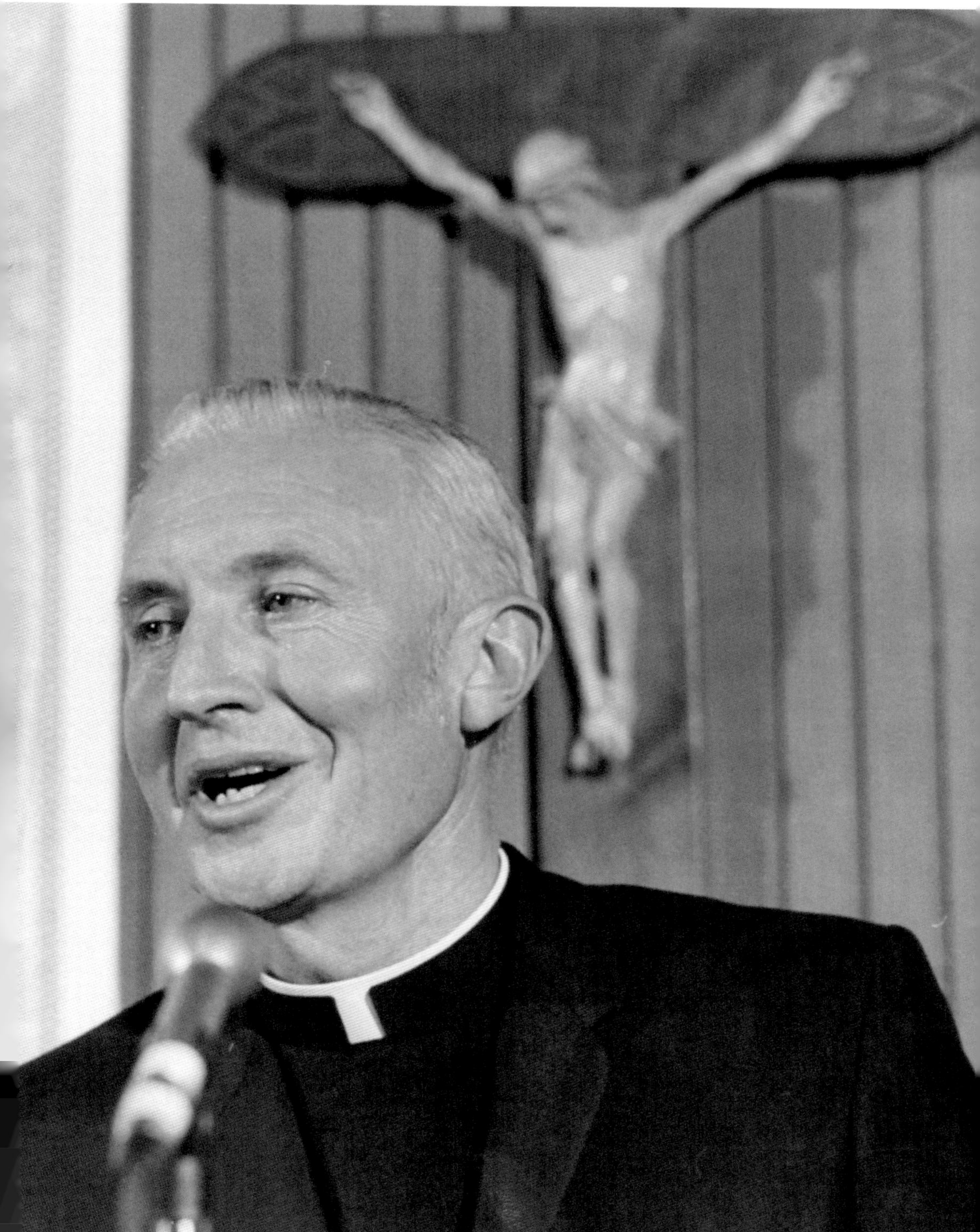

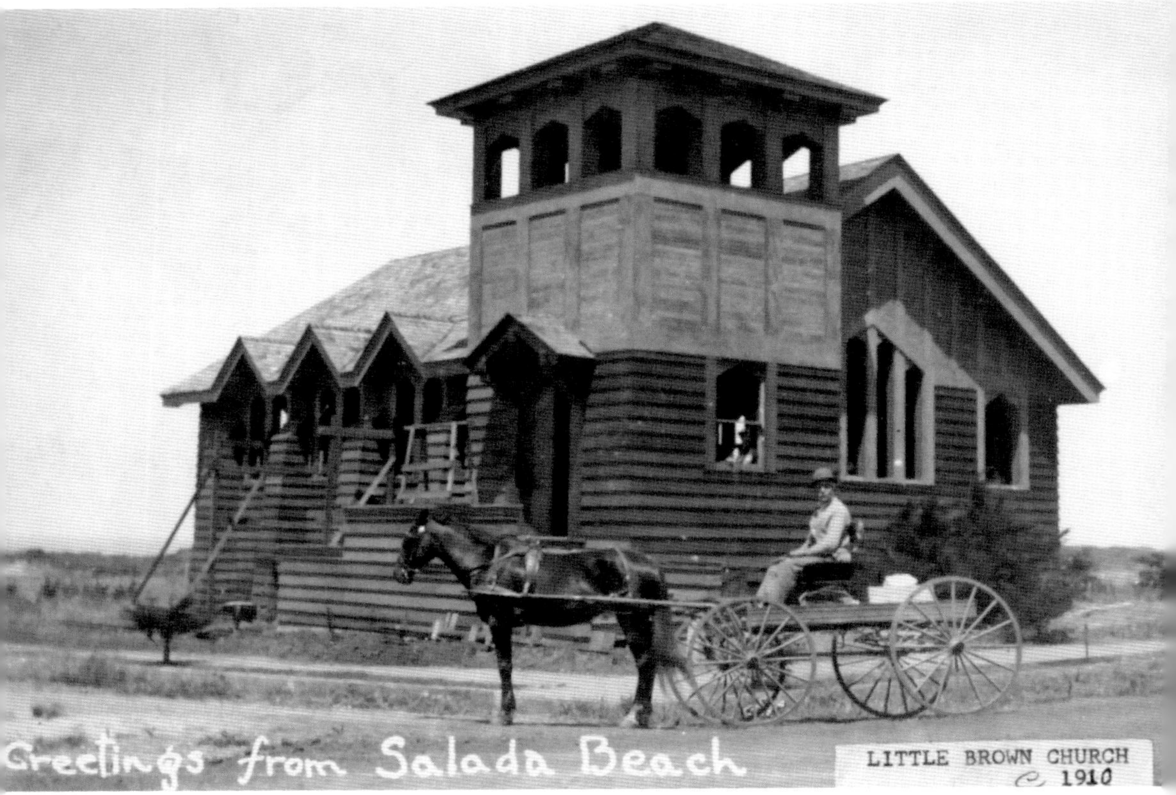

Rev. Herschel Harkins's "Little Brown Church"
The historic Little Brown Church, where Rev. Herschel Harkins preached, was built in 1909 and is being converted into a Pacifica History Museum.

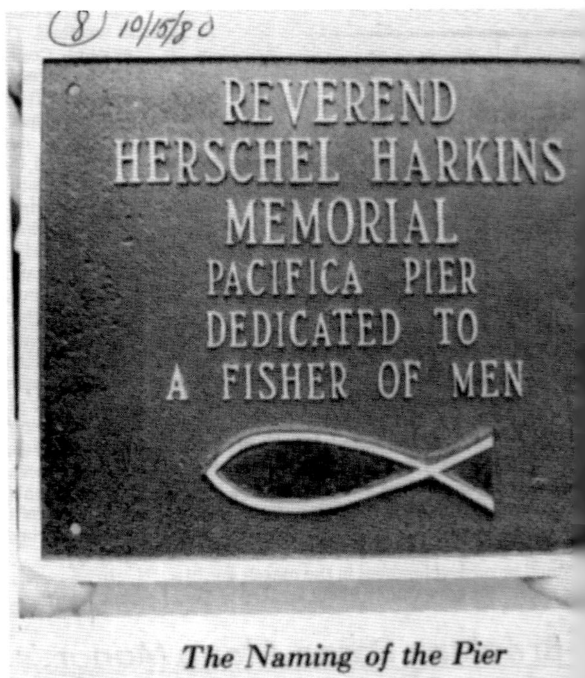

The Naming of the Pier

Pacifica's fishing pier becomes the "Reverend Herschel Memorial Pier" this week when a plaque received this week manufacturer is installed. The pier was named for the late the Little Brown Church who served it and was an unofficial ' of a community" during a lifetime of religious service here

Rev. Herschel Harkins Memorial
Rev. Herschel Harkins was honored by having the Pacifica Pier named after him. Built to support the wastewater treatment plant's outfall line, that original purpose is no longer needed now that Pacifica has built a newer sewer plant in the Rockaway Quarry. Funding for pier upkeep has become a challenge.

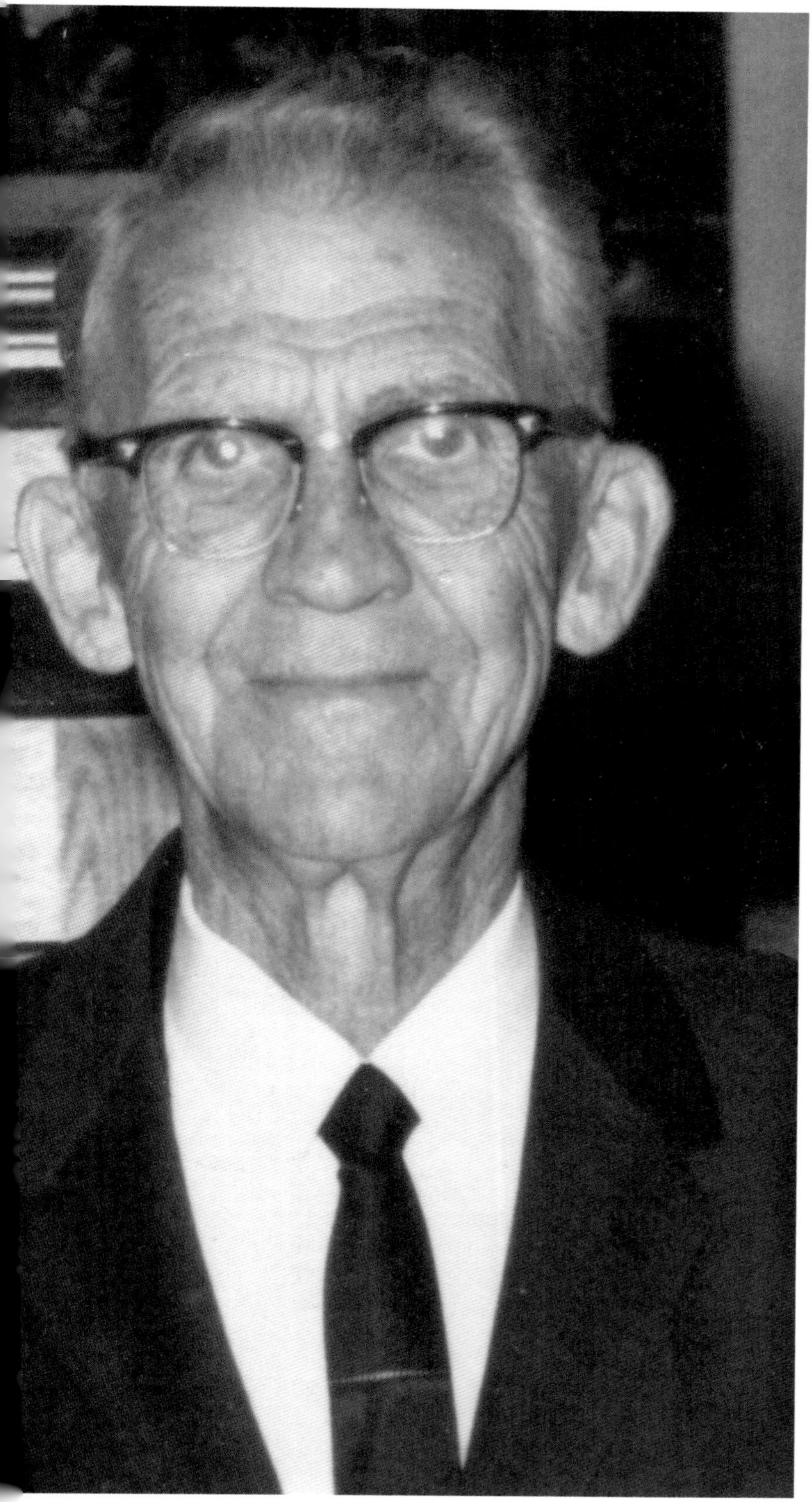

Rev. Herschel Harkins
An early Presbyterian minister who served as the pastor for the Little Brown Church from 1943 to 1965, Rev. Herschel D. Harkins was a pillar of the community and a powerful influence on the growing community of Pacifica. The pier was named the Herschel Harkins Memorial Pier. He once served the area on horseback, commenting often that when he started, the "area was run by bootleggers." Often called the "chaplain of the community," Reverend Harkins was an incredible influence on the community and when the pier was named for him in 1978, it was because it was "the strongest structure in Pacifica," and symbolic of the well-liked pastor.

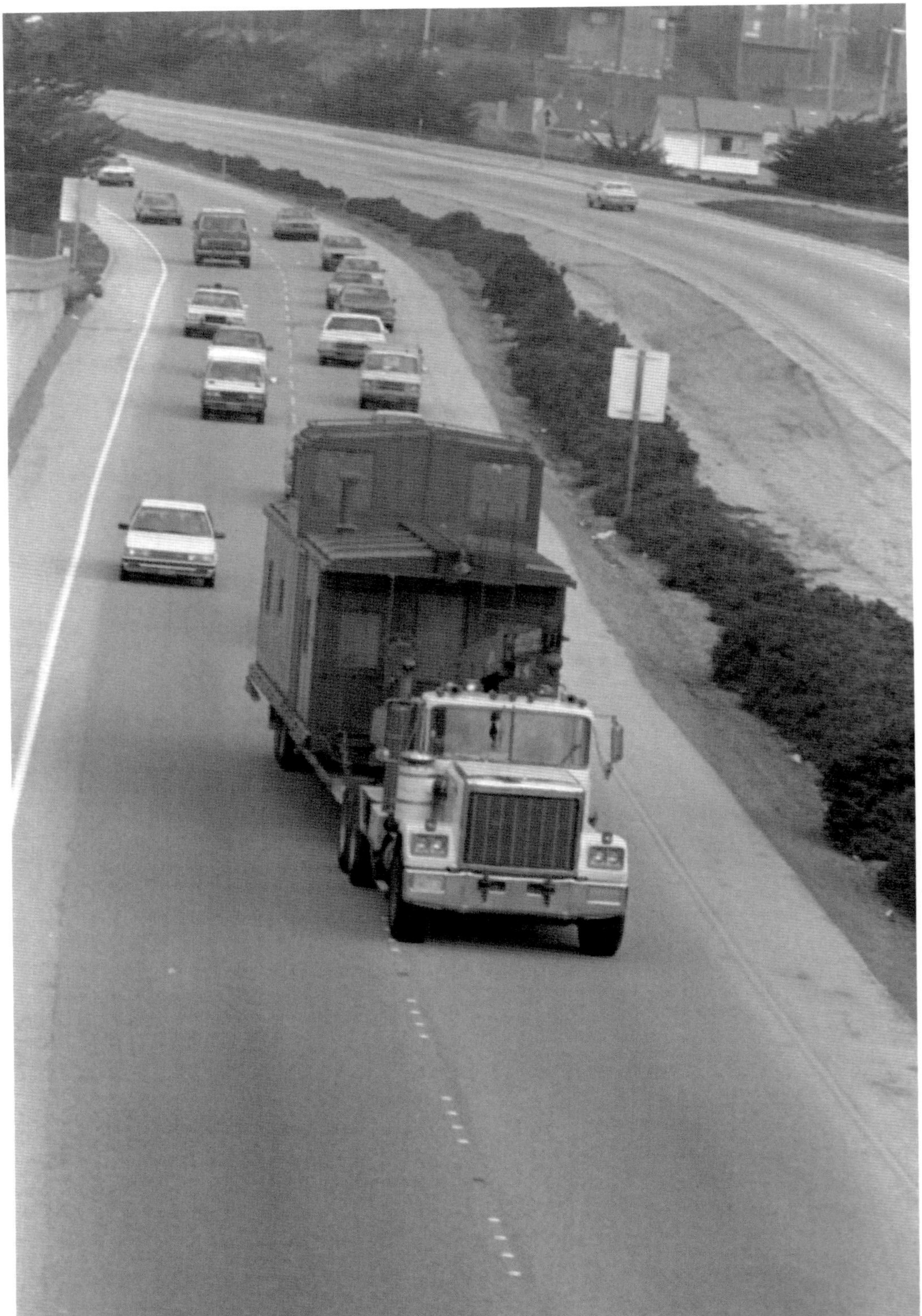

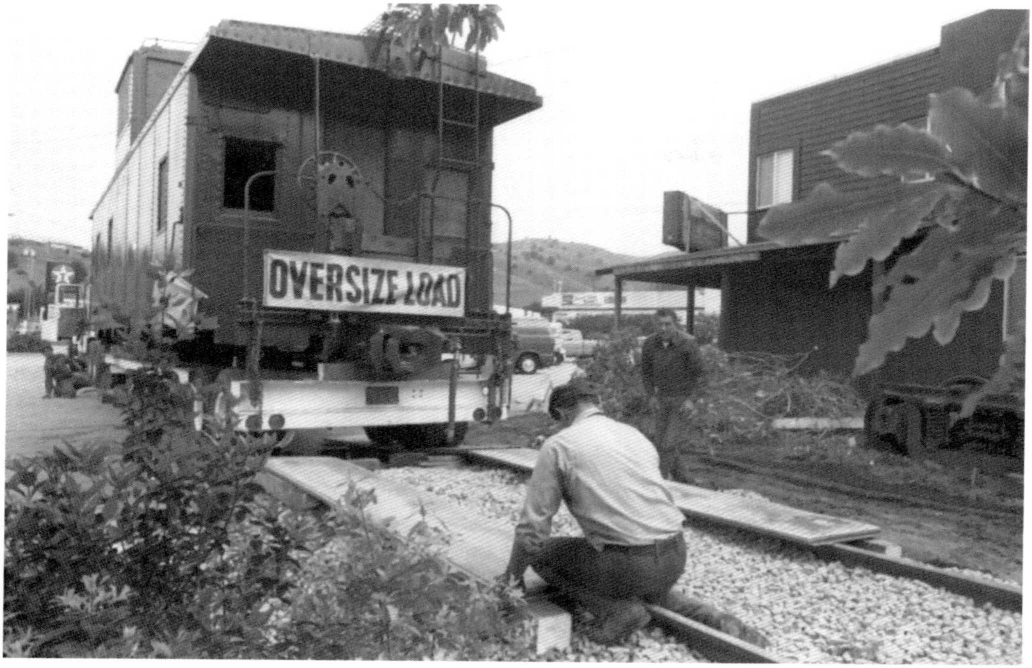

Pete Pereira

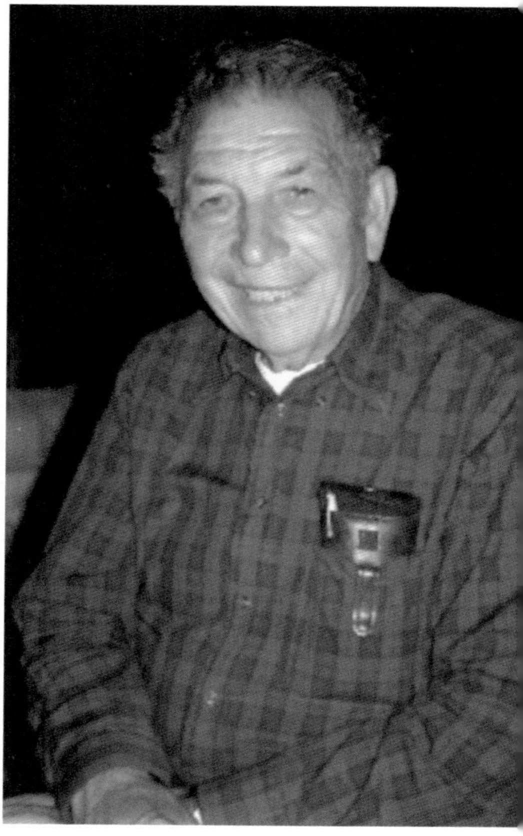

Pete Pereira is linked to the look and feel of Pacifica in a very unique way. He moved houses, churches, and railroad cars around town. Whether it was the church that became the city's community theater building in Oddstad Park or the caboose that has housed several businesses in Vallemar, Pereira combined a construction career with a specialized relocation expertise that brought him fame and fortune. His company, called Coast House Movers, was known throughout the Bay Area. Many of the historic Victorian houses in San Francisco were carefully moved from place to place by Pereira. Pictured at left, he rolls a train car down the highway on a truck. Pereira also developed and built custom homes, which sometimes brought him into conflict with city politics. A frequent critic of government regulations, Pereira wrote countless letters to the editor and was a regular speaker at city council meetings. More often than not, he was able to succeed in his projects and those who knew him personally fondly remember his playful nature. A houseboat he kept for decades on Lake San Pedro was where he entertained countless friends and family. As a landlord, he maintained most of the commercial area along Highway 1 at Vallemar, including the famous Vallemar Station.

Ian Butler

Ian Butler is not a politician, but he has had a growing impact on his adopted community of Pacifica. A tree trimmer by trade, Butler is more widely-known as an entertainer and in recent years, a public access television star. He moved to Pacifica in 1990, renting a beach house from comedian Rob Schneider's parents. Although his sister Margie is more well-known as a Celtic musician featured in the group Golden Bough, Ian is a musician in his own right, having played in the Celtic rock band Tempest through 1995. A sharp-witted bon vivant, Butler capitalized on his sense of humor and began to host a local cable access show called *Laugh Locally*, which enjoyed 42 episodes and earned six WAVE cable excellence awards. He also wrote a humor column in the *Pacifica Tribune*. While studying local issues to research his comedy, Butler found himself getting involved in those local issues, particularly anything involving environmental topics. He likes to say that some problems just cannot be solved by "making fun of them," although he did write song parodies for a popular Fog Bless Pacifica CD. Since 2010, Butler has become something of a news celebrity, producing a weekly commentary show called *Wavelength* during which he interviews local personalities. That public affairs program earned him a Producer of the Year award in 2012. In addition to his entertainment and commentary creativity, Butler is a dedicated environmentalist who is active in Pacifica's Environmental Family, nonprofit organization that acts as a fiscal sponsor to the Pacifica Beach Coalition and the Pacifica Gardens. Butler even announces the parade at the annual Fog Fest and coordinates beach and creek clean-up activities throughout the community. Perhaps his greatest attention-getting activity has been his discovery of 20,000-year-old Columbian Mammoth fossils while picking up trash at what has become known as the Secret Waterfall. Butler is a uniquely contemporary legend in Pacifica who has made his fame through humor, music, and simply cleaning up the beloved local environment. "My favorite part of a community event, whether it is a parade, a TV show or a beach cleanup, is watching the commotion as everyone works together as a team to make something special happen. That is what a community is all about, and what I love about Pacifica."

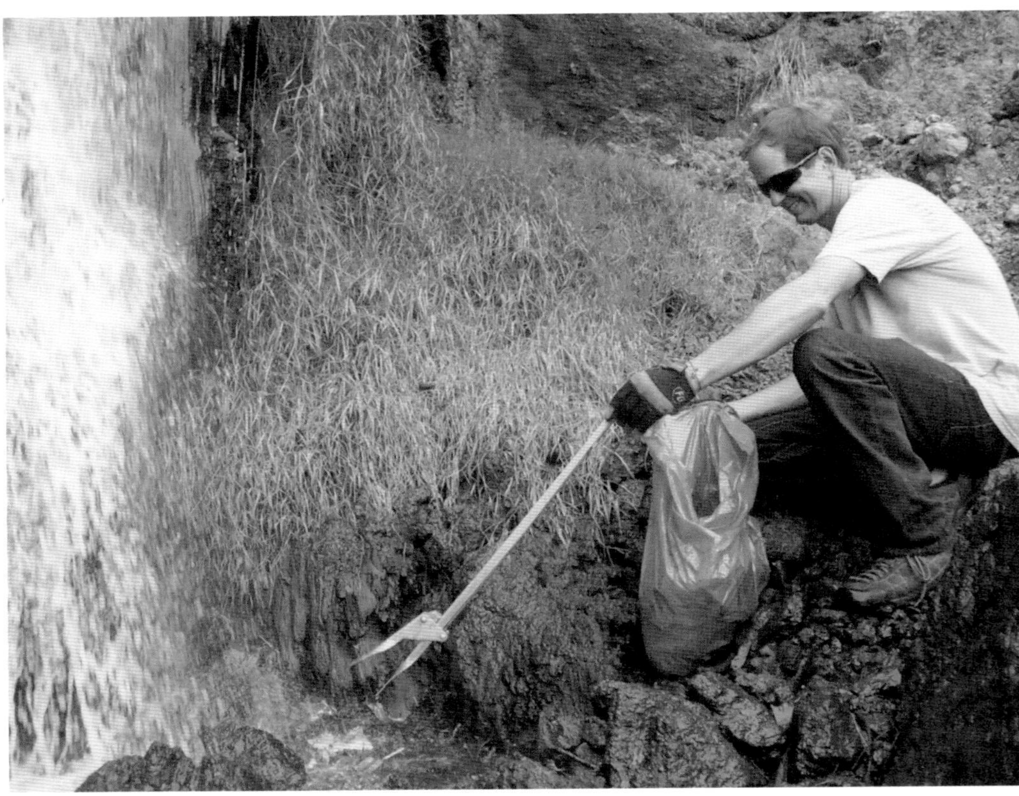

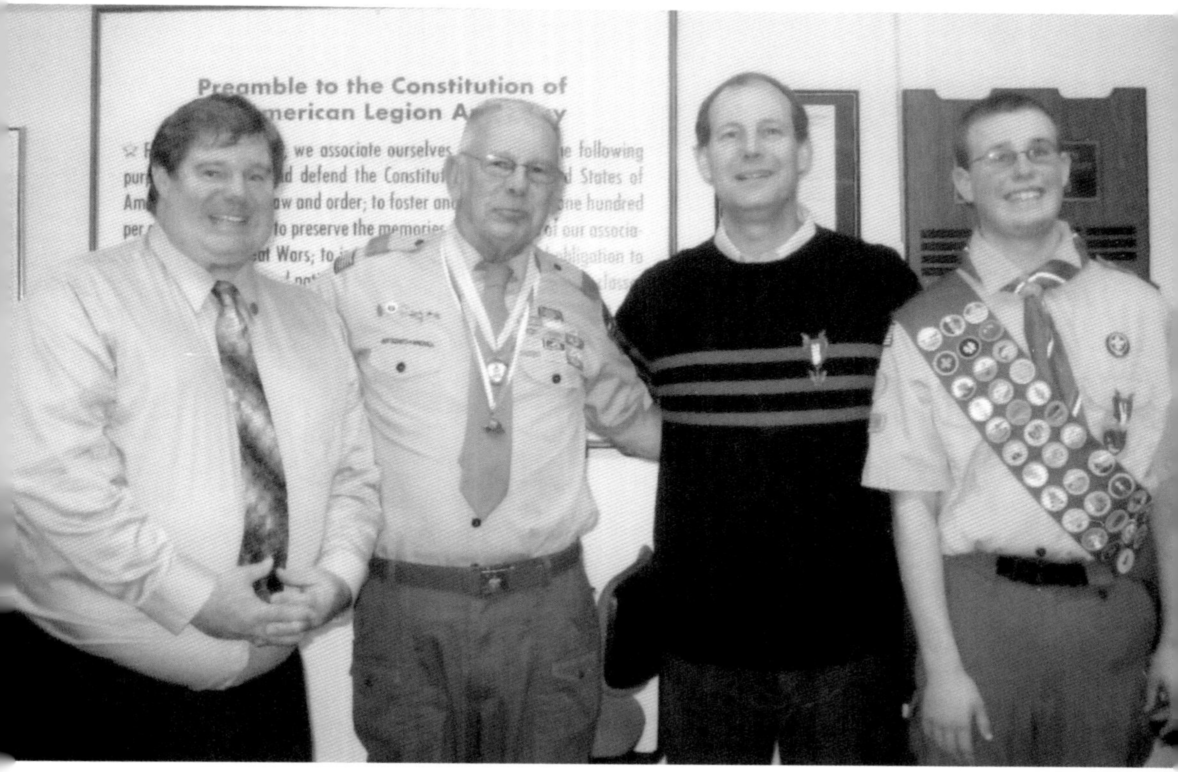

Allan Hale
A high school athlete at Jefferson High School in Daly City, Allan Hale moved to Pacifica in 1956 and worked at the family business called Accurate Appliance, which was known for years as one of the most supportive local companies sponsoring sports teams. Any school or community sports league that can be named had some involvement from Allan Hale and Accurate Appliance. He coached, managed, and played in adult leagues and helped create the image of Pacifica as an active sports community. No one ever heard Allan Hale say no to a request for help. As a Veteran, he became involved in the American Legion and the Veterans of Foreign Wars Post 10245, even serving as the Department of California American Legion vice commander. He manages the American Legion Hall and has been commander for both veteran groups. Perhaps his true legacy is as the Scoutmaster for Troop 264, which he has guided for more than four decades, leading many young men to Eagle Scout status. Hale is second from the left in this photograph, with a new Eagle Scout and other Scoutmasters. As a member of the St. Andrew Presbyterian Church, he has been invaluable in supporting the maintenance of that facility and tending a community garden there. (Courtesy of Allan Hale.)

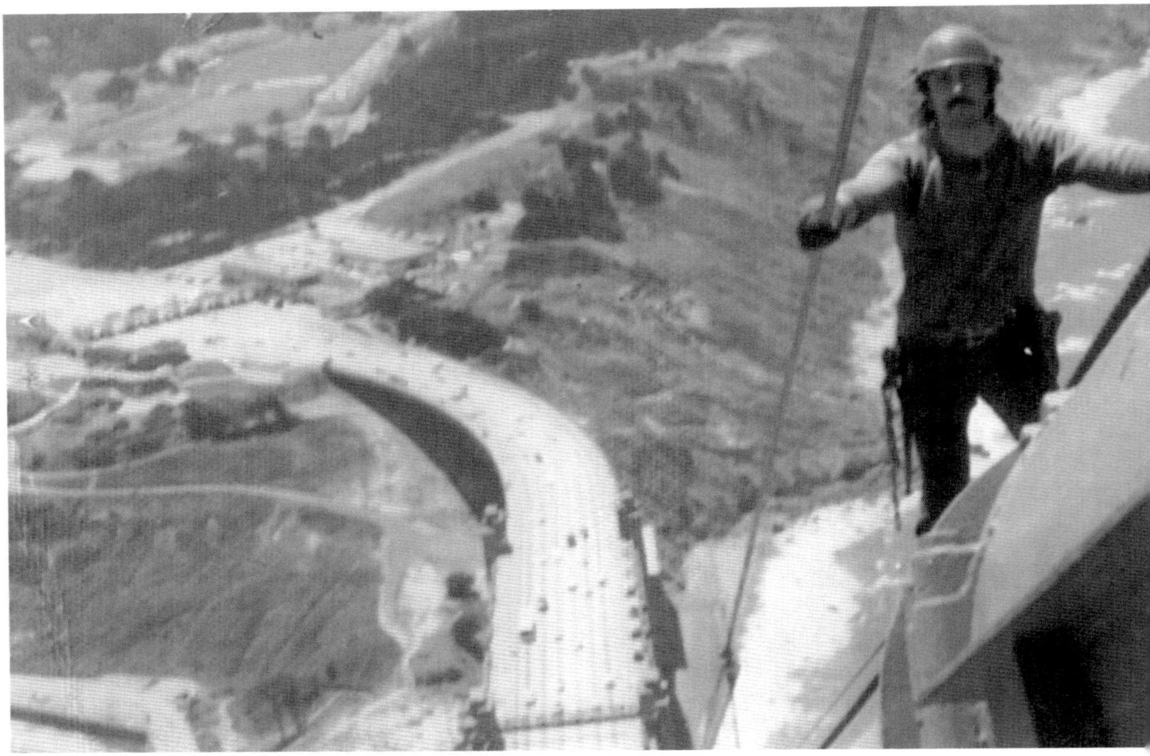

Frank Cimo

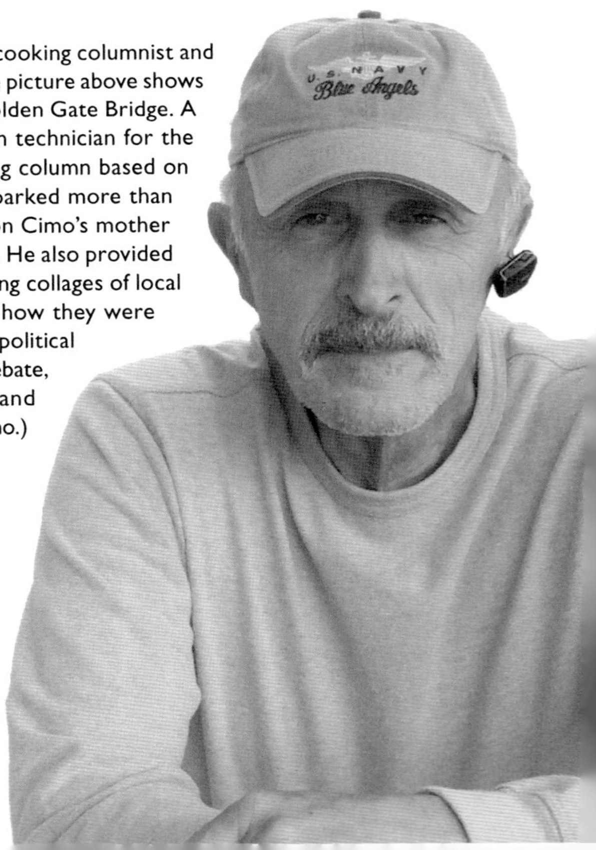

Frank Cimo was an ironworker who became a cooking columnist and eventually a right-leaning political columnist. The picture above shows 23-year-old Cimo climbing to the top of the Golden Gate Bridge. A jack-of-all-trades, Cimo worked as a darkroom technician for the *Pacifica Tribune* before asking to write a cooking column based on his mother's Italian recipes. That inspiration sparked more than a decade of popular weekly columns focusing on Cimo's mother and the Cimo family's history in New York City. He also provided photography services for the newspaper, creating collages of local families on holidays and letting readers know how they were celebrating. His second writing project involved political columns that stirred up constant comment and debate, mirroring national debates between liberal and conservative commentators. (Courtesy Frank Cimo.)

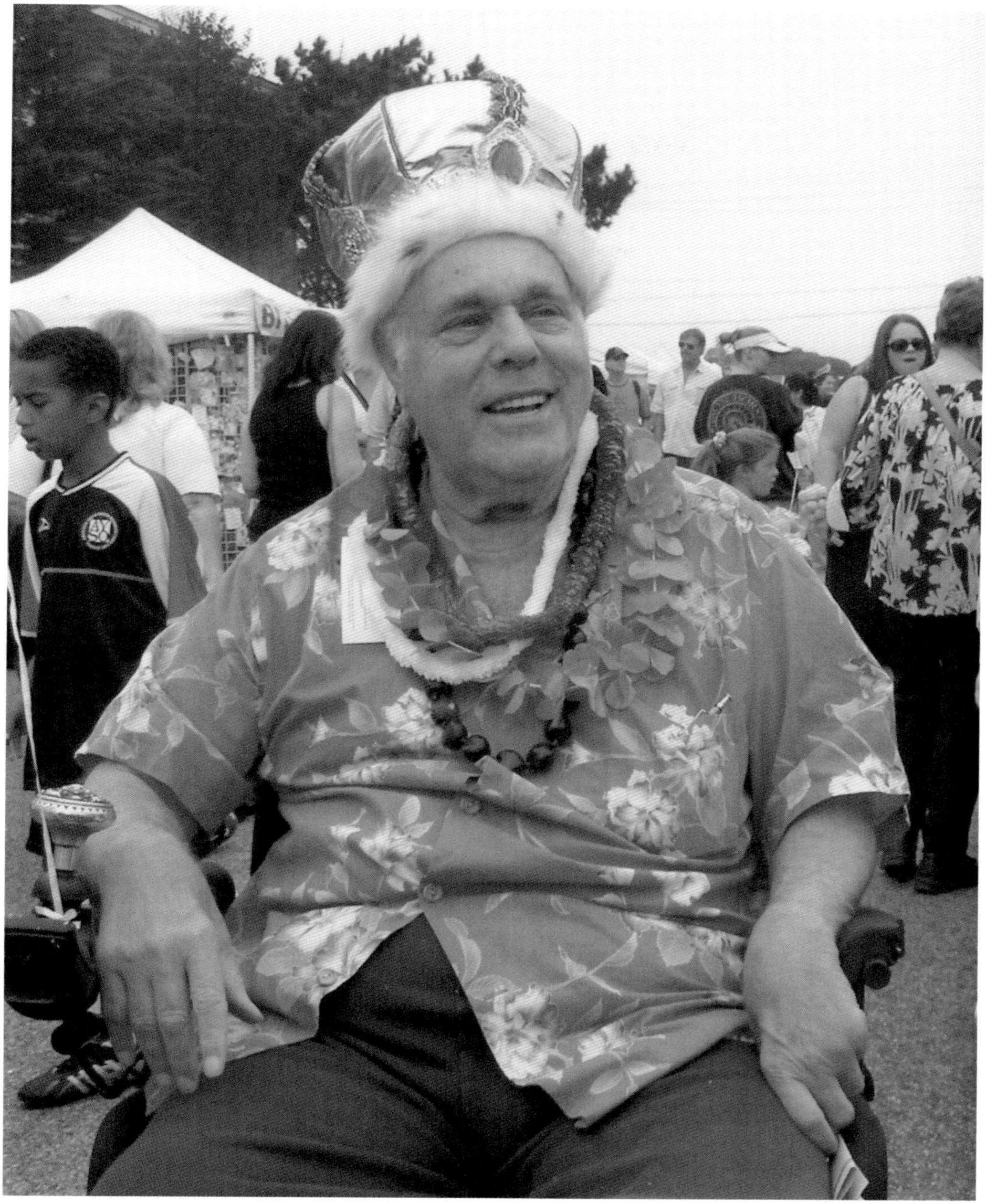

"frank d. winston"

Insisting that his name always be in lowercase letters, frank winston was a former immigration lawyer, law teacher, and creator of the Northern California Jewish Sports Hall of Fame, who was also disabled and spent much of his later life confined to a wheelchair. He brought his creativity to the Pacifica Historical Society when he retired. His enthusiasm for all things Pacifica was inspirational and people began to jokingly call winston the "Emperor of Pacifica." He helped lift the local history buffs into having a higher profile and worked tirelessly before his death to enjoy his adopted hometown and give others the same love of history that he had.

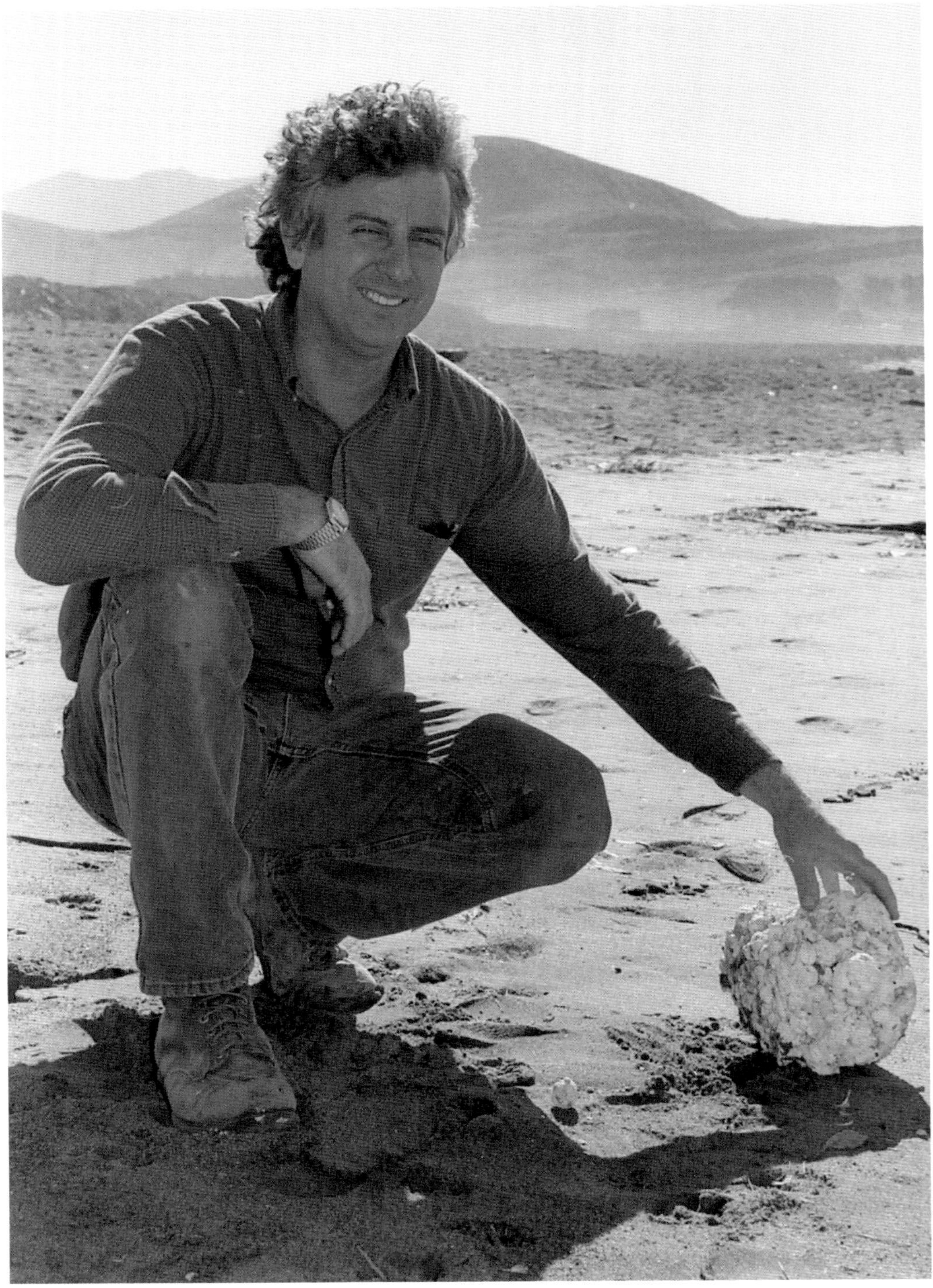

Scott Holmes (BELOW AND OPPOSITE PAGE)
The City of Pacifica's primary engineer for more than 20 years, Scott Holmes was an innovative public works director and creative developer of infrastructure projects. For many years, he was able to keep the old Sharp Park Wastewater Plant operating, even though it was obsolete for most of its years of existence. He was given free rein by city leaders to develop a sophisticated new tertiary treatment plant to replace the old one, and it was built in the Rockaway Quarry. Holmes crafted an environmentally friendly outfall for the new plant, which was able to release water directly in to the Calera Creek and then out to the ocean. The old plant had discharged water out in to the ocean by way of the pier. The new plant, while very successful in treating wastewater, was plagued by occasional odors and difficult overflow problems during heavy storms. Another project involved a comprehensive flood control plan in the Linda Mar valley. After Holmes retired, he became the designer and one of the developers of a proposed live work facility south of Pacifica, which would provide living quarters for developmentally challenged adults, one of whom is Holmes's daughter. The project created controversy, and although it was approved at the planning level of San Mateo County, it was rejected by the California Coastal Commission. Holmes has not given up and he continues to hope a revised project can be more successful.

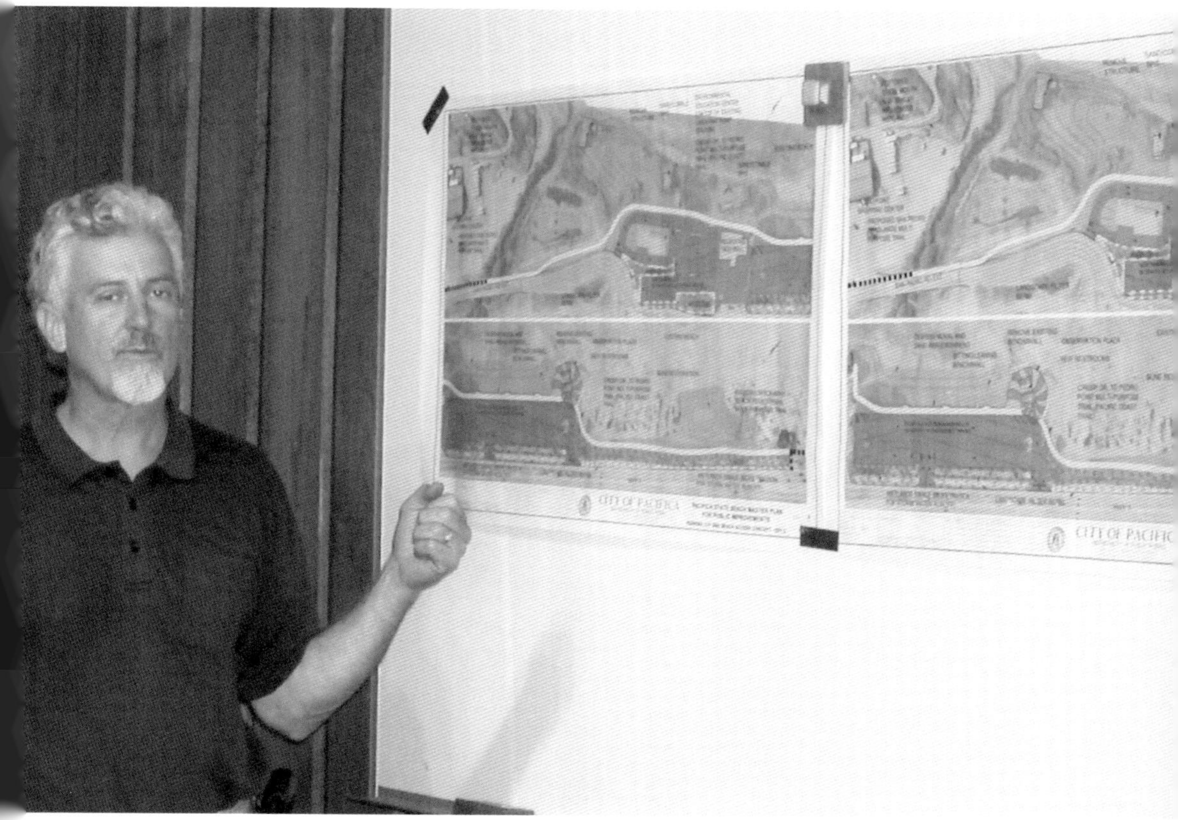

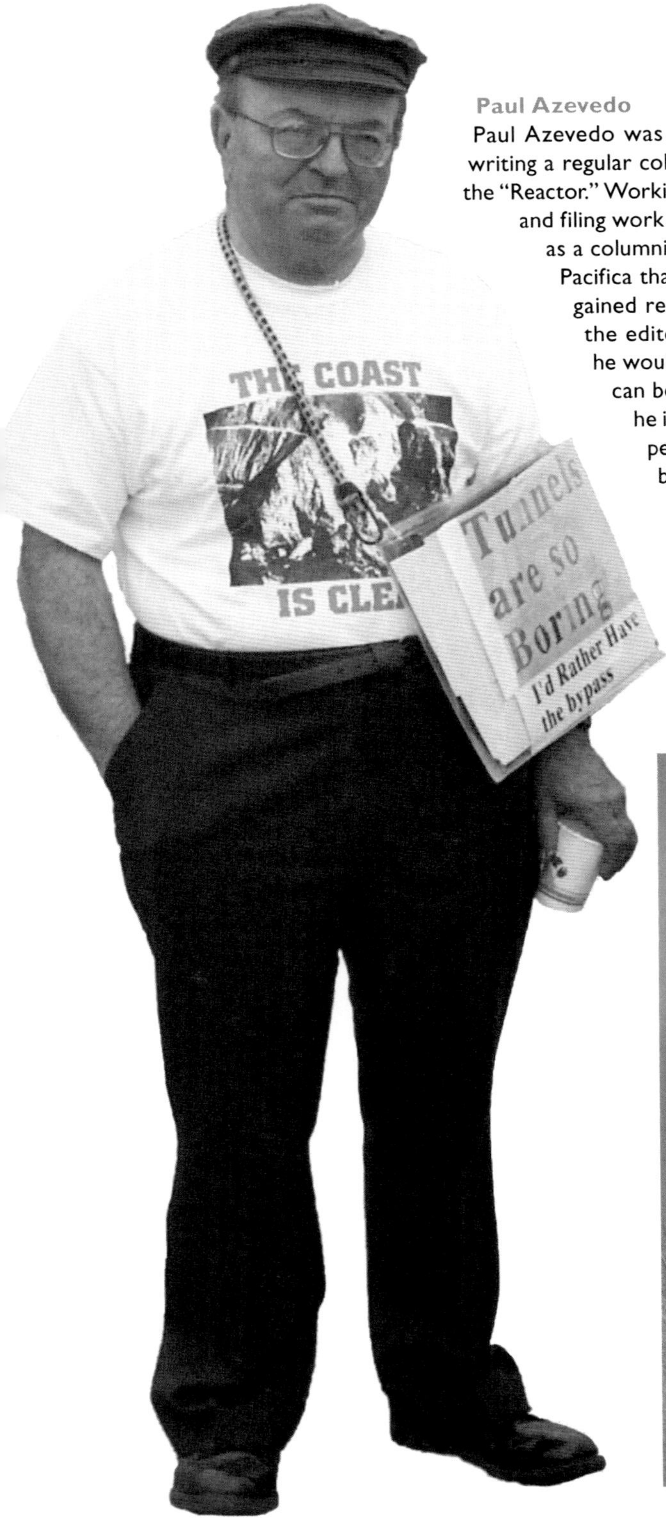

Paul Azevedo

Paul Azevedo was the conscience of Pacifica for many years, writing a regular column for decades in the *Pacifica Tribune* called the "Reactor." Working for publisher Bill Drake, Azevedo did clerical and filing work but was mostly known for his prolific abilities as a columnist. It seemed as though there was no topic in Pacifica that would not appear in the "Reactor." He also gained recognition for a constant stream of letters to the editor in the *San Francisco Chronicle*. Sometimes, he would go against the grain of the general public, as can be seen by the anti–Devil's Slide Tunnel T-shirt he is wearing in the left photograph. More than 75 percent of San Mateo County residents voted to build a tunnel on the coast instead of a highway bypass to avoid a crumbling cliffside, but he thought it was a bad idea (that tunnel opened in 2013). With his wife, Lydia, who was active in the Democratic party and an equally unique figure in Pacifica, Azevedo created a vivid perception of what made Pacifica tick. He died unexpectedly on a family trip to Chicago, leaving a void in Pacifica's heart.

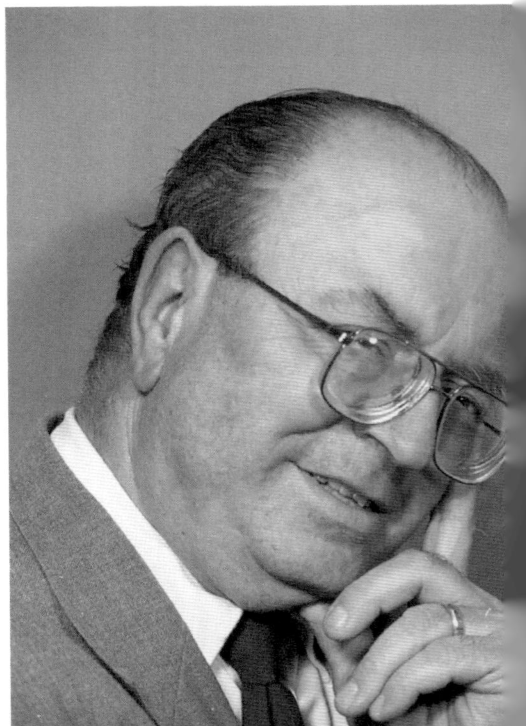

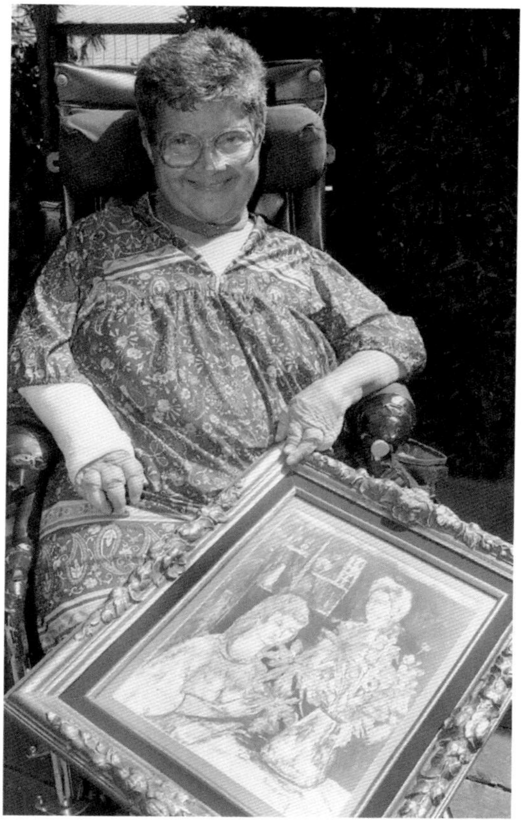

Lucy Muir
Lucy Muir did more from a wheelchair than most people without any disabilities accomplish in a lifetime. Having to deal with rheumatoid arthritis, she never let her physical disabilities dissuade her from her love of art, writing, and maintaining a sunny, supportive personality. She was also an incredible activist and advocate for disabled people. During the political campaign for the 1973 Rehabilitation Act, Muir went to Washington and lobbied Joseph Califano, the US Secretary of Health, Education, and Welfare, to sign it. Later, in 1977, she joined a month-long sit-in at the Federal Building in San Francisco in protest and to show solidarity with disabled activists doing the same thing in Washington, DC. In 1990, thirteen years later, the American Disabilities Act became law. Muir never stopped being an advocate for helping disabled people integrate into the general society. She was also known for the empathy training she provided to able-bodied people who worked as drivers for Caltrain and SamTrans, teaching them how to successfully interact with disabled passengers. A cofounder of the Center for Independence of the Disabled in Belmont, Lucy Muir was also the president of the San Mateo County Chapter of the California Association of the Physically Handicapped. She was also inducted into the San Mateo County Women's Hall of Fame in 1992. Lucy Muir was honored again in 1999 with one of the People Who Care Awards from San Mateo County, which honor those who enhance the lives of people with disabilities in San Mateo County. She took home the Lore Radisch Lifetime Advocacy Award. In addition to her work for disabled people, her energies were directed towards her artwork, and she was an essential member of the Pacifica Art Guild, displaying her paintings on a regular basis at Pacifica art shows. Lucy Muir seldom complained about her disabilities, providing strength and inspiration to all those who knew her, rolling through Pacifica in her motorized wheelchair. She died in 2013 and had told her fellow artist and friend Tom Jackson that she wanted to be cremated and her ashes scattered off the Pacifica Pier. "That way I can always be with you," she said, "and will be able to spiritually ride in on the morning fog to visit."

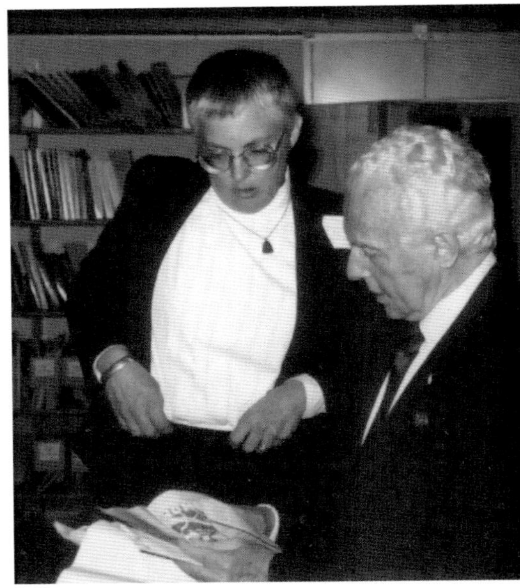

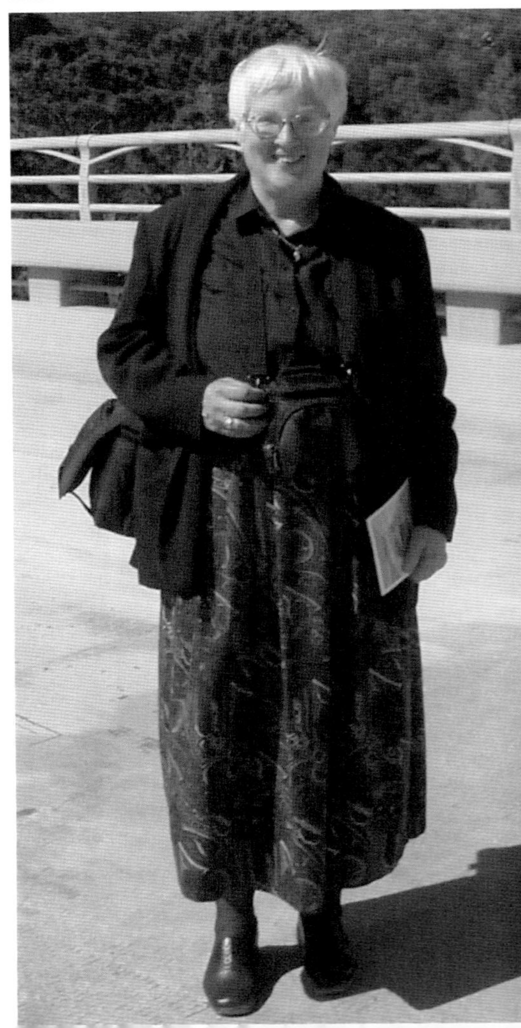

Margery Farrar

Margery Farrar's career as a human rights analyst for Congressman Tom Lantos might never have taken place had she not moved to Pacifica, where she read his town meeting bulletin and applied to work for him. A law school student at the time, she was hired as an intern in the Lantos district office and wound up staying as an employee for more than two decades, until Lantos died in 2008. Congressman Lantos, the only Holocaust survivor to be elected to Congress, had a strong commitment to human rights and founded the Congressional Human Rights Caucus, which inspired Farrar to want to work for him. She found her niche and built a career investigating and analyzing human rights issues for Lantos, becoming one of the few congressional aides to do that kind of work out of a district office instead of the Washington, DC, office. She was able to focus on constituent cases that often fell through the cracks of government assistance and were not viewed with the same importance that Margery Farrar viewed them, like local homelessness. In the early 1990s, Farrar developed the Theater of the Homeless project, bringing together stories about homelessness by homeless people in San Mateo County themselves. It was an innovative combination of art and social activism that helped homeless people connect with services while educating the broader public about the issue, and it is something Farrar views as one of her major accomplishments. "We began to respond more and more to human rights concerns," said Farrar. "There were dicey asylum cases that I would analyze within an inch of their lives." After Lantos died, Farrar took time to be with an ill brother and is now developing her own human rights think tank exploring the connection between human and global security. "There are always ways one can take one's own experience, mix and match what fits in one's own life, and find ways to support human rights," she said. (Courtesy of Margery Farrar.)

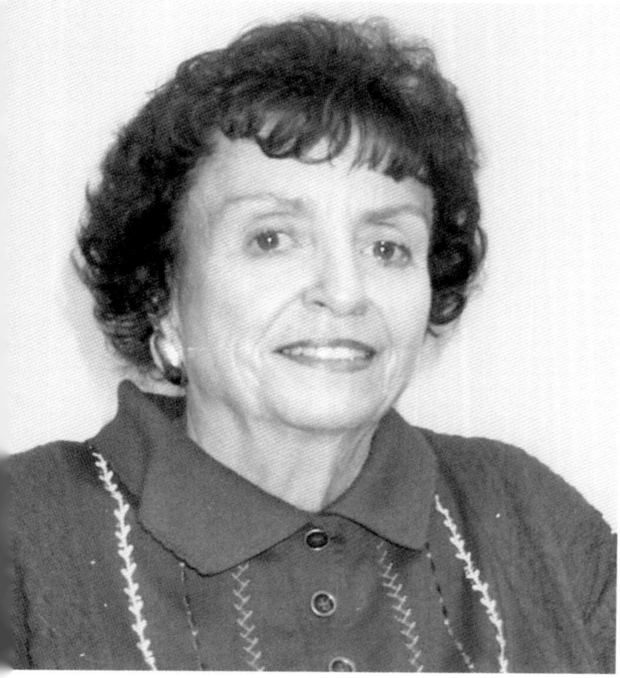

Mary Beauvais
For more than 50 years, Mary Beauvais was involved in the American Red Cross. She received a Red Cross scholarship in 1959 for training in first aid that would lead to her teaching others in Pacifica, where the newly incorporated city saw a demand for such training. Beauvais continued her association with the Red Cross, stepping up to help with every major disaster throughout the years and coordinating details for those injured or inconvenienced. Her consistent efforts on behalf of the Red Cross established her as well-known figure throughout San Mateo County. In the below photograph, she is seen at the Emergency Operations Center with Pacifica officials during an emergency drill.

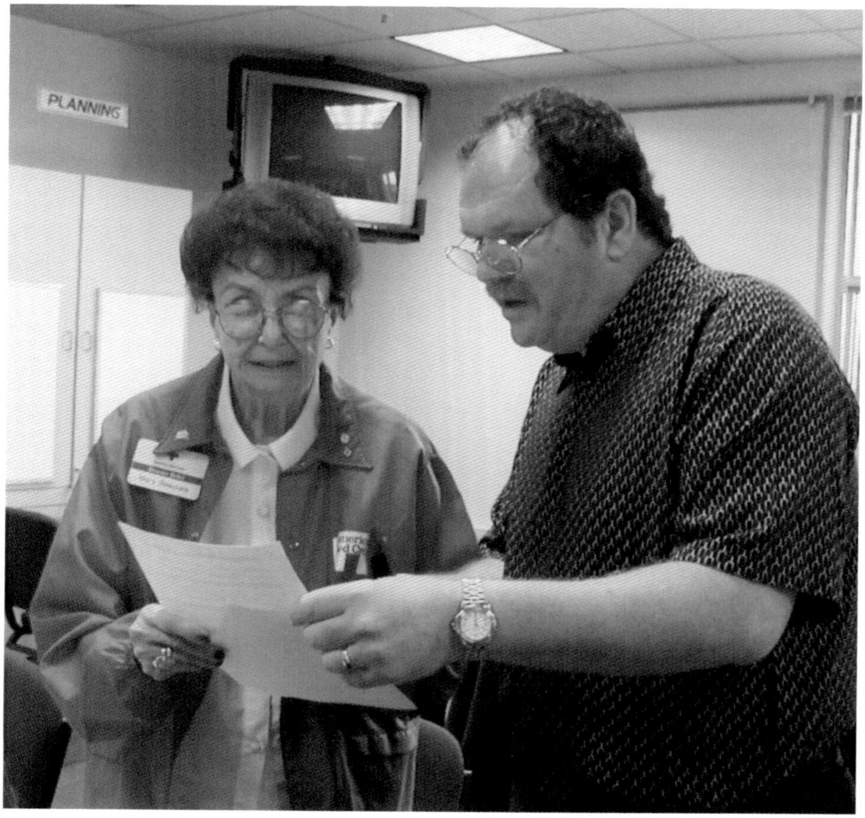

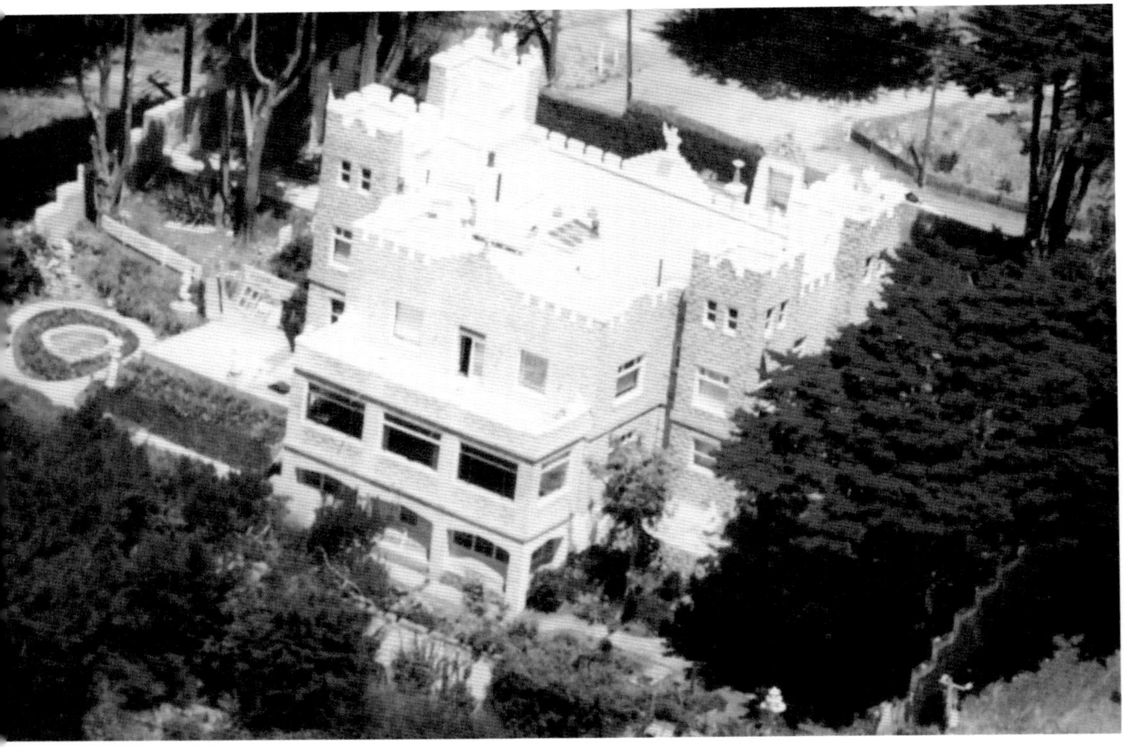

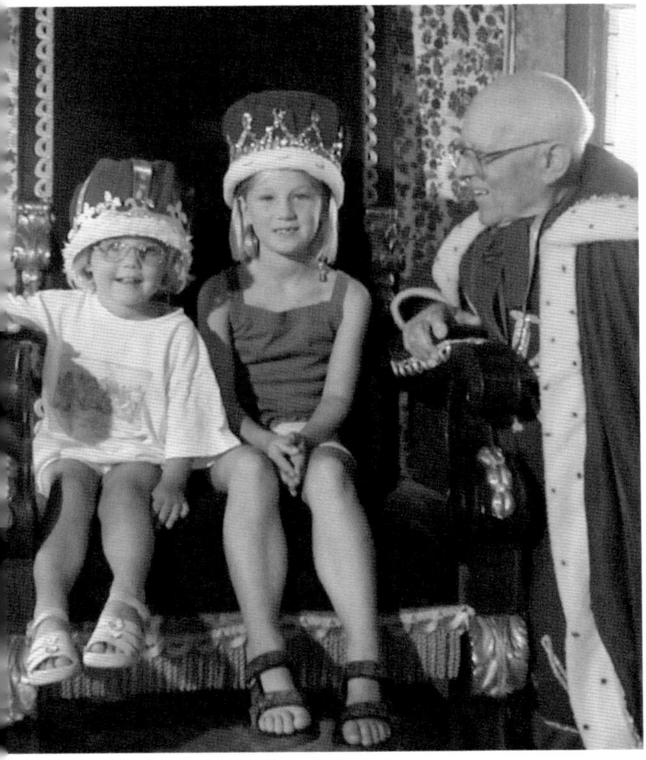

Sam Mazza

Owner of the famous castle in Pacifica, built after the 1906 San Francisco Earthquake as a safe haven for the McCloskey family, Mazza was an eccentric collector of memorabilia. Although he did not live in Pacifica, generations of people grew up fantasizing about the castle. He was fond of saying that he stopped in Pacifica for a gin fizz and bought the castle on a whim for $29,000. His playful nature manifested in the eclectic collection he kept at the castle, ranging from movie props to a real suit of armor. Once, he tried to turn the castle into a restaurant and sought to create a small incline railroad to carry customers up the steep hill in Sharp Park where it was built. Code restrictions prevented such a grand plan and he gave up the idea. Upon his death, the castle reverted to a family trust and is being maintained carefully. Although it is not open to the public, Sam's castle continues to be sought after as a unique location for private events. The Pacifica Historical Society is allowed to hold tours occasionally, which generate great interest and donations. Sam Mazza is pictured entertaining the author's daughters, Brae (left) and Mettlin, during a visit to the castle.

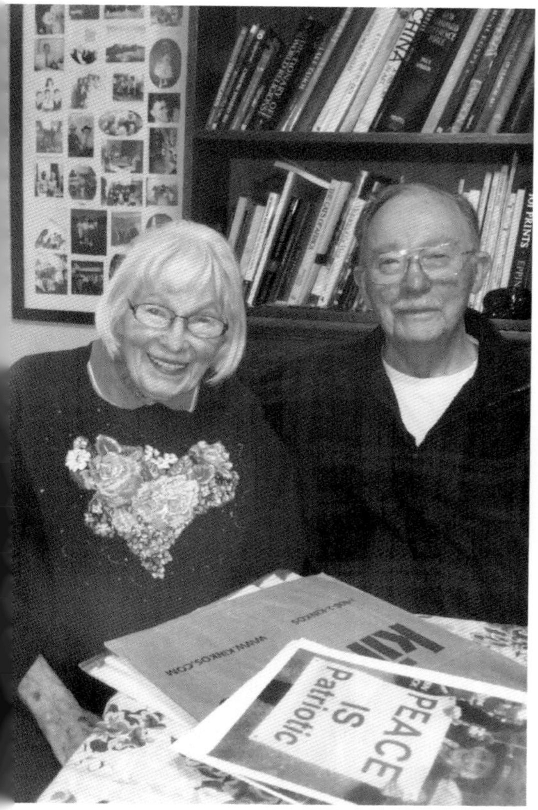

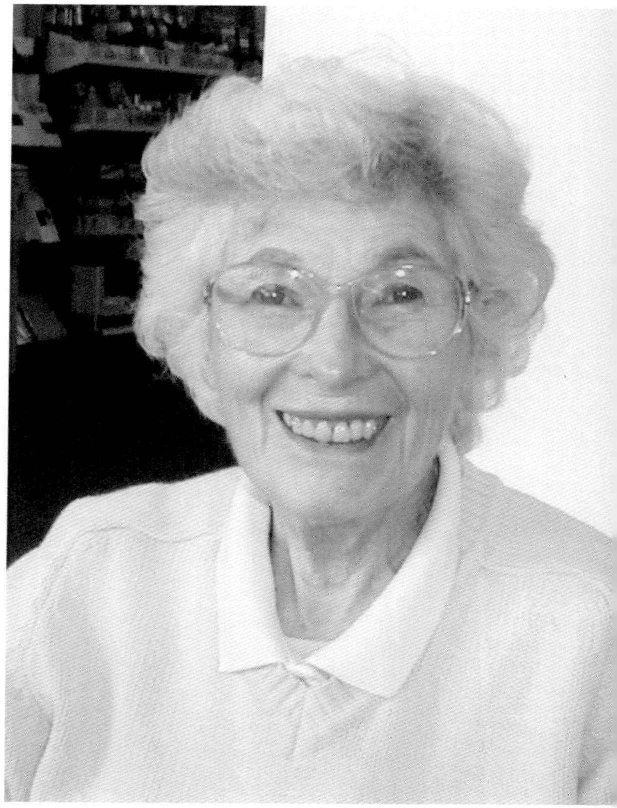

Helen James

There is no one in Pacifica who has not had some kind of encounter with Helen James. She and her husband, Lowell, moved to the coastal city in 1954 and she immediately set out to volunteer by exploring clubs and committees. She became the secretary of the local Democratic party right away, moving on to having an active involvement in nearly every organization in the local school district, where her three children attended. A Minnesota native, Helen James was happy to escape the bitter cold of her home state, like so many others. "We'd heard about these sunny places," she laughs. A teacher, James also attended Hastings Law School for a year-and-a-half before becoming a full time mother and then educator. "I do not have a good sense of time," she admits. "I sometimes think I can do more things than I have time for." She never ran for local office, although countless people urged her to do so through the years. While she worked as a teacher, she admits she has always thought wistfully about what her life would have been like had she continued to pursue a law degree. "In my early teens, I wanted to be a ballet dancer or an attorney," she says. "Or a social worker. What kind of life would I have had? I couldn't have had a happier life, although there was nothing spectacular." Her active participation in the early Pacifica community helped shape the new city and she created a golden reputation through her involvement. In addition to Mizpah, a philanthropic religious women's group, James maintained continuous engagement in the Pacifica Historical Society, the local cable television station and even the mobile blood bank. She learned how to use video equipment and worked as a cameraperson broadcasting school board meetings for decades. "I just did the things I enjoyed doing," she says, "with the people I enjoyed being with. On the whole, I think I have been pretty happy. When I turned 70, I decided I would learn to play golf." James turns 90 years old in 2013, and she tells people she will take the year off. No one really believes that.

Lynn Adams

A veritable force of nature herself, Lynn Adams is Pacifica's beach-cleaning inspiration. A dedicated environmentalist who leads the Pacifica Beach Coalition and works tirelessly to clean up the beaches, she has turned an annual Earth Day into one of the city's biggest celebrations. From a simple community clean up event, the local Earth Day has blossomed into a daylong festival of environmental education, entertainment, and public support for beach protection. She has brought in experts on sea turtles and sharks to speak, as well as making sure proper credit goes out to those who work all year to protect the environment. In 2007, she faced the death of her sister, eventually overcoming grief by focusing on the short time everyone has on earth. It inspired her to commit to doing something positive for the environment and her growing success with the Pacifica Beach Coalition is a remarkable example of someone actually changing their own life to try and change others. "We all need to know that we matter," she told the *Pacifica Tribune*. "By being connected, it is instantly clear how much we matter to each other and to the environment."

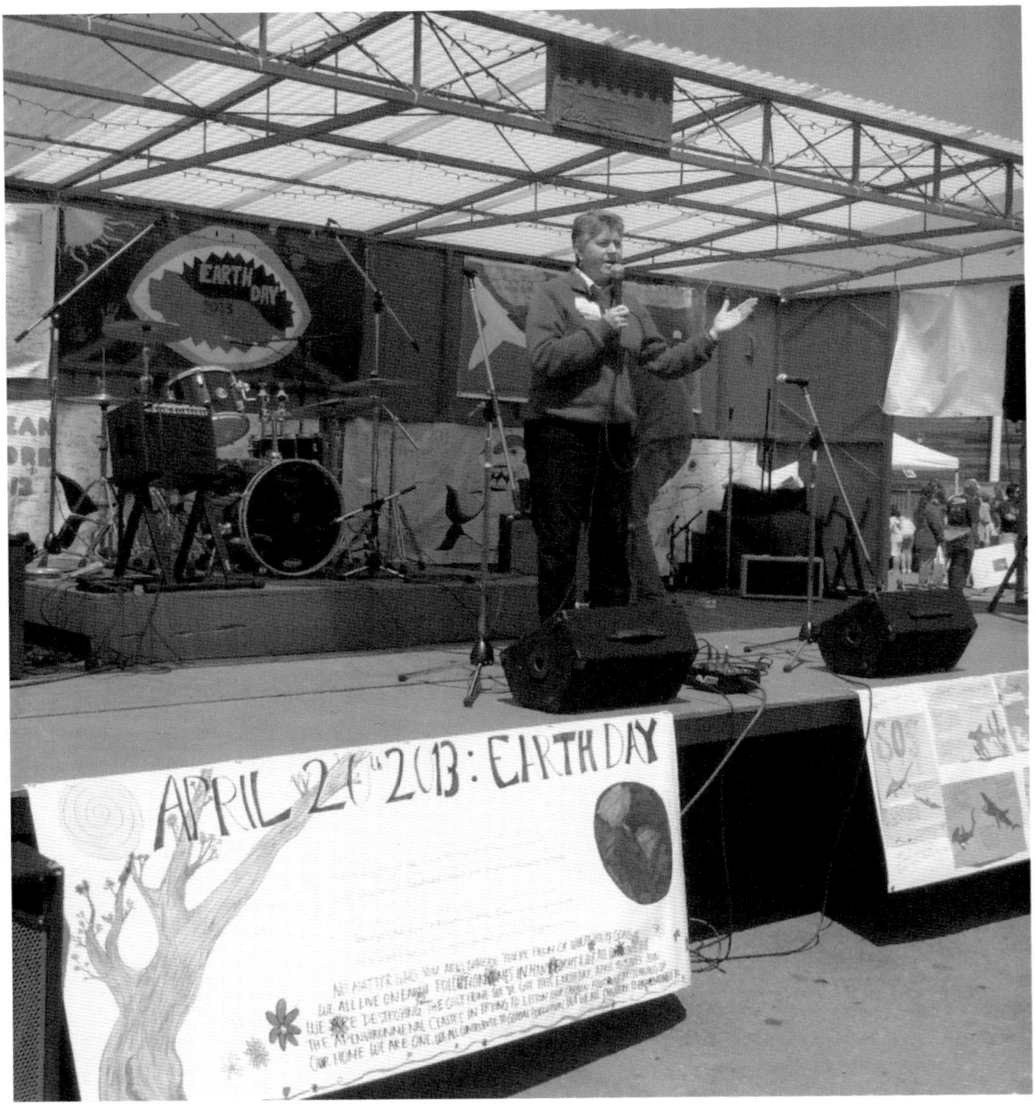

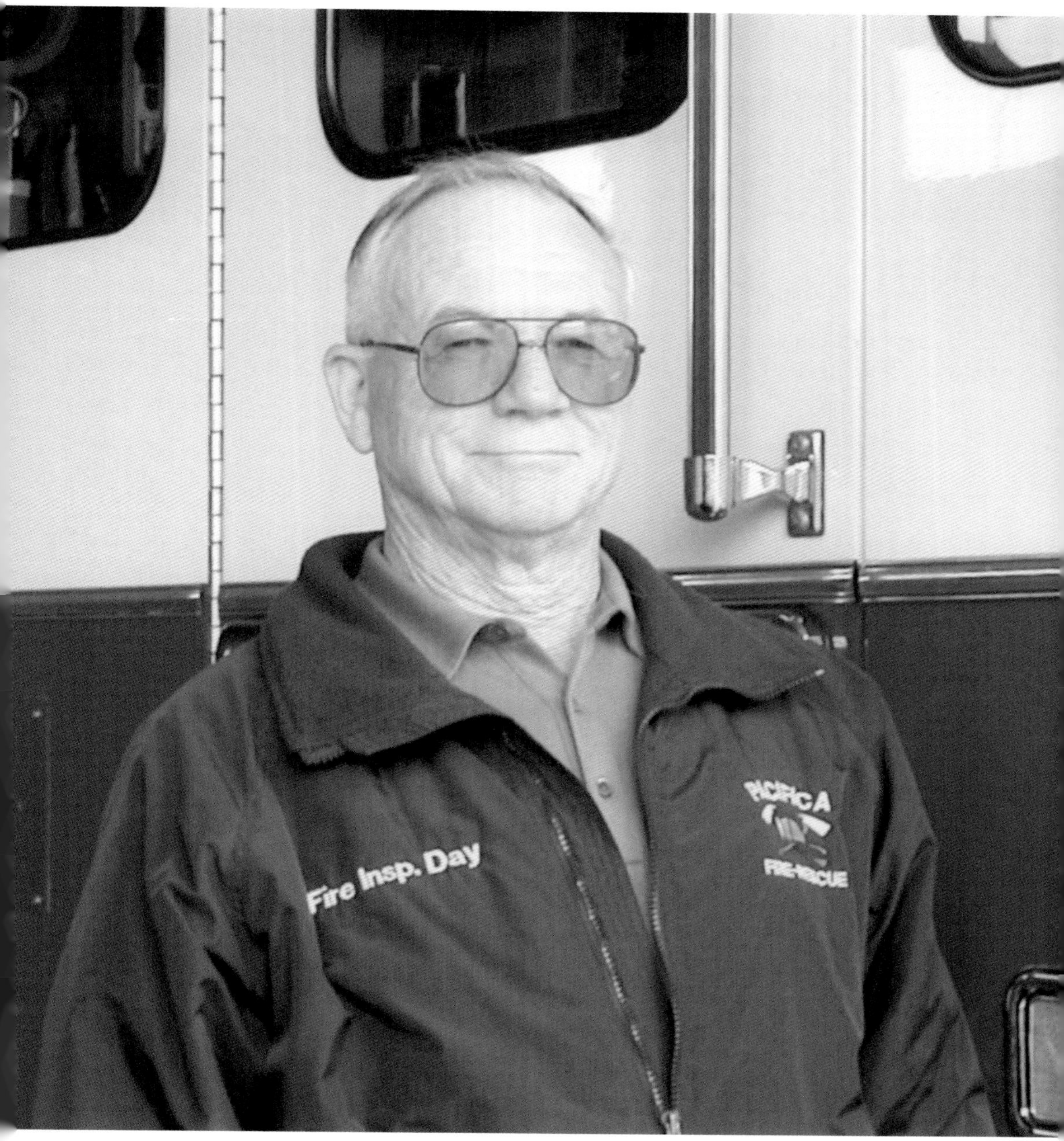

Eugene "Gene" Day

A career as a firefighter at the Presidio in San Francisco was topped by a second stint as a fire inspector with the Pacifica Fire Department, which eventually became the North County Fire Authority, a consortium made up of Pacifica, Daly City, and Brisbane. Day was at every incident, following up with his experience, lending a hand to younger firefighters and figuring out just what had happened at a fire scene. He was exceptional at communicating with the public and the media, often alerting the *Pacifica Tribune* to details. He retired a second time and headed out to the Dakotas, but the folks who enjoyed meeting him every morning at his favorite coffee shop do miss the stories.

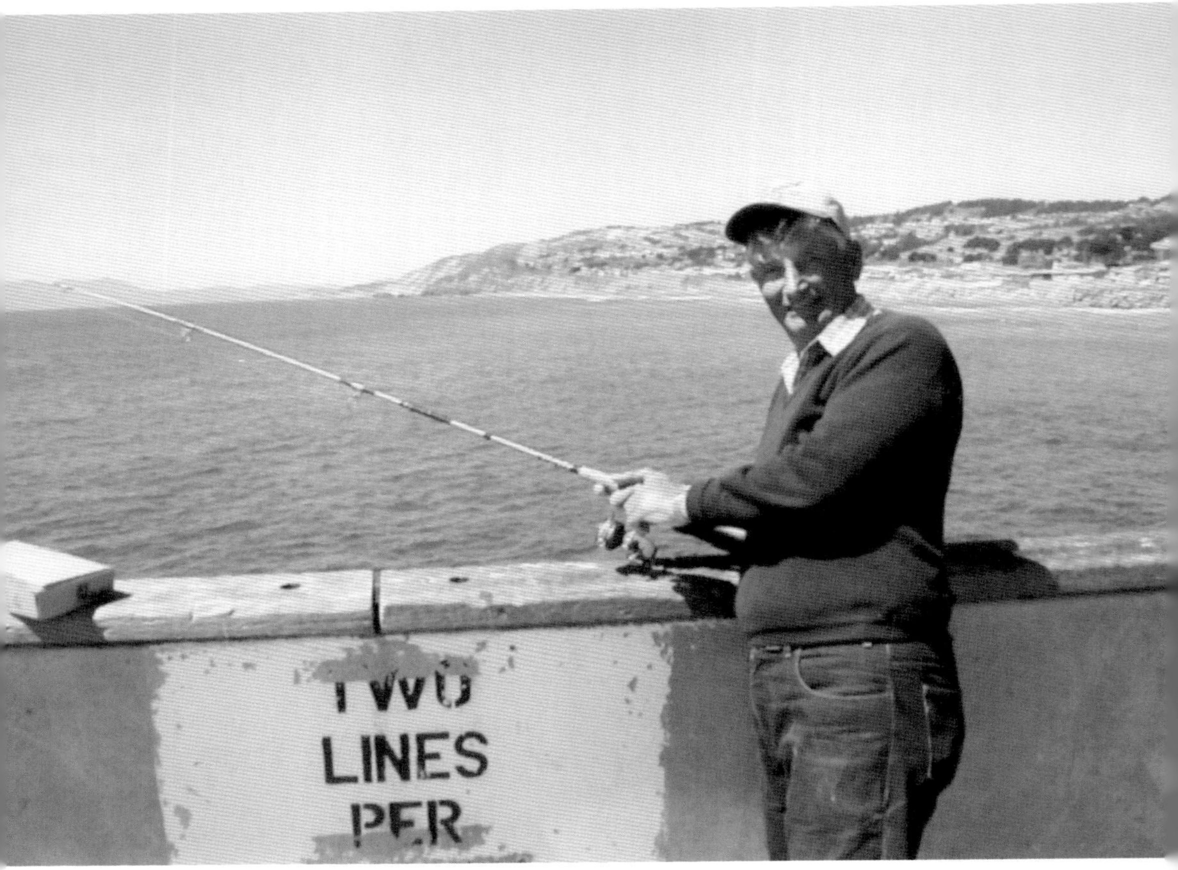

Andy Pappas

A champion of the Herschel Harkins Memorial Pier, Andy Pappas greeted every opening of every fishing or crabbing season with a brightly worded letter to the editor to the *Pacifica Tribune*, encouraging everyone to come out to the pier and enjoy nature's bounty. He taught anyone who was interested how to throw a crab pot or cast a line. For years, the beginning of crabbing season could be timed by the enthusiastic response of Andy Pappas as much as by the boats heading out to sea.

Helen Karr

Helen Karr managed beauty salons for 25 years and saw the troubling reality of elder people being taken advantage of by others. So, she went to law school at the age of 64 and eventually became one of the top champions of elders in the battle against elder abuse in the state. In 2013, at 78 years old, she now works part-time for the San Francisco District Attorney's office and has been responsible for tremendous strides in protecting older people, particularly against financial fraud. Active in San Mateo County as the former chair of the County's Commission on Aging, Karr has also served on the State Commission on Aging and helped to designate May as Elder and Dependent Adult Abuse Awareness Month.

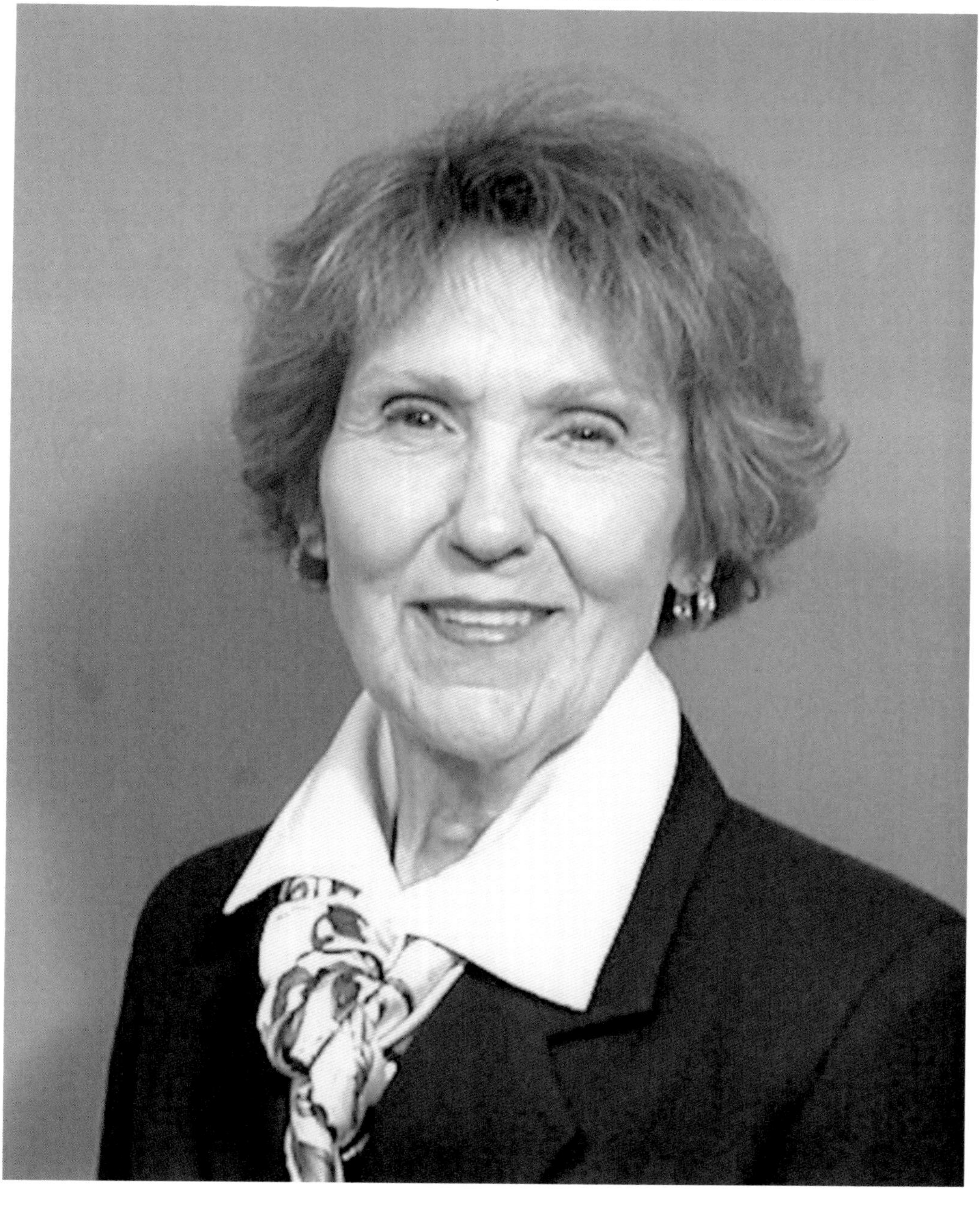

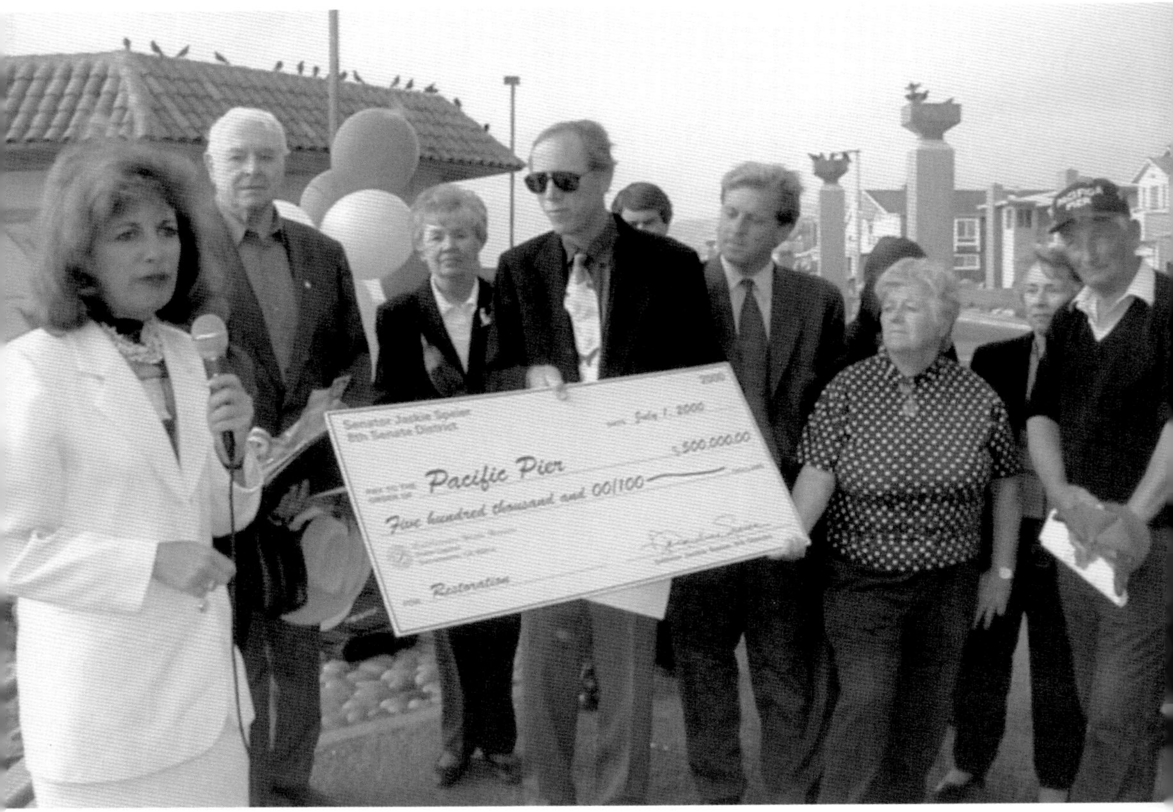

Jackie Speier

Although not a Pacifica resident, Congresswoman Jackie Speier has spent an enormous amount of time cultivating the coastal city as a home away from home. Here, she is shown with a group of prominent Pacificans as she announces a grant for repairing the Pacifica Pier. Speier, who was wounded when she traveled with then Congressman Leo Ryan on his fact-finding mission to investigate the Jim Jones community in Guyana, went on to become one of the most popular politicians in the Bay Area herself. She served as a San Mateo County supervisor, a member of the state assembly, and a state senator. When Congressman Tom Lantos died in 2008, she easily won that seat in the US House of Representatives.

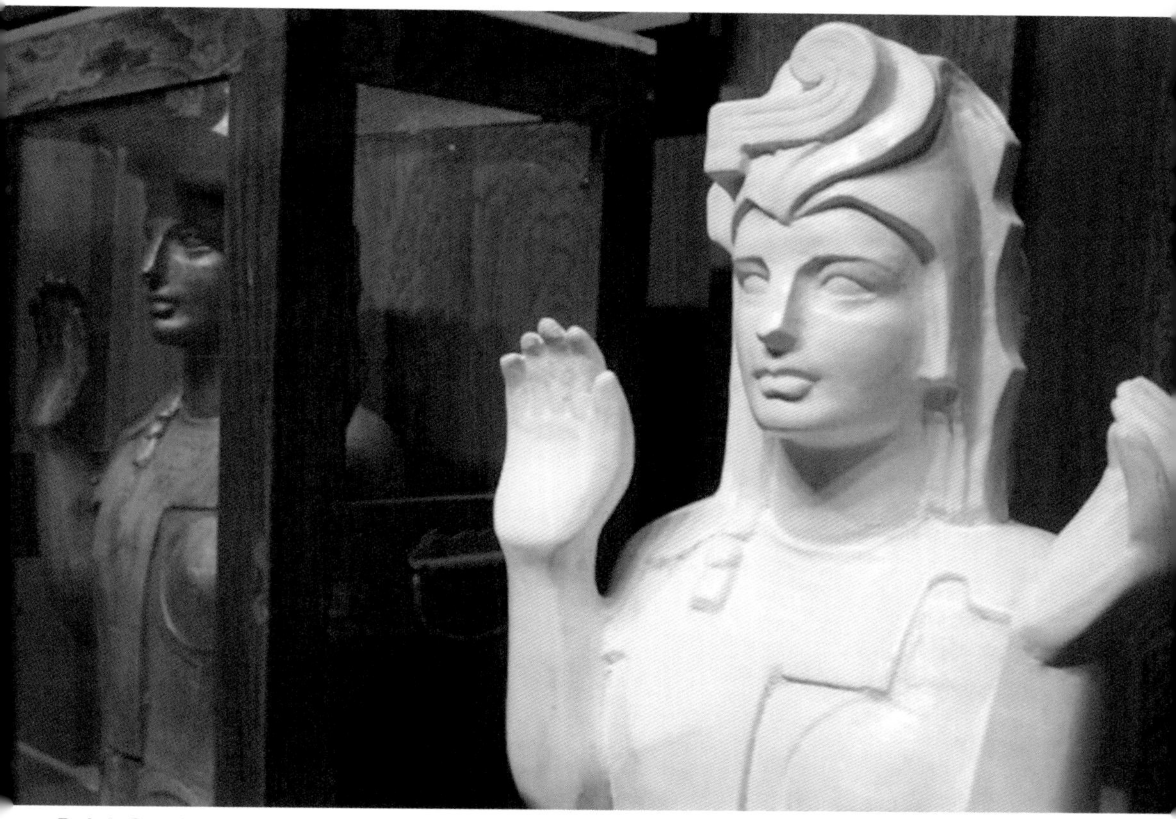

Ralph Stackpole

The unique symbol of Pacifica is the figure of a woman with her hands held up in front of her and a calm expression on her face. There is a three-foot-tall statue of this figure placed inside a glass-sided case in front of the city council dais. There is also an image of this unusual lady's face on the official seal of Pacifica. But who is she? In 1939, for the Golden Gate International Exposition, held on Treasure Island in the San Francisco Bay, the noted sculptor Ralph Stackpole was commissioned to make a sculpture that would embody the theme of the fair, which was "Pacifica." At the time, of course, no such city called "Pacifica" existed and the term had more to do with a conceptual encompassing of the world of the Pacific Ocean as well as a nod to "peace." Stackpole created an 80-foot statue that dominated the entrance to the exposition and captured the world's attention. *Life* magazine featured photographs of the sculpture, and 16 million people saw it themselves during the two years the exposition was open. Made of frame and applied stucco, the statue of Pacifica was destroyed at the end of the exposition, although there continues to be the dream that someday it can be recreated as a sort of "Western Statue of Liberty." Instead, the City of Pacifica will be home to the spirit of artist Ralph Stackpole's creation.

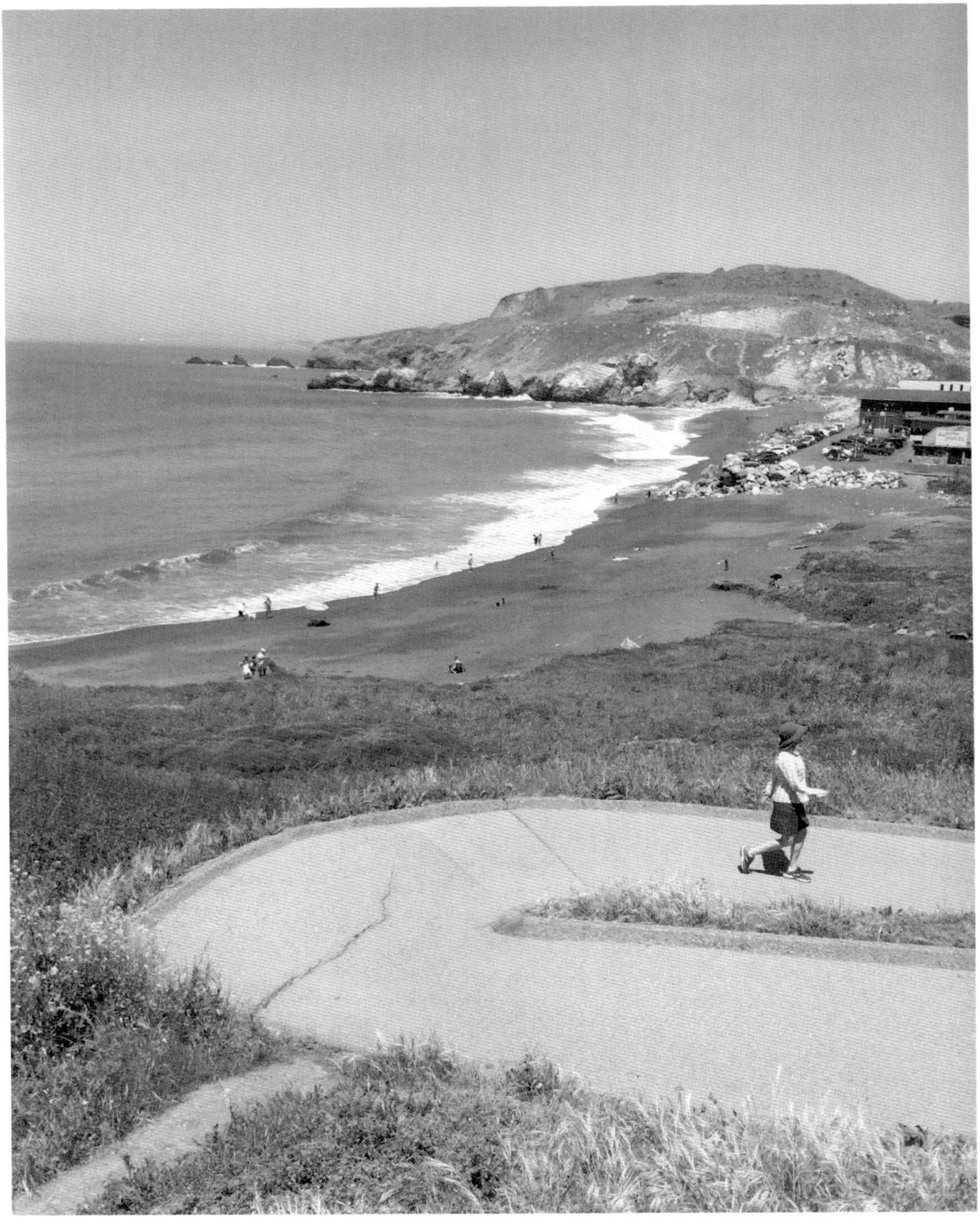

The Hiker

Pacifica has more open space than any other city in San Mateo County. There are federal, state and county parks and beaches along the nine miles of coastline that border the western edge of the city. People in Pacifica take pride in their city's natural beauty, dubbing it "Scenic Pacifica" and rallying to protect the hills and beaches whenever possible. Many people have championed the preservation of pristine Pacifica, but even more enjoy setting out on a hike whenever they like. "The Hiker" could easily have been the symbol of Pacifica.

INDEX

Adams, Lynn, 120
Ampola, Maria, 77
Ampola, Phillip, 77
Ash, Hal, 76
Azevedo, Paul, 114
Baldwin, Karl, 13
Barrish, Jerry, 38
Beauvais, Mary, 117
Beck, Don, 94
Berrner, Karina, 35
Bossier, Mike, 44
Boudinot, Ruth, 49
Brink, Jean, 49
Butler, Ian, 108
Byrne, Bill, 98
Cimo, Frank, 110
Colombo's Delicatessen, 64
Conroy, Russ, 22
Curtis, John, 16
Day, Eugene, 121
DeJarnatt, Pete, 15
Delman, Gretchen, 57
DiCello, Jackie, 46
Digre, Sue, 16
Drake, Bill, 72
Durst, Debi, 44
Durst, Will, 44
Duryea, Robert, 102
Ellis, Jackie, 72
Emde, Dale, 70
Emde, Enid, 70
English, Charlie, 21
Ewald, Roberta, 43
Farrar, Margery, 116
Fassler, Jean, 11
Florey, Mary, 65
Garrett, Duane, 33
Gee, May, 14
Genereux, Roger, 40
Glew, Sarah, 79
Gray, Bill, 82, 83
Gust, Charles, 18
Gust, Lena, 18
Gust, Lorraine, 18
Gust, Nick, 18
Hale, Allan, 109
Hall, Nancy, 36
Harkins, Herschel, 105
Harris, Elmer, 97
Harris, Mary, 29
Hazard, Manny, 92
Hill, Jerry, 58
Hinshaw, Horace, 85
Hinton, Cal, 19
Holmes, Scott, 112, 113
Horsley, Don, 58
Howard, Fred, 22
Jackson, Tom, 46
James, Helen, 119
Jaquith, Ginny, 23
Jimno, Cheryl, 68
Jimno, Joe, 68
Johnson, Keith, 62
Johnson, Stephen (photographer), 34
Johnson, Stephen (teacher), 35
Karr, Helen, 123
Kelly, Kevin, 61
Lancelle, Julie, 24
Larsen, Elaine, 73
Latimer, Bruce, 39
Lee, Matthew, 78
Leone, Andrew, 36
Lepeltak, Bill, 86
Loeb, Peter, 17
Lucas, Fred, 48
Mazza, Sam, 118
Mazzetti, Julie, 75
McCarthy, Grace, 20
Michaelis, Bill, 52
Miller, Lynn Ruth, 32
Miller, Warren, 71
Mineta, David, 51
Mineta, Norman, 51
Moe, Tonia, 95
Mueller, Loyle, 80
Muir, Lucy, 115
Nash, Frank, 67
Nava, Johnny, 100
Nichols, Jim, 31
Nichols, Morning, 30, 31
O'Brien, Ron, 71
Owen, Mildred, 30
O'Neill, Michael, 58
Paik, Pat, 56
Pantoleon, John, 41
Pantoleon, Kathy, 41
Pappas, Andy, 122
Pereira, Pete, 106, 107
Petersen, Fred, 71
Piccolotti, Jason, 91
Piccolotti, Johnny, 90
Piccolotti, Lou, 89
Piccolotti, Tom, 88
Pickell, Rudy, 93
Raskin, Jef, 60
Ribera, Ernest, 96
Rothenberg, Michael, 42
Ruchames, Eric, 54
Rush, George, 84
Schlieve, Aaron, 65
Schneider, Pilar, 26
Schneider, Rob, 26
Seavue Theater, 74
Sholin, Dave, 28
Sor, Elizabeth, 50
Speier, Jackie, 124
Stanley, John, 27
Stenstrom, Glenn, 67
Strom, Paul, 80
Torlakson, James, 37
Vallero, Carl, 99
Vinces, Ed, 66
Vinces, Stephanie, 66
Vreeland, Jim, 24
Wallace, Sandra, 55
Williams, Emmanuel, 45
Willis, Dennis, 69
Yap, Marian, 28
Winston, Frank D., 111

Consistent with our mission to preserve history on a local level, this book was printed in South Carolina on American-made paper and manufactured entirely in the United States. Products carrying the accredited Forest Stewardship Council (FSC) label are printed on 100 percent FSC-certified paper.